Paradigms in Political Theory

Paradigms in Political Theory

EDITED BY

STEVEN JAY GOLD

Iowa State University Press / Ames

TO MY PARENTS,
Richard and Pearl Gold,
for giving me their love of scholarship

Steven Jay Gold is assistant professor of philosophy at Southern Connecticut State University, New Haven.

Copyright is not claimed for Chapter 3, which first appeared in *At the Intersection of Legality & Morality* (New York: Peter Lang Publishing, 1990); Chapter 9, which first appeared in the *Canadian Journal of Philosophy;* Chapter 10, © Kathryn Pyne Addelson, which first appeared in Eva Kittay and Diana Meyers, eds., *Women and Moral Theory* (Towata, N.J.: Rowman and Littlefield, 1987); and Chapter 11, which first appeared in Seyla Benhabib and Drucilla Cornell, eds., *Feminism as Critique* (Minneapolis: University of Minnesota Press, 1989). These chapters are reprinted by permission of their original publishers.

Authorization to photocopy items for internal or personal use, or the internal or personal use of specific clients, is granted by Iowa State University Press, provided that the base fee of $.10 per copy is paid directly to the Copyright Clearance Center, 27 Congress Street, Salem, MA 01970. For those organizations that have been granted a photocopy license by CCC, a separate system of payments has been arranged. The fee code for users of the Transactional Reporting Service is 0-1838-1283-6 93/$.10.

♾ Printed on acid-free paper in the United States of America
First edition, 1993

Library of Congress Cataloging-in-Publication Data

Paradigms in political theory / Steven Jay Gold—1st ed.
   p.   cm.
   Includes index.
   ISBN 0-8138-1283-6 (alk. paper).
   1. Political science—Philosophy.   I. Gold, Steven Jay.
JA74.P343   1993
320.5—dc20   92-40789

Contents

Introduction   vii

I. LIBERALISM

1. Intuitions, Ideology, and Liberal Social Philosophy   3
   John Exdell

2. Fair Play and the Obligation to Obey the Law   11
   William Langenfus

3. Hard Cases and No-Right-Answer Answers   23
   Daniel Skubik

4. Personal Autonomy, Institutions, and Moral Philosophy   34
   Edward Sankowski

5. Sharing Responsibility: The Logic of We and We, Qua . . .   50
   J. K. Swindler

II. MARXISM

6. Michel Foucault, Analytical Marxism, and Functional Explanation   59
   Steven Jay Gold

7. Lukacs: Theory and Praxis   69
   Joseph Bien

8. Marx, Nietzsche, and the Voices of Democracy   79
   Fred Evans

III. FEMINISM

9. A Feminist Aspect Theory of the Self   101
   Ann Ferguson

10. Feminist Thought and Action   116
    Kathryn Pyne Addelson

11. Impartiality and the Civic Public: Some Implications of
Feminist Critiques of Moral and Political Theory   139
Iris Marion Young

IV. POSTMODERNISM

12. Postmodernism and Politics   165
Robert Hollinger

13. Lyotard as Political Thinker   174
David Ingram

14. Elements of a Derridean Social Theory   181
Bill Martin

15. The Critique of Marxism in Baudrillard's Later Writings   194
Tony Smith

Contributors   211
Index   215

Introduction

For the greater part of this century, political philosophy played a relatively minor role in Anglophone philosophical debates. Metaphysics, epistemology, ethics, and especially the philosophy of language dominated the tradition. In the last few decades, however, things have changed radically. Not only has political philosophy become a central, even dominant part of the philosophical dialogue; the diversity and richness of the emerging traditions has become staggering. The liberal tradition that prevailed in political philosophy throughout this century is alive and well. Marxism, long neglected in Anglo-American philosophy, has undergone a renaissance of unprecedented proportions. And new traditions like feminism and postmodernism have taken an extensive share in the discussion. With this in mind, I have attempted to put together a collection that represents the more important issues of current debates in the four main "paradigms" in political theory—liberalism, Marxism, feminism, and postmodernism.

Liberalism

The political theoretical position known as liberalism, like any theory that lasts over several centuries—and in the context of vastly different social, political, and religious situations—is notoriously hard to define. Put simply, liberalism sees politics as a human invention created to overcome the hardships associated with the natural human condition of total liberty. Politics, as a convention, serves to prevent the negative effects necessarily produced by competitive human nature. Governments, therefore, are legitimate only insofar as they secure the legitimate goals of peace and harmony while maximizing the autonomy of each individual. The three most important authors in the tradition are Hobbes, Locke, and Rousseau.

In 1651 Thomas Hobbes (1588–1679) produced *Leviathan,* one of the great works of Western political theory and the seminal work in the liberal tradition. Concerned with the problems of human nature, sovereignty, and political obligation, Hobbes was among the first to look to the imaginary "state of nature"—a state of total freedom and hence a "war of all against all." Rational agents in such a state of pure freedom would, of necessity, seek security in a "social contract," setting up a sovereign (or leviathan) who would be absolute in making law and protecting the security of the people. Such an arrangement would then be in accordance with reason.

John Locke (1632–1704) was next in line with his *Treatises of Civil Government* (1690). According to Locke, the law of nature, understood by reason and given by God, entails natural rights to life, limb, and free action, as well as the right to own anything with which one mixes one's labor. The role of the state, then, is to protect the individual's right to life and property. Rational individuals would then consent to limitations on their freedom to protect these natural rights.

Swiss-born Jean-Jacques Rousseau (1712–1778), in his *The Social Contract* (1762), starts from the position of man's natural freedom, though "everywhere he is in chains." As a naturally free "noble savage," each person needs a proper state to be truly free, though the unjust states about us make humans unfree. Direct democracy is the only form of government that can truly preserve liberty in individual choice. The active state or sovereign expresses the "general will" of the people as opposed to the aggregate will of individuals. That is, in addition to each individual's self-interest, or private will, each citizen has a collective interest in the future of the community. The foundations of legitimate authority for Rousseau, then, lie in political formulations of the general will; that is, the citizens acting as a whole and freely accepting rules that apply equally.

In modern times, John Rawls revived the state-of-nature reasoning by giving us the "original position" where participants, shrouded by a veil of ignorance, would select principles of social justice that provide equal rights to each. This freedom must be compatible with the most extensive liberty for all, so that individual liberty will be to the greatest advantage of the worst-off in the new society while opening all positions of power to fair and equal competition. In the contractarian tradition of Rousseau, Rawls develops rational principles of justice that allow us to determine when a state's authority is justified.

Along more libertarian lines, Robert Nozick argues for the traditional view of justice respecting legal rights and a "minimal state." By protecting citizens' private property and preventing harm to others, Nozick's minimal state purports to respect basic natural rights, as with

Locke, while caring little for Rawls's representative worst-off man. Although the political systems established on the liberal ideal have indeed expanded the range of individual freedom, especially when compared to feudal political arrangements, the nature of modern social structures is decidedly more oppressive than Locke or Rousseau could have imagined. Equality in political rights today, to the extent that it exists, seems more to legitimize as great a degree of inequality as was tolerated in feudal societies.

John Exdell critiques the analytical methods in American liberal social philosophy as it pertains to the moral legitimacy of legal paternalism. Exdell raises doubts about the fundamental methods used in analytical social philosophy, such as the commitment to "principles that capture common intuitions on the matter" or "the agreement with our linguistic habit and widely shared moral convictions." Raising doubts about the assumed society-wide consensus on fundamental values, Exdell exposes the underlying precepts of mainstream liberalism as the latent ideological imperative of what purports to be objective rational methodology.

William Langenfus brings us the well-established "fair-play" argument as the basis for political obligation. Critics of the view that those accepting the benefits provided by a cooperative enterprise are obligated in fairness to comply with the requirements of that scheme often suggest that there are no benefits of large-scale political systems that citizens generally can be said to "accept" in the appropriate sense. To this Langenfus argues that the problem can be resolved by placing the issue within the context of a plausible conception of law itself, a conception that regards it as essentially a cooperative enterprise. Given this, there is a benefit inherently associated with such an enterprise that citizens generally can be presumed to "accept" in the appropriate sense, and it can provide the basis for at least a prima facie obligation to obey the laws of any functioning legal system.

Daniel Skubik attempts a refutation of Ronald Dworkin's insistence that all hard cases have unique resolution. Treating Dworkin's "right-answer thesis" and the two versions of the "no-right-answer thesis" Dworkin purports to refute, Skubik delves into the formalized logical constructions and semantics of ordinary lawyers' adversarial discourse in an admirably lucid fashion. In the end, Skubik suggests that Dworkin misconstrues his opponents' positions and presents an argument that is reductive in nature and misses describing legal practice fairly. Ultimately, Skubik tells us, the debate can be settled only by reference to deeper moral and political theory, not by reference to linguistic or logical levels of argumentation.

In his critique of Joseph Raz's influential book *The Morality of Freedom*, Edward Sankowski argues that Raz's position on autonomy is damaged by an omission of a detailed description and defense of institutional arrangements and practices connected with his ideal of personal autonomy. Sankowski suggests that Raz's definition of autonomy, his treatment of tolerance, and his "basic principle of autonomy" are defective because of insufficient attention to institutions. Affirming the view that describing and defending the institutions of a community one holds to be authoritative vis à vis autonomy is fundamental to an adequate account of the concept, Sankowski finds Raz's conception of autonomy incomplete.

J. K. Swindler is concerned with the language and logic of collective agency. Swindler carefully sets out and critiques the three competing basic positions. He pursues John Ladd's view that organized collectives are not persons and have no moral properties. The view of Peter French that collectivities are persons and possess moral properties is considered, as is David Copp's position that collectives are personlike and their properties logically and causally reducible to their constituent members. Swindler then argues that by understanding moral ascriptions reductively, we can see that French is right to say that groups have moral properties but that Ladd is correct to suggest that they are not reducible to the group's individual members.

Marxism

The tradition in social theory known as Marxism originates in the writings of Karl Marx and Friedrich Engels in the nineteenth century. At the core of this vast tradition lies a commitment to Marx's theory of history, the rigorous criticism of capitalist social and economic formations, and the development of a project centered on strategies intended to move us from a class-divided society based on exploitation to a classless community where private property is eliminated and exploitation only a distant memory. That agreement on even these most basic claims about Marxism is hard to reach among the seemingly infinite number of types of Marxists makes clear the diversity of this school of thought.

The central aspect of Marx's work has to be found in his conception of history, which came to be known after his death as historical materialism. Put simply, this theory states that history is the development of human productive power where the productive forces set the functional requirements for a set of production relations that foster their development through class conflict. Marx divides history into different stages, or "modes of production," defined by a class division (production relations) based on ownership and control over the means of production (forces of production). Upon this economic base arises a social and political superstructure with corresponding ideological elements that reinforce and legitimize the system of exploitation. At a certain point in time, production relations cease being functional for developing the productive forces and become a fetter. At that point, revolution in the mode of production occurs, and the superstructure crumbles. The practical point, then, was to find the best strategy that would facilitate the demise of capitalism and aid in the transition to communism, where class divisions and exploitation would come to an end.

The relative coherence of Marxism from Marx's death in 1883 to the beginning of World War I was fairly short-lived. The split in the Second International between the determinist views of Kautsky, the reformist views of Bernstein, and the more radical position of Luxemburg made clear that Marxism was to head in many directions. With the revolution in Russia, the influence of Lenin and Trotsky, albeit in different paths, dictated much of the course of Marxism, even in the West at the time.

The beginnings of what we call Western Marxism start in the early twenties with Lukacs's work on class consciousness and Gramsci's development of the concept of "hegemony." After World War II, Sartre's existential Marxism brought out a new element of Marx's work, emphasizing the subjective psychological and "humanistic" Marx. He was succeeded by Althusser and the structural Marxists, who identified with the opposite side of Marx, namely the scientific, with an emphasis on "overdeterminations" and "contradictions."

In the seventies, structural Marxism had seen its better days, and Marxism was in a state of crisis. However, just after liberal social theory began to take off in the wake of Rawls and Nozick, Marxism saw a renaissance in the English-speaking world as never before. G. A. Cohen, Jon Elster, and John Roemer began a tradition in the late seventies that has come to be called analytical Marxism. This attempt at rejuvenating Marxism through the use of the tools of the philosophy of social science, analytic philosophy, and, for some, neoclassical economics has met with joyous praise and strong criticism. But for good or ill, it has sparked an intense interest in Marx in the English-speaking philosophical community that it never enjoyed before. This opened philosophers to a discussion of Marx in relation to other accepted philosophers like Kant, Mill, Aristotle, and those undergoing a rejuvenation of their own, like Nietzsche.

Steven Jay Gold attempts to take recent developments in analytical Marxism to show how Michel Foucault misunderstood essential elements of historical materialism. Using G. A. Cohen's defense of functional Marxism, Gold attempts to show first how crude functional explanation—that is, the naive assumption that merely pointing to the consequences of a phenomenon beneficial for the mode of production suffices to explain that the phenomenon—is not essential to historical materialism. Second, Gold shows that Foucault was wrong to see the Marxian conception of power as instrumental, that is, the possession of the dominant class. And last Gold disagrees with Foucault's contention that in functionally subordinating politics to economics, historical materialism reduces all elements of power to the economy.

Joseph Bien explores in depth the relation of theory and practice in Lukacs's *History and Class Consciousness*. Scrutinizing Lukacs's anti-idealist Marxist stand on the nature of theoretical justification, Bien attempts to make clear the resolution of social and historical validation with the logical ground for true judgments. This leads Bien to examine the nature of how class consciousness is developed in Lukacs's understanding of Marx. Class consciousness as a historical principle of Lukacs's system, and as an "ought" or demand that men act in a certain historically necessary fashion are synthesized and developed.

Fred Evans attempts a synthesis of Marx and Nietzsche, representing the diachronic and synchronic dimensions of democracy. Evans argues that any society, or "linguistic community," is an interplay of "voices," so that the synchronic dimension is always suppressed by the diachronic movement of the community toward the unification of "oracularity" required for production and governance. Democracy consists of the continual freeing of suppressed voices and the consequent reestablishment of their interplay or "creative tension." For Evans, Marx provides the oracle of a classless society that can best release the voices suppressed by capitalist and technocratic society, and Nietzsche's appeal to "chaos" serves as the necessary antidote to Marx's exclusive emphasis on the diachronic dimension of society—that is, to Marx's oracularity.

Feminism

For nearly twenty-five years feminists have played a major role in political theory. Taking more than merely philosophical position, contemporary feminists maintain an active voice for progressive political change beyond that of most of their male colleagues, Marxists included. Central to this eclectic tradition is the opposition to patriarchy, the system of male domination. Understanding this system and finding ways to deal with it, be it in women's equality (the liberal tradition) or undermining the system itself (the radical and socialist feminist traditions), feminists have provided a voice in philosophy for women's rights in opposition to the domination of men for decades. Much of the feminist tradition in political theory is of relatively recent origin, yet an incredibly diverse group of writings has developed that defies easy categorization. For the sake of simplicity, I will discuss contemporary feminist political theory in terms of liberal feminism, radical feminism, and socialist feminism.

Liberal feminism is as old as liberalism itself. For over two centuries, women, and some men, have advocated the application of liberal ideals to women. Traditional arguments regarding natural rights gave way over the years to a discussion of utilitarian conceptions of equality, and eventually to a concern for equal opportunity and social reforms by the welfare state. The liberal feminist is principally concerned with how discrimination on the basis of sex denies women equal opportunity and the ability to realize personal projects. Fighting for the equality of women, liberal feminists have fought legislation that puts differential burdens on women, pressing for reproductive rights, aid to families and children, job training, and more. Though liberal feminism remains a vital part of the liberal tradition, it represents some of the more progressive voices consistently advocating equality, freedom, and the value of the individual when other voices in the liberal tradition rang hollow.

Radical feminism arose in more recent times, principally as a product of the 1960s women's movement, the civil-rights movement, and New Left organizations. Fundamental to radical feminism is the belief that the oppression of women is the source of all forms of domination. Gender, for the radical feminist, is the fundamental explanatory category in terms of which all other forms of domination must be understood. Radical feminists attempt to set strategies to expose and destroy the patriarchal system, operating in both an active and creative theoretical tradition as well as maintaining a diverse involvement in women's political movements, especially in the United States. The essential project for radical-feminist political theory lies in exposing the way gender is socially constructed and helps to maintain the system of male domination. The mode of procreation—that is, the organization of reproduction, raising children, and managing the household—forms the central dynamic by which social life and male domination is constituted. Unfortunately, by attempting to show how "gender" is socially constructed in a fundamental unity found in the oppression of women, radical feminists initially suffered from a race-class bias. By assuming that there was an essential cross-cultural, cross-class boundary for the experience of women, radical feminists reified the status of middle-class white women. Though the majority of radical feminists are still white and middle class, a serious attempt is being made to include diversity in women's experience and integrate problems of race and class.

Socialist feminist analysis began about a decade after the radical-feminist movement. The project remains today an attempt at fusing a Marxist-feminist analysis in a fashion that respects the categories of race, gender, and class. Unlike the radical feminists, socialist feminists take the category of "gender" as on the same par as the category of "class." Understanding and finding ways to fight "capitalist patriarchy" necessitates historical materialism and the traditional Marxist goals of socialism and material equality as well as the fight against male domination. The analysis is more than Marxist in that "gender" plays a role equal to that of "class." The analysis is Marxist-feminist since the end of capitalism is necessary for the end of patriarchy, and vice versa. Socialist feminists emphasize the social construction of gender based on human production and reproduction, much like the radical feminists. The sexual division of labor plays as important a part of the general division of labor. Hence, the socialist feminist attempts to rework Marxism in a feminist fashion.

At the philosophical center of much of the debate in political theory, in all four paradigms discussed in this book, lie competing theories of self. Ann Ferguson critiques traditional "rational-maximizer" theories of the self, where humans are seen as unified agents who seek their own self-interest, and the "difference theory," which emphasizes social and biological differences between the genders. She rejects these traditional conceptions in favor of an "aspect" theory of the self. In this aspect theory selfhood progresses over time; unique individual concerns compete with social constraints for determining the nature of the agent. This subtler, more flexible theory of the self sets the foundations for a more progressive political theory.

Kathryn Pyne Addelson represents the best in political theory with her commitment to examining how the needs of political action can be informed by political theory. Given her materialist outlook, it is not assumed that feminist political theory is monolithic and applies to all cases at all times. Rather, Addelson examines how the need for theory can be derived from the actual problems faced in political action. She focuses partially on the formation of women's collectives as an alternative means of empowerment. When women attempt to create non-hierarchical structures within these collectives, Addelson shows how they face a contradiction between the goals of feminist collectivism and the need to aid the clients where "outside" patriarchal constraints insist on structures and behavior that undermine empowerment. Feminist theorists, we are told, can help to understand and find strategies for dealing with these contradictions. Addelson attempts to understand and conceptualize the structures of dominance in our society by critiquing the "voluntarist" model, where social problems (e.g., teen pregnancy) are seen as problems of personal choice to be treated by educating and dealing with the individual. In this article one will find an excellent blending of the empirical tradition in sociology with the best in feminist political philosophy.

Advocating a position where feminists must break with the modernist project, Iris Young argues that those committed to an emancipatory politics must set a new course. She rejects the traditional view that the emancipation of women entails full participation of women in political affairs on equal terms with men. Rather, Young questions the traditional liberal ideals as inherently representing masculine biases about society and human nature. She does this by developing a conception of normative reason that does not oppose reason to desire and affectivity. The impartial and universal nature of reason in the deontological tradition represses difference; hence she undertakes a critique of normative reason, in part dependent on Habermas, and develops it in terms of the feminist critique of modern political theory. The traditional ideal of the civic, as expressed in Hegel and Rousseau, takes the public and private dimensions as an essential opposition corresponding to the distinction between reason and affectivity. Young argues that the will to unity expressed here entails the exclusion of difference. Young concludes that this problem can be dealt with only by taking an emancipatory conception of public life that provides heterogeneity.

Postmodernism

The problematics central to postmodernism go well beyond philosophy. Indeed, postmodern political philosophy is a relative newcomer compared to the decades-old traditions of postmodernism in painting, sculpture, drama, literature, architecture, and music. Postmodernism was given its first philosophical expression in the 1970s by Michel Foucault, Jacques Derrida, and others. Appealing to the antifoundationalist, antiuniversalist philosophy of Nietzsche, postmodernists emphasize the fragmentary and discontinuous nature of reality. Denying the accessibility of any objective truth, postmodernists have come to reject any sense of the individual subject as the locus of "truth," relying instead on a decentered concept of the individual as the intersection of power-desire relations.

This repudiation of any sense of objective truth guides some, like Lyotard, to reject the metanarratives of the "modern" theories that according to Lyotard serve only to legitimize oppressive social structures and political institutions. Lyotard denies that there is any general pattern to history; hence there is no way to systematize society and provide a blueprint for social change.

The major target of most postmodern political theorists is Marx. Typically they suggest that attempts to identify positive laws of human development so that a program for revolutionary social change can be developed inevitably lead to social institutions that are just as oppressive as the ones they replace. For this reason, postmodernists reject even revolutionary social programs.

While postmodern political theory purports to move beyond Marx, the task of attacking capitalism remains central. Analysis of the postmodern condition, its contradictions and convergences, entails the project of understanding the oppressive nature of postindustrial capitalism. In the context of human agency, social interaction, and history, postmodernists attempt a radical critique of the human condition.

The central assumption of this critique is that society is undergoing an epochal transformation. The Western world, we are told, has now moved from a postindustrial capitalist society to a society where information and theoretical research drives us forward. Postmodernists hold that class conflict is no longer the motor for human development and that the working class is no longer the agent of historical change. Our attention must be turned to discourse and the diverse new modes of communication.

Robert Hollinger provides us with a basic explanation of postmodern political theory. He touches on the differences between modernism and postmodernism; the key philosophical, literary, and architectural senses of the term; and the question What is enlightenment? as it is found in the so-called Habermas-Foucault controversy. The political implications of postmodernism are raised by Hollinger in this postmodern attempt at describing the postmodern.

David Ingram examines Lyotard's dissatisfaction with modernity and its tendency to undermine the ethical integrity and autonomy of diverse ethnic, religious, social, political, and cultural communities and the fair distribution of influences among them. For Lyotard, these tendencies exhibit totalitarian features that result when the universalistic ideas of modern rationality become ideologies or all-encompassing blueprints for large-scale social engineering. Despite Lyotard's critique of totalitarian rationalism, Ingram argues that he is not an antirationalistic philosopher. Ingram suggests that like Kant, Lyotard undertakes a critique of theoretical reason in the name of a higher practical reason. Though Lyotard appeals to universal ideals, Ingram understands him not to present concrete blueprints for social engineering (and hence totalitarianism) but regulative ideas in the Kantian sense, ideas that establish legitimate limits that are essentially indeterminate and fluid, varying from context to context. In this fashion, Ingram tells us, Lyotard can appeal to the universal ideals of community, autonomy, and justice without falling into the totalitarian trap that he finds hegemonic today.

Bill Martin presents us with an outline of a social theory that uses Derrida's work as its methodological foundation. Though Derrida is not a social theorist, his work, Martin tells us, has significant implications for social theory in two broad respects. First, as the basis for the critique of contemporary social theories, especially that of Habermas, Derrida's method can be most useful. Second, as the basis for a theory uniquely suited to a social theory that is postmodern, Martin tells us that Derrida's method can produce more than the "style" of postmodernism; it addresses the particularities of societies that are moving away from, or beyond, modernity.

Tony Smith attacks the attempts at moving beyond Marx that are common to postmodernists and exemplified in the later writings of Baudrillard. Smith addresses and attempts to refute the claims that (1) in contrast to Marx's focus on modes of production, Baudrillard holds that societies should be examined in terms of symbolic exchange (codes); (2) Baudrillard believes that the Marxist emphasis on class struggle at the point of production does not provide an adequate account for the present social order; (3) he holds that the Marxist call to revolution in its own way involves a repressive sublimation as dangerous as that imposed under capitalism. In a lucid and direct style, Smith attempts to show how each of these claims fails even to dent the Marxian approach to social theory.

ACKNOWLEDGMENTS

This collection owes much to many of my colleagues. I would personally like to thank Tony Smith, Robert Hollinger, Milton Fisk, and members of the Society for Social and Political Philosophy for their help in making this volume possible.

I

Liberalism

1

Intuitions, Ideology, and Liberal Social Philosophy

T his essay is a critical review of what we may fairly call the
analytical method in American social philosophy as we find it in the
debates among liberal philosophers over the moral legitimacy of "legal
paternalism." A dominant position in this literature holds that justified
paternalism is in some sense based on the voluntary consent of those
subject to it, whereas unjustified paternalism imposes a good on
individuals and thereby fails to respect persons as choosers of their own
ends. Although differences remain over what version of this position is
to be preferred and what specific laws and policies are warranted by it,
one finds wide agreement that discussion on these points continue within
boundaries set by the Kantian categories of "respect for persons" and
the "dignity of the individual" as a being capable of rational choice. The
liberal framework itself is justified by a presentation of examples and
analogies, often hypothetical and sketchy, that are offered as a way of
testing proposed principles against the intuitions of the author and his
or her readers.

We find this approach first joined to liberal political conclusions in
Joel Feinberg's influential 1971 article "Legal Paternalism." Feinberg
accepts the general presumption against state paternalism articulated by
Mill but wishes to accommodate what he considers a widely held view
that paternalistic interference is sometimes justified. The legitimacy of
some paternalistic legislation is evident in "common sense and our long
established customs and laws."[1] The problem, then, is where to draw the

line. Feinberg promises us that his approach to the problem "will not be particularly ideological." Rather, he will "organize our elementary intuitions by finding a principle that will render them consistent."[2] Thus Feinberg's discussion eschews any sustained philosophical investigation into controversies about the nature of the human good and conditions essential to human dignity. We can discover rational criteria for identifying cases of legitimate paternalistic interference in our laws, customs, and the ordinary good sense of reasonable men.

On this basis Feinberg affirms the venerable legal maxim *volenti non fit injuria*, which he interprets to mean that it is wrong for the state to interfere paternalistically in the "fully voluntary choice or consent of a mature and rational human being." For Feinberg, a crucial criterion of a "rational" and "voluntary" choice is that the risks it involves are proportionate to the value or importance of the goal sought for the individual who makes it. We may interfere with an individual's actions when he or she, presumably because of compulsion or ignorance, misunderstands the relationship between the risks assumed and "his or her settled values and preferences." If, however, we make the judgment that the individual's settled values and preferences themselves are misguided, our paternalistic interference moves beyond the *volenti* maxim and assumes "an acrid moral flavor." We are now judging the actions of individuals by an alien conception of the ethical good, not by their "interests," which is how their well-being is properly defined.[3]

Feinberg therefore opposes legislation prohibiting the sale of cigarettes because it would override the "informed judgments" of "voluntary risk-takers." On this basis he rejects Mill's position on voluntary enslavement. When considering issues of principle and not expediency, we must affirm the right of voluntary enslavement, says Feinberg, because it is perfectly conceivable that a rational human being might in some circumstances freely choose enslavement for the sake of some special benefit. To deny an individual the liberty to do so is again to override the "informed judgments" of "voluntary risk-takers." It is to embrace paternalism of a "strong" kind, in violation of "our ultimate principle" of "respect for a person's voluntary choice *as such*." What is at stake for Feinberg is our commitment to a liberal individualist conception of justice—"the principle . . . that every human being has a right to 'voluntarily dispose of his or her own lot in life' whatever the effect on the net balance of benefits (including 'freedom') and harms."[4]

What, then, grounds "our ultimate principle" of "respect for a person's voluntary choice *as such*"? Apparently nothing other than "our elementary intuitions," as these are discovered by a review of accepted legal precedent and prevailing custom. Feinberg notes that in our society most employment contracts require employees to abandon their liberty to do as they please for a daily period and to obey their boss's commands in exchange for a salary. Likewise, college students may choose to live in dormitories regulated by a curfew and other parietal rules in exchange for the enjoyment of order, quiet, and the absence of temptation. Through these examples we are brought to realize our acceptance of the idea that we should not "deny people the liberty of trading liberties for other benefits when they voluntarily choose to do so." Selling oneself into slavery is "only an extreme case of contracting away liberty, but not altogether different in principle."[5]

This manner of argument—i.e., the settling of philosophical issues by appeals to law, custom, and prevailing convictions—recurs as the primary modus operandi throughout the subsequent literature on legal paternalism. Thus John Hodson conducts a search for a "principle which captures common intuitions on this matter" and avoids "counterintuitive consequences." The principle he proposes is justified because "its application yields conclusions that are in agreement with common intuitions about what sorts of cases are such that paternalism should be allowed."[6] Some philosophers supplement such appeals to law and custom with hypothetical examples intended to reveal to the reader an unconscious conviction. Richard Arneson invites reaction to imaginary robot guardians to reveal "our underlying commitment" to the concept of autonomy as a right to free choice, a commitment that is also apparent in "our linguistic habit of complaining that certain state or societal incursions against individual freedom constitute denials of autonomy."[7] Nor does the appeal to intuitions or habits always favor the libertarian position. Robert Young argues that "a policy only of weak paternalism lacks comprehensiveness in that it fails to do justice to certain widely shared and deeply entrenched moral convictions relevant to paternalistic intervention."[8] Finally, Donald VanDeVeer introduces a lengthy work on the subject with the promise of "analytical advance beyond the disputes over the large 'isms.' " He will assess "explicit and well-defined specific principles" by noting "their implications for comparatively specific cases" and "their accordance with certain of our pretheoretical convictions about what is permissible and the . . . apparent lack of seriously counterintuitive implications—in contrast to the principles rejected."[9]

These appeals to "common intuitions," "our underlying commitment," "widely shared moral convictions," and "our linguistic habit" attempt to link a controversial position on policy to an alleged consensus in fundamental values. It is assumed that disagreement about the rightness of, for example, antidrug laws can be resolved by determining which position is most in harmony with conceptions of justice scarcely anyone in our society would dispute.

Here we should pause to raise some doubts about the assumed society-wide consensus on fundamental values. Is a nation beset by emotionally charged differences over such issues as abortion rights, military intervention in the third world, school prayer, pornography, the equal-rights amendment, and comparable worth for women nevertheless united at some deeper level in its understanding of justice? Or do these divisions actually reflect incompatible ways of life and antagonistic moral visions struggling for dominance in the body politic? What philosophical intuitions are shared by Jerry Falwell, Noam Chomsky, Jesse Helms, Jesse Jackson, Larry Flynt, David Rockefeller, and Andrea Dworkin? Given the obvious ethical heterogeneity represented in their constituencies, shouldn't the assumption of consensus strike us as a convenient illusion nurtured by a philosophical profession composed mainly of white middle-class males schooled in the precepts of mainstream liberalism?

When members of this profession appeal to "common intuitions" to settle the status of "autonomy" as a fundamental ethical value, they clearly do not include the intuitions of those millions of Americans whose moral convictions rest on faith in the absolute validity of the Old Testament, the idea of submission to God the Father, and who organize their lives under the guidance of right-wing clergy. When they announce "our underlying commitment" to the principle that each person has a right to "voluntarily dispose of his or her own lot in life," they are not speaking for those Americans who support revolution in Central America because it is moved by the vision of socialism and radical democracy rather than the norms of competitive free-market capitalism.

Even assuming the reality of ethical consensus in our civilization, the liberal philosophers cited above must confront a fundamental logical flaw in their discussion of moral rights and legal paternalism—the glaring contradiction between their philosophical objective and their method of achieving it. Feinberg and his followers pose the question, What acts of paternalistic interference in his or her affairs would a rational person affirm? Their inquiry is clearly framed as a quest for a universally valid position on the limits of permissible social interference in the liberty of individuals. At the same time, they attempt to answer the question by appealing to the "elementary intuitions" implicit in the social and legal conventions of *our* society. Feinberg thinks he finds a consensus in favor of the *volenti* maxim. Others do not. Regardless of who is right on this point, the crucial error is in their shared assumption that a philosophical position—for example, one favoring a utilitarian conception of the good or a Kantian conception of individual rights—can be justified by an appeal to the conventional legal doctrines or ethical consciousness of a particular civilization.

The classical liberalism of Locke, Smith, Kant, and Mill made no such mistake. Indeed the original champions of liberty saw custom and convention as obstacles to the triumph of a libertarian doctrine based upon a universally valid conception of human nature, individual dignity, or the general good. They confidently advanced a revolutionary philosophy based upon the conviction that established law and morality are subject to criticism insofar as they embody a flawed philosophical understanding of human life. Hence their ideas empowered an emerging ruling class hostile to traditional values to take command of society in the face of great resistance from both reactionary aristocratic elites and popular majorities moved by a more egalitarian and communal vision of the future. Although eighteenth- and nineteenth-century liberals celebrated the principle of noninterference, they installed their principle relentlessly by repeated acts of force. While they argued for a world in which people would be forever free to pursue their interests by their own lights, they imposed their vision of liberty upon unwilling societies and social classes without hesitation. This was a project that disdained prevailing legal and ethical norms.[10]

By contrast, one finds in the writings of most contemporary analytical liberals either simple indifference to alternative worldviews or the facile assumption that liberal values are universally recognized. For example, Rolf Sartorious, writing an introduction to a recent volume of essays he edited on paternalism, comments curtly on the only entry in his collection that sympathetically discusses cultures built upon feudal forms of paternal authority: "That paternalistic practices may fit in more comfortably with the underlying political morality of societies quite different from our own is more, rather than less, reason to subject them to close moral scrutiny."[11] In other words, cultures based on nonliberal values are alien and suspect, whereas those founded on liberal principles are assumed to be essentially in order. It is hard to read this response to the phenomenon of cultural difference as anything more than simple chauvinism.

Donald VanDeVeer, on the other hand, confidently claims universal validity for the principle that "each competent person has an equal right to direct the course of his or her life by choosing any alternative within the sphere of acts not wronging others." Recognition of this right, says VanDeVeer, "explains the importance which is commonly attached to valid consent," which "plays a fundamental role in ordinary moral assessments (moral assessments common, I would claim, to all cultures). To suppose their importance then is not to appeal to some special, and perhaps controversial moral point of view." Thus, as VanDeVeer proceeds with his analysis of cases, analogies, and intuitions, he is not merely examining the moral consciousness of his own civilization, or some portion of it, but something quite transcendental—"the 'deep

structure' of ordinary moral thought." He will "identify in an antirelativ-
ist manner rather basic principles as rationally defensible, universal
guides to deciding fundamental questions about the justifiability of
intervention with persons on paternalistic grounds."[12]

VanDeVeer sees no need to offer cross-cultural evidence to support
his claim about the universal importance of consent in human society.
Nor does he discuss the formidable body of historical and anthropologi-
cal evidence that can be directed against the idea of a universally
recognized right to "direct the course of his or her life." To discover the
"deep structure" common to the "ordinary moral thought" of all human
beings, it is enough to analyze "our pretheoretical convictions" and to
avoid principles with "counterintuitive implications" for the likely readers
of his book.

Given the striking lack of argument on this point, what gives
Feinberg, VanDeVeer, and others the confidence that they have seen
beyond their own culturally constituted values and discovered a
universally valid right to liberty? It is apparently the belief that "ordinary
moral thought," as we encounter it in the convictions of those who read
professional philosophy, manifests something genuinely universal.
VanDeVeer (quoting Ronald Dworkin) identifies this truth with "the
vague but powerful idea of human dignity." It is assumed, in other
words, that prevailing "intuitions" reveal a concept of "dignity" that is
not culturally conditioned but rooted in a timeless understanding of
essentially what we are as human beings. We are "persons"—choosers
of means and ends. It is this unique natural capacity that establishes each
individual's "moral equality" by contrast with "objects," "animals,"
"machines," and "incompetents." The task for philosophers, then, is to
"illuminate" this "vague but powerful" idea of dignity by connecting it
to liberal ideas of justice and human rights.[13]

I will not offer here any of the arguments available to refute this
position. Suffice it to note that the most prominent analytical philosopher of our time has finally given up on the idea that ontological truths
can serve as the foundation for liberal political institutions. His own
theory of justice, says John Rawls, is "political" and "practical, not
metaphysical or epistemological." It "tries to draw solely upon basic
intuitive ideas that are embedded in the political institutions of a
constitutional democratic regime and the public traditions of their
interpretation." Rawls frankly concedes, in other words, that the idea of
equal liberty in his theory of justice "is not intended as the application
of a general moral conception to the basic structure of society" but
formulates the moral conceptions that are *relatively valid* for the
institutions of liberal democracy.[14]

For Rawls, modern liberal democracies are founded on deeply

rooted social and historical conditions. They encompass intractable religious and moral differences that cannot be reconciled by philosophical doctrine. In this context, toleration of diverse conceptions of the good is the only alternative to autocratic state power: "Given the profound differences in belief and conceptions of the good at least since the Reformation, Philosophy as the search for truth about an independent metaphysical and moral order cannot provide a workable and shared basis for a political conception of justice in a democratic society. . . . No political view that depends on [a metaphysical doctrine of the nature of the self] can serve as a public conception of justice in a constitutional democratic state." A conception of justice suitable for liberal democracies, says Rawls, "deliberately stays on the surface, philosophically speaking."[15]

The literature on legal paternalism surveyed above began in the early 1970s with unselfconscious appeals to an alleged consensus in conventional intuitions. Belatedly, some liberal philosophers have enunciated the implicit Kantian ontological premises about "persons" and "dignity" needed to support universally valid libertarian objections to paternalistic interference. John Rawls, the dean of analytical social philosophers, now counsels against a quest for a realist ontological foundation. Liberal principles can be justified, says Rawls, only in relation to the historically grounded practice of pluralist democracy. Rawls's relativist turn does not, however, escape the questions posed earlier in this essay about consensus in conventional intuitions. Is there an established coherent practice of liberal democracy that requires a commitment to antipaternalist principles of liberty? Or is the nature of liberal democracy itself contested by diverse and incompatible moral visions, interests, and traditions? If the latter, then it will be necessary for philosophers to dive below "the surface, philosophically speaking" and to undertake a more serious and wide-ranging debate about the nature of the human good and the conditions of life essential to human dignity.

NOTES

1. Joel Feinberg, "Legal Paternalism," in *Paternalism,* ed. Rolf Sartorius (Minneapolis: University of Minnesota Press, 1983), pp. 3–17. Originally in *Canadian Journal of Philosophy* 1(1)(1971):106–24.

2. Ibid., p. 4.

3. Ibid., pp. 4–5, 7, 11.

4. Ibid., pp. 15, 16.

5. Ibid., pp. 15, 17.

6. John D. Hodson, "The Principle of Paternalism," *American Philosophical Quarterly*

14(1)(January 1977), pp. 62, 69.

7. Richard J. Arneson, "Mill vs. Paternalism," *Ethics* 90(4)(July 1980), p. 476.

8. Robert Young, "Autonomy and Paternalism," in *New Essays in Public Policy, Canadian Journal of Philosophy,* Supplementary vol. 8 (1982), p. 49.

9. Donald VanDeVeer, *Paternalistic Intervention: The Moral Bounds of Benevolence* (Princeton, N.J.: Princeton University Press, 1986), pp. 9, 88.

10. See, for example, Karl Polanyi, *The Great Transformation: The Political and Economic Origins of Our Time* (Boston: Beacon Press, 1957), and Edward Countryman, *The American Revolution* (New York: Hill and Wang, 1985).

11. Rolf Sartorious, ed., *Paternalism* (Minneapolis: University of Minnesota Press, 1983), p. xii.

12. VanDeVeer, *Paternalistic Intervention,* pp. 8, 20, 60.

13. Ibid., pp. 5, 8.

14. John Rawls, "Justice as Fairness: Political Not Metaphysical," *Philosophy and Public Affairs* 14(3)(Summer 1985), pp. 223–51, 225.

15. Ibid., pp. 230–31.

2

Fair Play and the
Obligation to Obey the Law

WILLIAM LANGENFUS

I

In an exemplary paper on rights, H. L. A. Hart states that "when a number of persons conduct any joint enterprise according to rules and thus restrict their liberty, those who have submitted to these restrictions when required have a right to a similar submission from those who have benefitted by their submission."[1] The moral obligation to obey these rules is said to arise because those who have benefited from the enterprise have done so only because others participating in the enterprise have done *their* part by submitting to the rules. John Rawls developed this idea, (at one time) called the underlying principle fair play, and proposed that it was the moral basis for the obligation to obey the law. According to Rawls, the principle is defined by a number of suppositions: (1) "that there is a mutually beneficial and just scheme of social cooperation, and that the advantages it yields can only be obtained if everyone, or nearly everyone, cooperates"; (2) "that cooperation requires a certain sacrifice from each person, or at least involves a certain restriction of his liberty"; (3) the benefits produced by the cooperative scheme are to a certain extent "free" in the sense that "if any one person knows that all (or nearly all) of the others will continue to do their part, he will still be able to share a gain from the scheme even if he does not do his part."[2] Rawls states that "under these conditions a person who has accepted the benefits of the scheme is bound by a duty of fair play to do his part and not take advantage of the free benefit by not cooperating."[3]

The whole point behind the appeal of the principle of fair play as a ground of political obligation—and its novelty—is that the obligation is alleged to be generated by merely voluntarily "accepting" certain benefits of the cooperative political enterprise. And this is held to be significantly different from explicitly or even implicitly giving one's "consent" to the scheme as a whole. Thus, the fair-play account is to be regarded as proposing a ground for political obligation that is independent from "consent-based" approaches. Although the acceptance of legally generated benefits must be regarded as "voluntary" according to the fair-play approach, it is the acceptance of such benefits that generates the alleged political obligation, not giving one's consent to be governed by the political scheme.

II

It is often held that one condition of an adequate account of political obligation is that it supply the basis for an obligation to obey the law that is applicable to all (or nearly all) the individuals operating within the confines of a particular legal jurisdiction. For it seems that if the moral obligation to obey the law is to apply to *any* individuals to whom the laws are addressed, it must also (subject to various mitigating considerations) apply to *all* such individuals. Otherwise, there would appear to be a sort of moral inconsistency involved—an inherent inequity concerning the application of the moral obligation.

How can the principle of fair play satisfy this generality condition? One initially plausible approach is to center the obligation upon the acceptance of a special type of benefit that law provides. It might be claimed that restricting the application of the principle to those *public* goods that are provided by legal enterprises will suffice to ensure that all (or most) citizens affected by the operation of such systems will be brought within the scope of the political obligation. A public good can be characterized, for our purposes, by two features: (1) the good can be provided only by individuals working in cooperation with each other—it is a good generated by social cooperation; (2) once the good is provided for any individual within the group, it cannot, without significant difficulty, be excluded from other members of the group—it is a nonexcludable good.[4] Since a public good is a cooperatively generated good, it is highly relevant to the principle of fair play, which focuses exclusively upon goods generated by cooperative enterprises. And since a public good is nonexcludable, once it is provided for *any* members of the cooperative scheme, *all* such members must be regarded as benefiting from it. Thus, if we center the discussion upon the provision of legally generated *public* goods, the fair-play account might satisfy the generality condition of an adequate account of political obligation. All individuals affected by the cooperative scheme could be said to receive such public benefits of the scheme and thus, according to the principle of fair play, incur an obligation to comply with its requirements in the provision of such benefits.

It is at this point, however, that the virtue of this approach seems to be its major vice when applied to large-scale legal systems. The most serious problem here lies in the difficulty of providing a sense to the idea of individuals generally "voluntarily accepting" public benefits of a legal order. A. John Simmons has noted that the voluntary aspect of the acceptance of benefits is indeed essential to the application of the principle of fair play and goes on to suggest two ways this voluntary *acceptance* of benefits can be accomplished. To have accepted a benefit, Simmons suggests, an individual "must either (1) have tried to get (and succeeded in getting) the benefit or (2) have taken the benefit willingly and knowingly."[5] It seems that public benefits cannot be acquired in the first way (i.e., trying to get and succeeding in getting the benefit). It is hard to make sense of the idea that one "tried"—made some specific effort—to get a benefit that is gained by everyone regardless of any such effort.

We are thus led, according to Simmons, to consider the second way (i.e., taking the benefit willingly and knowingly) if we are to make any sense of accepting such public benefits. Simmons allows for the possibility of accepting public benefits in this way; however, this involves a number of restrictions which explain what it means to take a benefit "willingly" and "knowingly." He states:

> We cannot, for instance, regard the benefits as having been forced upon us against our will, or think that the benefits are not worth the price we must pay for them. And taking the benefits "knowingly" seems to involve an understanding of the status of those benefits relative to the party providing them. Thus, in the case of [public] benefits provided by a cooperative scheme, we must understand that the benefits *are* provided by the cooperative scheme in order to accept them.[6]

Once these restrictions are taken into account, Simmons believes the principle of fair play is not generally applicable in the political context. He states, "Surely most of us do not have these requisite attitudes toward or beliefs about the benefits of government. At least many citizens barely notice (and seem disinclined to think about) the benefits they receive."[7] If this is so, then the "acceptance conditions" necessary for this application of the principle of fair play with regard to political obligations cannot be expected to be *generally* satisfied, and the fair-play account is thereby undermined. Unless it can be shown (contrary to Simmons) that such legally generated public benefits *are* capable of being generally "accepted" in the proper sense by individuals affected by the operation of such legal enterprises, this fair-play account, which relies exclusively on the acceptance of such public benefits, must be regarded as a failure.

III

We must be able to *presume* generally that citizens in fact satisfy the "acceptance conditions" (noted by Simmons) with regard to some public benefit a system of law provides. What is required in the present context is that a further restriction be placed upon the *type* of benefit to which the fair-play account must appeal. A good beginning is to center the discussion on a public benefit of legal enterprises that can be presumed to be important enough to the satisfaction of a vast array of individuals' needs and wants, regardless of whatever other specific needs and wants they happen to have. In other words, if the public good can be regarded as akin to what Rawls has called a *primary good*—something that every person can be presumed to want regardless of his or her other specific desires or life plans—then we can at least presume that such a benefit will not have been forced upon individuals against their will and that it is (at least generally) worth the cost to gain it.[8] In this way, at least the first two acceptance conditions noted by Simmons might plausibly be regarded as presumptively satisfied by citizens generally with respect to any legally generated public goods that have, to use a term coined by George Klosko in this context, a "presumptively beneficial" character.[9] Whether individuals must also have a clear consciousness that the particular good is provided by social cooperation—whether the *third* acceptance condition mentioned by Simmons can be satisfied generally by citizens—will depend upon what specific candidate(s) we propose for this role. Specifying the appropriate presumptively beneficial public goods, then, is a major part of the burden that the proponent of the principle of fair play must overcome.

Are there any legally generated public goods that can satisfy these conditions? To answer this question, we must look not to certain particular goods that some or most governments provide but to a public benefit that functioning legal systems *as such* necessarily provide. In other words, one must correlate the obligation to obey the law with a presumptively beneficial public good that "law" necessarily provides. But to do this we will need a plausible conception of "law" itself. I believe we have at least the rudiments of what is needed in this regard in the legal theory presented by Lon L. Fuller in his *The Morality of Law.*

IV

One of the enduring values of Fuller's legal theory is the view that a legal system as such is essentially a purposive cooperative enterprise.[10] Law is defined by Fuller as "the enterprise of subjecting human conduct to the governance of rules." Its primary function is to provide a sound and stable framework for the interaction of citizens with one another. He states that "law furnishes a baseline for self-directed action, not a detailed set of instructions for accomplishing specific objectives." Note that Fuller is taking a view of law diametrically opposed to a view that conceives law on the model of a one-way projection of authority (from lawgiver to citizen). Law is not primarily a matter of an authority simply prescribing legally recognized rules but whether the legal enterprise is fulfilling its primary purpose. This "purposive" criterion for the existence of such systems is what is most distinctive about Fuller's theory.[11]

The way such systems operate to guide human conduct is to set up a general systematic framework of mutual expectations upon which individuals themselves can direct their actions and attain various ends without disrupting the stability of the society. Given some recognized rule and general compliance with it, an expectation concerning the actions of others will arise that can be the basis upon which one's own actions are directed. This phenomenon is clearly seen in the coordination provided by rules of the road. But it is also an element in any effective legal rule. It provides the basis for predicting what others, both citizens and government officials, can be expected to do. And this knowledge is essential for individual planning in any large-scale social context. Fuller is calling attention to the point that the primary legal purpose of *all* the rules of a legal system is to provide the overall societal framework of expectation within which stable social interaction is effected by self-directed individuals pursuing a wide variety of interests.

This systematic and widespread "framework of mutual expectations" pertains not only to mutual expectations between citizens (*as* citizens) but also to those between a government and its citizens. As Fuller states, "The existence of a relatively stable reciprocity of expectations between lawgiver and subject is part of the very idea of a functioning legal order."[12] An individual's ability to guide her own conduct by way of expectations arising from rules presupposes not only general compliance by other citizens but also a general cooperation on behalf of the government (the officials who enact, administrate, and enforce those

rules). If lawmakers did not enact and adequately promulgate rules or
the rules were confusing or inconsistent in some way or were continually
being administered and enforced in a haphazard or inconsistent fashion,
the citizens would not be in a position to guide their conduct successfully
according to rules. Compliance with such traditional principles of the
rule of law (what Fuller calls the principles of legality) is essential to the
fulfillment of the lawmakers' task. Without this, citizens would again be
at a loss as to how to conduct their affairs in socially interactive
situations with any semblance of stability or order because it would be
difficult if not impossible for them generally to obey them and thus set
up the necessary general framework of social expectations.[13]

Thus, we have a conception of law that is essentially a cooperative
enterprise not only between a citizen and other citizens but between
citizens and their governmental officials. A significant breakdown in the
cooperation between citizens and other citizens and/or between citizens
and their government will result in a failure to attain this purpose. And
any significant failure to attain this purpose, according to this conception
is a failure to maintain the very *existence* of the legal system.

Fuller's answer to the question of what legal systems do (as legal
systems and not some other means of social control) and what it
necessarily takes to fulfill this function is highly plausible. The twin
claims (1) that law has a primary function of providing the general basis
for a wide variety of self-directed action in a socially interactive context
and (2) that the fulfillment of this function depends essentially upon a
significant degree of cooperation on the part of both citizens and
lawmakers are not at all suspect. Indeed they appear to be eminently
true. It is this cooperative aspect of a functioning legal system, emphasized by Fuller, that provides the key to the appropriate application of
the principle of fair play and its ability to ground a *generally applicable*
moral obligation to obey the law. And that is the importance of this
aspect of Fuller's theory for our present purposes.

V

What benefits does a functioning legal system as such provide? What
benefits are provided for individuals simply in virtue of the fact that they
conduct their affairs in the context of an effectively functioning legal
system? One type of benefit can be seen in the following case. Suppose
some individual (call him Harold) wishes to have a peaceful, quiet picnic
with his family. Now Harold just happens to know of an ideal location
nearby where by city ordinance motor vehicles (such as motorcycles, etc.)
are forbidden. Loud motor vehicles have become quite prevalent in

Harold's community, and the number of quiet picnic spots has become correspondingly scarce. Because the ordinance is in effect and the expectation of general compliance by others and enforcement by officials is generated by the (promulgated) law, Harold and his family have their outing in that location and enjoy a quiet afternoon.

What Harold has done is to use part of the overall framework of expectations set up by the legal system to attain certain benefits (in this case, the benefit of a quiet afternoon picnic). The law (this particular ordinance and its systematic and coherent relations to the rest of the system) has been instrumental in attaining this benefit. For it is upon the expectations set up by the city ordinance that Harold was able to satisfy his desire for a quiet picnic. And this type of use of the framework of expectations set up by the system is not to be relegated to a minority of cases. On the contrary, it is commonplace in our legal experience.

Such benefits, actively gained by using the expectations generated by effective rules of the system, could be called *secondary benefits* of the system. This is because they are associated with various specific individual wants that are generally satisfied (or at least *able* to be generally satisfied) in a social setting only because the system as a whole provides a certain *primary benefit*. The primary benefit of a functioning legal system lies in the widespread framework for self-directed social interaction provided by the legal system itself. This framework, as Fuller has noted, provides the *baseline* from which the self-directed actions of the individuals are coordinated and the ground upon which so many of one's individual wants are satisfied within the context of social interaction.

This general framework for social interaction is, I believe, a "presumptively beneficial" good (to use Klosko's term). It precisely fits the definition of a *primary good* given by Rawls upon which Klosko grounds his notion. It is something any rational person can be presumed to want regardless of the person's other (specific) wants or life plans. This is because such a systematic and widespread framework for stable social interaction seems to be essential in gaining in any consistent or stable fashion what I have called the secondary benefits of a legal system. Without the primary benefit of a legal order, it would be extremely difficult to gain the vast array of personal wants in a stable manner when this is to be done in a context of broad social interaction. Knowledge of the expected behavior of others—provided by an effective legal framework—is essential for this. Thus, it can be presumed that (rational) individuals desiring to gain a variety of such personal "secondary" benefits *also* want the basic "primary" benefit provided by an effectively functioning legal system that allows them to do this.

The primary benefit of an effective legal system also appears to be a public good. First, it is clear that it is provided only as a result of the significant *cooperation* of individuals—citizens generally and lawmakers. The cooperation that is needed by lawmakers to effect and maintain such a framework is (at least) a significant compliance (in the making and administration of laws) with what Fuller called the principles of legality. The cooperation that is needed by citizens, on the other hand (once the lawmakers have properly done their task), is general obedience to such laws. A significant systemwide failure of cooperation in either of these ways results, as we have seen, in the failure to effect a functioning legal system and thus a failure to provide its primary benefit. Hence, the primary benefit of a functioning legal system is essentially a result of significant social cooperation.

A second condition of a good having a "public" character is that the good be nonexcludable. The primary benefit of a legal system also seems to satisfy this condition. It is clear that the primary benefit of a legal system, once it is provided for anyone in society, cannot without great inconvenience be avoided by anyone else in that society. One can deliberately refuse to use the social expectations set up by the system (and thus minimize one's acceptance of secondary benefits), but one cannot without considerable trouble avoid the general order and framework for mutual expectations maintained by it. One would have to refuse deliberately to take note of certain adequately promulgated and administered laws and the general expectations of the actions of others that are based upon them. This will be difficult with respect to any (recognizably just) legal system that significantly complies with the principles of legality. It is difficult to remain ignorant of such widespread grounds of social expectation generated by such a functioning system. In this way, the primary benefit cannot be easily avoided once it is provided socially.

VI

The relevance of calling attention to both the presumptively beneficial and the public nature of the primary benefit of a functioning legal system is to indicate that this particular scheme of cooperation provides a special benefit that all (or nearly all) individuals affected by the operation of the system can be presumed to "accept." The task at this point, however, is to make some sense of the idea of voluntarily accepting such a public benefit in this context. It will be recalled that Simmons has suggested three restrictions to "willingly and knowingly" accepting a public benefit: (1) it must not be regarded as having been forced upon us against our will; (2) we must not think that the benefit is not worth the price we must pay for it; (3) in the case of a public benefit provided by a cooperative scheme, we must *understand* that the benefit is provided by the cooperative scheme. Are these three conditions satisfied (generally) by citizens with regard to the primary benefit of a functioning legal system?

The ground upon which we can presume that this is so with regard to the first two conditions lies largely with the fact that the primary legal benefit has a presumptively beneficial character. Any minimally rational person can be presumed to want it regardless of any other specific wants (especially, as in the present context, where such wants must be satisfied in the context of broad social interaction). And individuals who are deemed candidates for political obligations can indeed be expected to have a minimally rational character—where this is taken to mean having a rationality of no greater degree than having some regard for the satisfaction of one's particular needs and desires and the means by which they can be satisfied. Thus, we can presume that such individuals generally do desire the widespread framework for social expectations provided by a legal system to satisfy so many of their other individual wants. It would seem irrational for individuals living in a social context *not* to want this benefit, at least not without some further special reason. This being so, it is not too much to presume that such a benefit is not in general forced upon such individuals against their will.

Also—barring unjust or repressive systems, which in Rawls's formulation do not come within the province of the principle of fair play anyway—it is not too much to presume that such a benefit is worth the price of at least general obedience to the rules of the system. It seems clear that rational persons would not give up the essential basis for the satisfaction of so many of their desires simply because this involves their *general* compliance with the rules of a (nonrepressive) system. There may be particular rules or perhaps whole systems where the burdens of such compliance are too great and the general presumption toward acceptance overturned. But I do not think that this casts doubt upon the general rationality of an initially favorable weighting of the primary legal benefit over the cost of general compliance to the rules of a reasonably nonrepressive legal system. The primary benefit is just too important for the satisfaction of so many other interests in a socially interactive context for it to be regarded as not worth the price—general compliance with the reasonably just rules of the system—we must pay for it.

Simmons's third condition for the acceptance of a public benefit—that we understand that the benefit is provided by the cooperative scheme—is the one that cannot be satisfied by merely pointing out the presumptively beneficial character of some good. The mere fact that some good is presumptively beneficial does not imply anything about whether the individuals acquiring such a good have a clear consciousness that it is provided by social cooperation. The objection pressed by Simmons, it will be recalled, is that with regard to large-scale cooperative enterprises like present legal systems there is no clear consciousness that social cooperation is providing the benefits. However, it is not too much to presume that adult citizens who do not suffer from some form of mental incompetence have the requisite understanding of the cooperative nature of a legal system's primary benefit. There is no need for one to be a social scientist or political philosopher to have this understanding. It demands merely an understanding that the usefulness of functioning laws in the pursuit of various individual wants is inherently tied to whether *others* (both citizens and lawmakers) are complying with the requirements of the system. Clearly, this knowledge is not so esoteric that it cannot be presumed to be possessed by nearly all mentally competent persons. Indeed, the use of such laws by citizens to gain secondary benefits of the system presupposes this knowledge. It is only because Harold *expected* social cooperation (i.e., general obedience by other citizens and enforcement by officials) with the city ordinance against loud motor vehicles in his picnic spot that he gained the benefit of a quiet picnic. Otherwise, he would have looked elsewhere. His action is premised upon his knowledge (or at least the reasonable expectation) of this type of social cooperation. And there is no reason to think that rationally competent individuals attempting to guide their actions within such systems cannot also be presumed to be aware of this.

This knowledge is not some "communitarian consciousness" in which individuals have a sense that they are closely bound together in solidarity for the achievement of some social goal. But this type of consciousness is not what is required for an individual to accept a public cooperative benefit in a knowing fashion. The understanding that the benefit is gained (only) as a result of the cooperative acts of others is all that is needed. And this can be presumed to be generally satisfied with regard to the framework for self-directed social interaction provided by an effective legal system.

Hence, the "acceptance conditions" stated by Simmons can be regarded as generally satisfied by citizens when we consider them in relation to the primary benefit of a functioning legal system and view the issue in terms of a general *presumption* regarding mentally competent citizens toward acceptance. Thus, it can be presumed that all (minimally rational) individuals operating in a reasonably just and effectively functioning legal system accept its primary benefit. And since this special benefit can be supplied only if there is general compliance with the overall requirements of the system, it follows according to the principle of fair play (at least as a matter of general presumption) that all such individuals have at least a prima facie moral obligation to comply with such requirements.

This presumption can be overturned on the basis of evidence to the contrary in particular cases, or other moral considerations might be relevant that could override such an obligation in such cases. But these possibilities for escaping the actual obligation in particular cases do not count against the general presumption of obligation established here. This being so, the fair-play account can account for at least a prima facie political obligation that is generally applicable to those individuals operating in an effective legal jurisdiction and thus, contrary to the type of attack pressed by Simmons, remains a viable basis for the general obligation to obey the law.

NOTES

1. H. L. A. Hart, "Are There Any Natural Rights?" *Philosophical Review* 63(1955), pp. 185–86.

2. John Rawls, "Legal Obligation and the Duty of Fair Play," in Sidney Hook, ed., *Law and Philosophy* (New York: New York University Press, 1964), pp. 3–18.

3. Ibid.

4. Two further features are sometimes associated with public goods: (1) once the good is gained by any individual in the group, there is no less available for the other members of the group—it is a good characterized by "jointness"; (2) all the individuals of the group are provided with (roughly) the same quantity or degree of the good. These are presented and discussed by Richard J. Arneson in "The Principle of Fairness and Free-Rider Problems," *Ethics* 92(1982), pp. 616–33.

5. A. John Simmons, *Moral Principles and Political Obligations* (Princeton, N.J.: Princeton University Press, 1979), p. 129.

6. Ibid.

7. Ibid., pp. 138–39.

8. Rawls's presentation of his notion of a "primary good" can be found in *A Theory of Justice* (Cambridge, Mass.: Harvard University Press, 1971), pp. 62, 92.

9. George Klosko, "The Principle of Fairness and Political Obligation," *Ethics* 92(1982), pp. 616–33, and especially, "Presumptive Benefit, Fairness, and Political Obligation," *Philosophy and Public Affairs* 16(3)(Summer 1987), pp. 241–59. I follow Klosko here in emphasizing the *importance* or *indispensability* of the goods in question. I do *not* follow him with regard to his apparent claim that this allows us to downplay the importance of showing that citizens generally satisfy certain "acceptance conditions"—even for presumptively beneficial goods. I believe, as Simmons has stated in response to Klosko, that the real importance of stressing the indispensability of certain public goods is not to preclude reliance upon showing such "acceptance" of the benefits but to give an indication of when it is most likely that all (or nearly all) citizens can be presumed to *satisfy* such conditions. See A. John Simmons, "The Anarchist Position: A Reply to Klosko and Senor," *Philosophy and Public Affairs* 16(3)(Summer 1987), pp. 270–75.

10. See especially Lon L. Fuller, *The Morality of Law*, rev. ed. (New Haven: Yale University Press, 1964).

11. Fuller, *Morality of Law,* pp. 106, 207–8, 210.

12. Ibid., p. 209.

13. Fuller lists eight "principles of legality" applicable to lawmakers that he believes are essential to the effective functioning of such a cooperative legal order. There must be general rules; they must be promulgated; there must not be too much retroactive legislation; the rules must be clear and understandable; they must not be contradictory; they must not require the impossible; they must not be changed too frequently; and there must be a congruence between the enacted legislation and its administration (Fuller's extended discussion of these principles is at *Morality of Law*, pp. 46–91). These principles combine to make up the "internal morality of law." Fuller was severely criticized for holding that these are in any way "moral" principles; they are more plausibly regarded as only principles of good legal craftsmanship. See H. L. A. Hart, "Book Review: *The Morality of Law* by Lon L. Fuller," 78 *Harv. L. Rev.* 1285–86 (1965); Marshall Cohen, "Law, Morality and Purpose," 10 *Villanova L. Rev.* 651 (1965); and Ronald Dworkin, "The Elusive Morality of Law," 10 *Villanova L. Rev.* 635 (1965). There is no need, for our purposes, to follow Fuller concerning the *moral* status of these principles. The claim that they are principles of good legal craftsmanship defining the essential forms of cooperation that lawmakers must adhere to if they are going to be able to ensure an *effective* and *functioning* legal system is all that is needed. It is an important, and enduring, value of Fuller's theory to have emphasized this aspect of the existence and maintenance of such systems.

3

Hard Cases and
No-Right-Answer Answers

DANIEL SKUBIK

Right Answers?

Does every dispute submitted for adjudication have a unique resolution that can be said to be the "right answer"? Alternatively, do judicial officials ever need to exercise a "strong" discretion to resolve a hard case just because no right answer exists? Put simply, do hard cases always have right answers?

In the contemporary jurisprudential debate on judicial decision making, Ronald Dworkin has stood virtually alone as an academic and lawyer asserting time and again that judges do not have to have discretion because there are right answers, even in hard cases.[1] In "Is There Really No Right Answer in Hard Cases?"[2] Dworkin defends his right-answer thesis against his construction and formalization of two versions of no-right-answer (NRA) theses. To develop this defense, he turns from previous tactics involving ordinary language analysis and critiques of judicial opinions to formalized logical constructions and the semantics of ordinary lawyers' adversarial discourse.

The following arguments attempt to show that

1.   Dworkin has misconstrued the meaning and force of his own construction of the bivalence thesis of dispositive concepts;

2.   he has misconceived his two no-right-answer theses, for there is only one significant NRA thesis embedded in his essay;

3.   because of these misconstructions, Dworkin has improperly formalized and explicated their arguments; and thus

4. he has failed to address successfully the conceptual challenges raised against his right-answer thesis. He cannot so simply dismiss NRA answers on logical or linguistic grounds, leaving his own right-answer thesis the only viable candidate.

Consequently, let it be clear that what follows is not an attempt to refute directly Dworkin's right-answer claims. The point is to demonstrate the inappropriate moves in his argument when employing logical formulas to construct and to refute NRA alternatives.

Bivalence Thesis of Dispositive Concepts

Dworkin begins his analysis with a characterization of "the 'bivalence thesis' about dispositive concepts: that is, that in every case *either* the positive claim, that the case falls under a dispositive concept, *or* the opposite claim, that it does not, must be true even when it is controversial which is true."[3] Thus, according to Dworkin, following ordinary lawyers' discourse, it can be said that (1) an exchange of promises either does or does not come under the dispositive concept of contract; (2) damage-causing action either does or does not come under the dispositive concept of tort; (3) specified conduct either does or does not come under the dispositive concept of crime; and so on. Bivalence might then be formalized

$$\forall x: (x \in L) \lor \sim(x \in L) \tag{1}$$

where for every "exchange of promises" either it is true that the exchange is an element within the legal set (contract) or it is true that it is not the case that the exchange is an element within the legal set (contract) (and so forth—making respective substitutions) with the understanding that this disjunction is not only obviously to be read exclusively (i.e., one disjunct or the other can be true, and not both: $[\alpha \lor \beta] \land \sim[\alpha \land \beta]$ where $b \equiv \sim\alpha$) but exhaustively as well (i.e., the two disjuncts are not simply contraries, but contradictories: $[\alpha \lor \sim\alpha]$ is necessarily true).[4]

But Dworkin then proceeds to make a stronger claim about the duty of a judge subsequent to the judge's determining whether, say, an exchange of promises does or does not come under contract: "If it does, then judges have at least a *prima facie* duty to enforce these promises if so requested within their jurisdiction; but if it does not, then they have at least a *prima facie* duty not to do so on contractual grounds."[5] This is mistaken. And it is an important mistake regarding a proper explication of the legal and logical relations underlying bivalence.

Let D_1 represent the function "the judge has a *prima facie* duty (pfd) to enforce," and let D_2 stand for the function "the judge has a pfd not to enforce." Thus

$$\exists x: (x \in L) \wedge D_1(x) \tag{2}$$

which can be read: For some exchange of promises found to come under contract, the judge has a pfd to enforce that exchange.[6] Similarly

$$\exists x: \sim(x \in L) \wedge \sim D_1(x) \tag{3}$$

which can be read: For some exchange of promises where it is not the case that it is found to come under contract, it is not the case that the judge has a pfd to enforce that exchange. But (3) is not truth-functionally equivalent to

$$\exists x: \sim(x \in L) \wedge D_2(x) \tag{4}$$

where the judge has a pfd not to enforce the exchange since D_2 is not the simple negation of D_1; it is a distinguishable duty.[7] Consider the functional difference from the judge's viewpoint: he lacks a pfd to enforce in (3) still leaves the question of enforcement open; his pfd not to enforce in (4) *prima facie* disposes of the question of enforcement, though that disposition is defeasible on balance or all things considered. Conversely, consider the tactical difference from the other side of the bench—from the litigants' viewpoint: (3) calls for reasoned argument from both sides before the disposition of the case goes either way; (4) requires a negative disposition unless the party for whom that disposition is adverse legally carries its burden of proof to overcome the judge's pfd of nonenforcement.

Now, $\sim D_1$ *might be rendered* functionally equivalent to D_2 in a particular legal system. It is certainly conceivable that judicial decision making might be subject to the rule " 'lack of a pfd to enforce' dictates that the judge 'has a pfd not to enforce.' "[8] But such notions of duty and interpretative bindingness must be part of a deeper, or at least parochial, theory of law and cannot be assumed in theoretic discussion.[9] Thus, contrary to Dworkin's interpretation,[10] while one can argue per the bivalence thesis *simpliciter* that every case in which the dispositive concept applies has *an* answer, it is not open to declare that every case in which the issue of whether the dispositive concept supplies dispositive reason for a particular judicial duty has even a *prima facie* answer, much less a right answer. As observed by Tony Honoré:

A system can be complete in a strong or weak sense. In the strong sense it is complete if it has rules which prescribe the answer to every problem that may occur, so that all the law is wholly predictable. We could make a legal system complete in this sense by inventing far-fetched rules: that every action which a rule does not forbid is permitted, that every transaction which is not validated by a rule is invalid, and so on. Armed with implausible gap-filling rules of this sort, we should have a complete but inflexible system. . . . If in the real world legal systems are complete, their completeness does not depend on the claim that the solution to every problem can be known in advance. It resides rather in the fact that the system has the resources to provide [I would interpolate "construct"] a solution to every problem.[11]

No-Right-Answer Theses

After constructing and setting forth his interpretation of the bivalence thesis, Dworkin moves to distinguish two NRA theses.[12] Both theses are said to reject the bivalence thesis as developed, but for significantly different reasons. Yet it can be shown that these two theses (NRA$_1$ and NRA$_2$), properly understood, merge into each other, and the resulting NRA thesis is quite compatible with the bivalence thesis as set out above. What *is* confuted is Dworkin's extended interpretation of duty, given his analysis of two-disjunct exhaustiveness.

NRA$_1$

According to Dworkin, the first version denies that the two-disjunct bivalence thesis is exhaustive. That is, NRA$_1$ holds the two disjuncts, $(x \in L)$ and $\sim(x \in L)$, to be contraries rather than contradictories. Thus, NRA$_1$ must hold some sort of trivalence thesis of the form $(p \lor \sim p \lor r)$, where r is a third possible position to hold given the facts of the case presented for judgment. He analogizes this analysis to the query "Is Tom a young man or an old man?" Since "old" is merely the contrary, and not the contradictory of "young," the question might be answered: "Tom is neither; he is middle-aged."[13]

Turning the analogy back to law, Dworkin argues that this first NRA version must then posit a three-variable response to, say, contractual validity: The contract is valid (i.e., the exchange of promises in question comes under the dispositive concept of contract); the contract is not valid (i.e., the exchange of promises in question does not come under the dispositive concept of contract); or the contract is inchoate (i.e., the contract is neither valid nor invalid). Since concepts such as "inchoate contract" are not to be found in lawyers' ordinary discourse or practice, he argues that a supporter of NRA_1 is hard-pressed to make a case against the exhaustive character of his bivalence thesis.[14]

But these moves are much too quick and are quite misleading. While a supporter of NRA_1 will surely deny Dworkin's assertion that his two-disjunct bivalence thesis is exhaustive as regards duty, the actual character of the posited third disjunct here is obscured by Dworkin's introducing an incongruous third category for r and his ignoring important types of legal discourse and the effect of shifting perspectives.

Let Δ represent "it is clear that," and p represent "the promises at bar do come under contract." Thus, Δp represents "it is clear that the promises at bar do come under contract" [i.e., "it is clear that $(x \in L)$"]. Similarly, $\Delta \sim p$ represents "it is clear that it is not the case that the promises at bar come under contract" [i.e., "it is clear that $\sim(x \in L)$"]. A supporter of NRA_1 will then assert that there may be a third category, $\aleph p$, where $\sim(\Delta p \vee \Delta \sim p)$, which represents "it is not the case either that it is clear that the promise(s) at bar do(es) come under contract or that it is clear that it is not the case that the promise(s) at bar do(es) come under contract" [i.e., $(\Delta p \vee \Delta \sim p)$ is significantly indeterminate antejudgment]. Thus, to the query "Does x constitute a promise or exchange of promises coming under contract?" a proponent of NRA_1 may respond: $(\Delta p \vee \Delta \sim p \vee \aleph p)$.[15]

Does this situation ever obtain? Consider the plight of an attorney who is attempting to advise a client with reference to a unilateral promise that on the one hand appears to come within the ambit of the conceptual category quasicontract (not inchoate) but on the other hand is not itself dispositive of legal obligation under currently developed doctrines of contract. That the attorney qualifies any advice "it generally appears that . . . , but it should be kept in mind that . . ." need be neither simply a legal realist's warning that no standards bind an arbiter on the point nor a rights-based concern that though there may be a right answer; judges, being fallible, sometimes get it wrong. Rather, such advice (regularly given) is a function of the lawyer's recognition and acceptance of a position as counselor and advocate whose office does not include the authority to dispose of contentious issues or cases.

Should it be feared that this way of putting the point is somehow question-begging, we need not rest the case here. Consider too, given ordinary legal discourse and practice, that $\aleph p$ is otherwise quite common. Is this not the very reason for much if not most litigation? Setting aside those few bad-faith cases where the defending litigant entertains no doubts regarding the validity of a contract, the illegality of its breach, and the certainty of a monetary judgment against him or her but who nonetheless forces the other party into court to delay collection, is not almost every good-faith case proceeding to trial and judgment a function of the inability of either party to persuade the other of the clarity of its respective (dispositive) position?[16] And is not the prime task of the judge to resolve $\aleph p$ into p or $\sim p$ for purposes of judgment?[17] Granted, the resolution of this disjunction and the subsequent judgment based upon some selected and justified categorization is a result of the judge's evaluative determination of the law and facts of the case.[18] Neither is it denied that the theory of adjudication this evaluative determination entails is the subject of extensive debate. But it should suffice to note there are no logical or practical incongruities in this NRA_1 position as Dworkin supposes he constructed.

NRA_2

According to Dworkin, the second version also denies that the two-disjunct bivalence thesis is exhaustive. Yet "it does not suppose that there is any third possibility" but simply denies "that one of the two available possibilities always holds, because it may not be true that either does."[19] Following the formalization of the bivalence thesis, we may write that NRA_2 holds

$$\forall x: (x \in L) \lor \sim(x \in L) \lor \sim[(x \in L) \lor \sim(x \in L)] \tag{5}$$

While formulating, *arguendo,* a substantive position grounded upon the concept of vagueness which might support NRA_2 Dworkin makes the following observation: "If 'ϕ' is a vague term, then there will be sentences of the form 'x is ϕ' that are true, others that are false, and still others that are neither true nor false. (This is different from the claim, which would be made by someone supporting the first version of the thesis [NRA_1], that in some cases 'x is ϕ' and 'x is not ϕ' are both false.)"[20]

Now, this is a curious observation. For unless he means to put the assertion " 'x is ϕ' is neither true nor false" in the at-judgment mouth of the judge,[21] what could it be taken to assert in the mouth of the litigants and their lawyers if not prejudgment $\aleph p$? That is, at time t_1 preceding the judge's declaration of judgment,

$$t_1: [NRA_2] \sim[(x \in L) \lor \sim(x \in L)] \equiv \aleph p \ [NRA_1] \tag{6}$$

which is resolved by the judgment at time t_2

$$t_2: [NRA_2] \ (x \in L) \ \text{or} \ \sim(x \in L) \equiv \Delta p \ \text{or} \ \Delta \sim p \ [NRA_1] \tag{7}$$

Similar semantic confusion surfaces again in Dworkin's argument *contra* mutual-entailment and truth-functional equivalence positivism where an attempted formalization goes awry: "If 'p' represents a proposition of law, and 'L(p)' expresses the fact that someone or some group has acted in a way that makes (p) true, then positivism holds that (p) cannot be true unless L(p) is true."[22] Mutual-entailment positivism then requires "for example, that Tom's contract is valid if a sovereign has commanded that contracts like his be enforced, and vice versa," while truth-functional equivalence requires "that whenever Tom's contract is valid it will always also be true that some sovereign has commanded judges to enforce contracts like his, and vice versa."[23]

This symbolization and explication is not quite right. If it were correct, Dworkin would be forced into a position wherefrom he quite rightly recognizes he might have to concede a form of semantic positivism (where p just means or is identical to $L[p]$), which would support NRA_1 against his interpretation of the bivalence thesis,[24] though he off-handedly dismisses semantic positivism as "indefensible."[25] Since it has been shown that the surface linguistic behavior of lawyers is perfectly explicable on the NRA_1 thesis, the debate must move to deeper adjudicative theories—a debate which Dworkin also admits may reveal the nonexistence of a right answer "in virtue of some more problematic type of indeterminacy or incommensurability in moral theory."[26]

For formalization of mutual-entailment or truth-functional positivism that is not reducible to semantic positivism, it will not suffice for p to represent a proposition of law. Rather, p must represent the statement "x is a proposition of law"; only then can we escape reverting to semantic positivistic formulae. Thus,

$$L(p) \otimes (x) \tag{8}$$

can be cashed out in entailment or truth-functional form[27] as

Rex has acted in a way that makes p true *entails* x is a proposition of law, and x is a proposition of law *entails* Rex has acted in a way that makes p true (8a)

or

It is true (false) that Rex has acted in a way that makes p true *iff* it is true (false) that x is a proposition of law (8b)

Also

$$L \sim(p) \otimes \sim(x) \tag{9}$$

which can be cashed out as

> Rex has acted in a way that makes p false *entails* it is not the case
> that x is a proposition of law, and vice versa   (9a)

or

> It is true (false) that Rex has acted in a way that makes p false *iff*
> it is not the case that it is true (false) that x is a proposition of law   (9b)

But just as D_2 was seen not to be equivalent to the simple negation
of D_1 in (3) and (4), the internal negation $L\sim(p)$ is not equivalent to the
simple external negation $\sim L(p)$ since the latter should be formalized

$$\sim L(p) \otimes \sim(x \lor \sim x) \tag{10}$$

and which should be interpreted

> It is not the case that Rex has acted in a way that makes p true
> *entails* it is not the case that either x is or x is not a proposition of law,
> and vice versa[28]   (10a)

or

> It is not the case that it is true (false) that Rex has acted in a way
> that makes p true *iff* it is not the case that either x is or x is not a
> proposition of law   (10b)

And (10), on either interpretation, *supports* NRA_2, contrary to Dworkin's
insistence that these internal and external negations necessarily collapse
and thereby provide an argument against NRA_2.[29] Neither need this
argument put NRA_1 in jeopardy, for as previously indicated (in [6])
proponents of both NRA_1 and NRA_2 are actually making the same
argument against a right-answer thesis modeled on Dworkin's interpretation of bivalence.

Concluding Observations

Now, Dworkin anticipates a variation on the argument last produced
and admits that his own argument fails against it. He notes that
propositions of law might be classed "inherently positive" or "inherently
negative" and that whatever is not prohibited is thereby permitted,

though he also claims that this is a reductionist program not fairly descriptive of legal practice.[30] Be that as it may, the argument proffered above is *not* identical to this anticipated one, though a positivist might so attempt to extend it (e.g., by arguing that prejudgment indeterminacy equates with civil permissions). We need not entertain the feasibility or fairness of such a project here. My point of our text is that Dworkin's argument is reductive in nature and misses fairly describing legal practice, however else it might fail.[31]

In short, Dworkin has not yet made his case secure for a determinate answer, much less a right answer, in every case from the lawyer's perspective. Nor has he made his thesis firm against the ascribed exercise of significant discretionary power in those classical and Hartian positivistic accounts so providing from the judge's perspective. At best, his failed attempt to devise and defeat a significant NRA thesis reveals that the disagreement envisioned is finally a deep one of moral and political theory and not one to be resolved at surface linguistic or formal levels of argument.

NOTES

1. See the series of essays and reply to critics collected in R. Dworkin, *Taking Rights Seriously* (Cambridge: Harvard University Press, 1977) with particular reference to essays 2–4, 13: "The Model of Rules I & II"; "Hard Cases"; and "Can Rights Be Controversial?" This strong right-answer thesis should be distinguished from various weaker theses exhibited in the legal theoretic writings of authors otherwise sympathetic to Dworkin's ordinary-language and case-law analyses. *Cf.* R. Sartorius, "Social Policy and Judicial Legislation," 8 *American Philosophical Quarterly* 151 (April 1971) ("judges should always reason *as if* there is a right answer, even when one does not exist," pp. 158–59); G. Fletcher, "Some Unwise Reflections about Discretion," 47 *Law and Contemporary Problems* 269 (Autumn 1984) ("we need not decide whether there is a 'truth' about the law—a right answer, as Dworkin claims" in order to attribute a commitment to justification, p. 285); and P. Weiler, "Two Models of Judicial Decision-Making," 46 *Canadian Bar Review* 406 (1968) (there may be a *"reasoned* way of *justifying* one solution as more *probable* than another," but the "creative work" of judging does not produce "demonstrably *the* right answer," p. 436).

2. In R. Dworkin, *A Matter of Principle* (Cambridge: Harvard University Press, 1985), p. 119. This chapter is a revised version of his article "No Right Answer?" 53 *New York University Law Review* 1 (April 1978), which is itself a revised and expanded version of his essay "No Right Answer?" in *Law, Morality, and Society: Essays in Honour of H. L. A. Hart,* eds. P. M. S. Hacker and J. Raz (Oxford: Clarendon Press, 1977) p. 58.

3. Dworkin, *Principle,* p. 120.

4. Dworkin makes this formal point in *Principle,* pp. 121–22. *Cf.* Michael Dummett's explication of four semantic principles and their corresponding logical laws in relation to his understanding and use of the terms "principle of bivalence," "principle of *tertium non datur,"* and "law of excluded middle": (i) the principle of bivalence, that every statement is either true or false, corresponds to the law of excluded middle; (ii) the principle of

exclusion corresponds to the law of contradiction; (iii) the principle of stability corresponds to the law of double negation; and (iv) the principle of *tertium non datur* corresponds to the law of excluded third. M. Dummett, *Truth and Other Enigmas* (Cambridge: Harvard University Press, 1978) p. xix. Thus, our formalization (1) corresponds to (i); the exclusivity reading corresponds to (ii); while Dworkin's rendering of his necessary-truth proposition is a functional combination of (iii) with (iv).

5. Dworkin, *Principle*, p. 120.

6. The stronger implication, $D_1(x)$ *because* $(x \in L)$, is often implicit, sometimes explicit, in legal discourse. But the weaker form here used in (2)–(4) suffices to illustrate our point.

7. This nonequivalence in deontic logic is basic. Indeed, it is so basic, it is thought pedantic to raise it. The point of introducing it here is just that Dworkin has ignored this distinction in his analysis.

8. *Cf.* Dworkin's remarks in *Principle* regarding a general theory of statutory interpretation that might include a rule of just this type, beginning at p. 129.

9. For a strong claim that some such closure rules are analytic from within at least one deeper theory of law, see J. Raz, "Legal Reasons, Sources and Gaps," *Archiv für Rechts und Sozialphilosophie:* 11 *Beiheft Neue Folge* 197, 215 (1979); revised and reprinted in his *The Authority of Law: Essays on Law and Morality* (New York: Oxford University Press, 1979), pp. 53, 77.

10. *Principle*, p. 120.

11. T. Honoré, *Making Law Bind: Essays Legal and Philosophical* (New York: Oxford University Press, 1987), p. 29.

12. These theses should be distinguished from the rather different summaries of NRA claims canvassed in Dworkin, *Taking Rights Seriously,* pp. 331–32. There Dworkin allows that one NRA claim might hold: In the rare case within even a developed legal system it is possible for no litigant to have a right to a decision when no prior rights exist; thus, there may be no right answer in any strong sense. But this concession has little to do with the NRA positions sketched here, where the (non)existence of prior rights is not at issue.

13. *Principle*, pp. 121–23.

14. *Principle*, pp. 123, 126.

15. A similar point is made in S. F. D. Guest, "Two Theories of Adjudication," in *Anglo-Polish Legal Essays,* ed. W. E. Butler (New York: Transnational Publishers, 1982), p. 1; though the form offered there is misleadingly conjunctive and the "slight modification" presented (at p. 8) seems to lack appreciation of the antejudgment time factor. More on this time factor below.

16. Criminal law as founded and practiced in common-law jurisdictions is excepted here; the prosecutor in all cases must overcome the initial presumption of innocence in favor of the criminal defendant with evidence of guilt beyond reasonable doubt; no defendant has a good-faith duty imposed by law to plead guilty. But it is a normative exception that proves the rule.

17. Note that this need for resolution is not to be confused with any subsequent controversy which may surround a "right answer" once a dispositive category is identified. Rather, the prior resolution is whether the dispositive category(-ies) put by the parties is(are) the appropriate one(s). Thus, a Dworkinian argument that any second-stage controversy can exist without impugning a right-answer thesis, correct as it may be, is no support for the further claim of logical incongruity within the NRA position here sketched.

18. See, e.g., J. Wróblewski, "Legal Language and Legal Interpretation," 4 *Law and Philosophy* 239 (1985), for a set of formalizations (similar to some of those offered here) covering "hard," "soft," and "fuzzy" language and a standardized form for justified interpretive decisions when some semantic or other form of fuzziness exists requiring normative evaluation to reach judgment.

19. *Principle,* p. 121.

20. *Principle,* pp. 129–30.

21. A placement he never makes, having all along presumed that a judge is settling the case one way or the other, rather than, say, declaring the dispute nonjusticiable; the putative controversy surrounds the judge's answer being "right."

22. *Principle,* p. 131.

23. *Principle,* pp. 132–33.

24. *Principle,* p. 132.

25. *Principle,* p. 405, n. 4. For more detailed construction and criticism of a semantic positivism that is "indefensible," see Dworkin's opening chapters in *Law's Empire* (Cambridge, Mass.: Belknap Press, 1986). But *cf.* recent criticisms of this approach in R. Gavison, "Legal Theory and the Problem of Sense," in *Issues in Contemporary Legal Philosophy* ed. R. Gavison (New York: Oxford University Press, 1987), p. 21 (claiming "Dworkin is constructing a straw man" and that positivism is not a semantic theory of law [at p. 23]), and B. Jackson, *Semiotics and Legal Theory* (Boston: Routledge and Kegan Paul, 1985) (claiming Hart's positivism is "a theory of legal pragmatics, dressed up in semantic clothing," while Dworkin is the one who provides "a semantic theory, masquerading as pragmatics" [at pp. 268–69]).

26. *Principle,* p. 144.

27. ⊗ being an empty placeholder for inserting entailment or truth-functional operators.

28. E.g., consider *q,* which might also represent the statement "*x* is a proposition of law," perhaps on other justificatory grounds and upon which Rex acts.

29. *Principle,* p. 133.

30. *Principle,* p. 406, n. 4.

31. The argument here should also be distinguished from the analysis and technically more complex formalizations advanced by Raz (e.g., through introduction of modal operators) against Dworkin's claims in his essay noted in note 9. There, a variety of NRA-type gaps are shown to be logically inescapable on a proper interpretation of Raz's sources thesis. While those demonstrations are of considerable interest, they seem to sidestep the thrust of Dworkin's challenge by requiring acceptance of some controversial theses to motivate the proofs (e.g., Raz's position on the concept of vagueness in his §3.2). Here, NRA answers are shown to be logically consistent with Dworkin's understanding of law and common-law legal systems and that his proffered formalized challenge has missed the mark.

4

Personal Autonomy, Institutions, and Moral Philosophy

EDWARD SANKOWSKI

I

Joseph Raz's *The Morality of Freedom* ranges over many topics, often illuminatingly. One concept important in Raz's contribution to the "political theory of liberalism" is the "ideal of personal autonomy." This essay is primarily about Raz's use of this concept. My main criticism is that Raz's position on autonomy and related matters is damaged by an omission: There is no detailed description and defense of institutional arrangements and practices connected with his ideal of personal autonomy.[1]

Raz does not think that he must extensively integrate his discussion of individual autonomy with a discussion of institutions. He accepts a distinction that implies that the avoidance of institutional issues in most of his current argument is a permissible strategy.

> Political theory can conveniently be divided into two parts: a political morality and a theory of institutions. Political morality consists in the principles which should guide political action. It provides the principles on the basis of which the theory of institutions constructs arguments for having political institutions of this character rather than that. Political morality also sets a goal as well as limits to the actions of those political institutions. But the principles of political morality themselves grow out of the concrete society with its own institutions. Their validity is limited by their background. In this way institutions shape the principles which are designed for the guidance and re-molding of these institutions. . . . In this book . . . we will not have the space to examine

34

the way the principles we will canvass should be translated into political institutions.[2]

Although Raz does not say this, at least two things may be meant by implying that principles might be "translated" into institutions. One sort of translation would involve explaining what institutional practices would satisfy the principles. Another sort of translation would involve justifying principles by setting out institutionally based considerations. That is, one justifies by (1) setting out arguments for the desirability and authoritative character of certain institutions and (2) showing that the dominant tendency among participants in the institutions would endorse those principles. Perhaps calling this latter activity translation is a bit odd, but whatever term we use, Raz seems to have such a justifying activity in mind in some parts of the book.[3] When Raz postpones development of a theory of institutions, he seems to postpone translation in both senses.

Raz suggests that a theory of institutions would be needed for some purposes to supplement the political morality he offers.[4] Such a two-part approach (this essay will contend) is very problematic. Political morality and the theory of institutions are so intimately connected that the philosopher must continually deal with issues in both areas. One cannot complete a major argument in one area without having recourse to an argument in the other. Raz himself sometimes finds it necessary self-consciously to disregard his bracketing of the theory of institutions. This is so, for example, in his discussion of the collective aspect of rights. Here he considers and favors the possibility of justifying some constitutional rights by appealing to the desirability and authoritative character of political institutions in which there is a division of powers between branches of government.[5]

In general, Raz deprives himself of an indispensable way of explicating the meaning of his claims about autonomy and justifying many of his moral views about autonomy when he postpones the critical discussion of institutions.

In Raz's account of autonomy, there are at least five major components: a verbal definition (or definitions) of *autonomy,* a list of "conditions of autonomy," examples to illustrate conceptual points about autonomy, a linkage of a virtue-concept (tolerance) with respect to autonomy, and discussions of principles and other moral generalizations (primarily about action) involving autonomy. In what follows I present a brief explanation of what is meant by *institution* and what is meant by my insistence that an account of autonomy should be connected with an account and defense of specified institutions. In the remainder of the chapter, I examine the five components of Raz's account of autonomy, showing how the absence of an institutional perspective damages each.

I describe and criticize the first three components of Raz's account in section III. I show in more detail in sections IV and V how the absence of an institutional perspective damages the fourth and fifth components.

Note that principles and generalizations involving autonomy are counted as a component of Raz's account of autonomy. This may seem peculiar. It should be realized, however, that Raz's concept of autonomy is a moral ideal valued by him, so it seems natural to include in his account of autonomy some of his views about how autonomy ought to be valued morally.

II

Raz offers no definition of an *institution*. Here I refer to an area of social life with a demarcable set of concepts and standards that function in coordination of interpersonal activity in that area.[6] There is much latitude about what institution-concepts could be selected for philosophical use or analysis. Examples of institutions as conceived here are the state in general; the contemporary Western liberal self-avowedly democratic state in particular; basic economic arrangements, including specific forms of capitalism or socialism; the family; schools; scientific activity; the art world; shared religious practices; medical practices. There are many other more or less specific institution-concepts, their specificity varying with place, time, or other aspects of social life.

Raz neglects the connection between autonomy and institutions in a way that damages his position. By *connection* I mean the following: First, suppose that a philosopher conceives of the autonomous person, thinking of autonomy as a politically significant ideal of character. Normally some assumptions must be made about the institutional circumstances that would render possible or facilitate the development and exercise of autonomy. Sometimes these assumptions are very general, such as assuming some morality. Sometimes these assumptions are more specific, such as assuming participation in particular forms of political or economic organization. To make it clear what is meant by autonomy and what is advocated when one advocates an ideal of autonomous character or a principle about autonomy, one needs to spell out and justify the institutional assumptions.

Second, more controversially, I maintain that the best way to defend one's moral principles (about autonomy or anything else) requires one to give an account of a appropriately constituted authoritative community, composed of individuals interacting within institutions. One must argue in support of the view that the dominant judgment of this community should be decisive about some range of moral questions. One must then assemble empirical, conceptual, and moral considerations to show that the dominant judgement of this community would be such and such. My criticism of Raz will for the most part not depend on accepting this approach to moral theory. It will be apparent, however, that on such an approach it is important to have an account of those institutions that supposedly provide the best imaginable social conditions for moral judgments (of a specific type) and important to have a justification of one's endorsement of such institutions.

Third, in connection specifically with what autonomy is and what moral attitudes we should take toward it, one needs to argue why this or that form of community will be best able to judge such matters. This point commends itself to reason whether or not one accepts the approach to moral theory advocated above. By mostly bracketing institutional questions, Raz dodges the genuine philosophical problem why Western liberal societies of the present should be thought of as best able to judge both what autonomy is and what moral attitudes we should take toward it. We may criticize Raz for neglecting to show *why* the principles of his political morality, and in particular his views about autonomy, are appropriate for the guiding and remolding of the institutions of Western liberal societies or any other society. Raz has no overall theory or similar device to answer these questions. He has arguments, often subtle ones, on particular moral questions but no overall foundation and no foundation for his views about autonomy. It is hardly enough to say cryptically about the ideal of autonomy, "Its suitability for our conditions and the deep roots it has by now acquired in our culture contribute to a powerful case for this ideal."[7]

III

In defining *autonomy,* Raz distinguishes personal from moral autonomy. He is primarily concerned with the former. He apparently regards the latter as a Kantian concept.[8] Yet what Raz means by personal autonomy is not very different from what some philosophers (including Kant-inspired philosophers) have meant by moral autonomy. Raz offers this definition: "An autonomous agent or person is one who has the capacity to be or to become significantly autonomous at least to a minimal degree. (Significantly) autonomous persons are those who can shape their life and determine its course. . . . In a word, significantly autonomous agents are part creators of their own moral world."[9]

This definition alternates between autonomy as a capacity-concept and autonomy as an exercise-concept. But it is clear that in most of the book Raz has in mind an exercise-concept; that is, one must actually choose autonomously to be autonomous. Thus Raz writes about "the conditions of autonomy" as preconditions that may render possible someone's actual autonomous decisions. Among the conditions of autonomy, Raz mentions these:

> If a person is to be a maker or author of his own life then he must have the mental abilities to form intentions of a sufficiently complex kind, and plan their execution. These include minimal rationality, the ability to comprehend the means required to realize his goals, the mental faculties necessary to plan actions, etc. For a person to enjoy an autonomous life he must actually use these faculties to choose what life to have. There must in other words be adequate options for him to choose from. Finally, his choice must be free from coercion and manipulation by others, he must be independent.[10]

So the major conditions of autonomy for Raz are appropriate mental abilities, adequate options, and independence.

In the course of explaining what he means by autonomy, Raz discusses some hypothetical examples.[11] The Man in the Pit is a person who has fallen into a pit from which he cannot escape in which there is enough food to survive. He can do little. He has certain choices, but these are obviously very circumscribed. The Hounded Woman, on a desert island hunted by a carnivorous animal, must devote her energies to staying alive. Both of these cases are used to illustrate what is not an autonomous life. Raz discusses other examples as well, but all told, examples do not play a major role in his account of autonomy.

Now, what Raz says in his definition, his conditions, and his examples is plausible. It is, however, woefully insufficient. One thing it lacks is realistic concreteness about background institutions alleged to be partially constitutive of the ideal of autonomy. Raz might perhaps agree with this criticism to some extent.[12] The root of the problem, however, is Raz's forswearing a discussion of institutions, a point Raz gives no indication of appreciating. Presumably the definition assumes (without explicitly designating) some range of background political institutions, economic practices providing for possibilities in job choices and property, possibilities in family or other personal aspects of life, schooling options, and so on. Phrases such as "autonomous persons . . . shape their life and determine its course . . . are part creators of their own moral world" must be applied. In applying them to individuals, one will be committing oneself to a moral attitude toward the institutional context of choice and action. One will commit oneself about answers to such questions as the following. Could one be "shaping one's own life" in a social environment dominated politically by American or Western European democracy? Soviet Marxism? Whatever one says about this (and eventually one will have to say something), it commits one to a way of connecting autonomy and institutions, to moral attitudes for or against the institutions. Even Raz's definition, if it is to have content and is to be applied to real-world examples, must be explicated in terms of which institutions are preferable to which (on grounds of the ideal of autonomy).

The conditions of autonomy also invite interpretation in terms of some institutional background, suitably evaluated. Take, for example, the "options" of which Raz writes. These seem to be objective conditions that allow for possible choices by an individual. Clearly, applying this idea of options to the real world requires confronting or at least committing oneself on moral questions about institutions. For example, is one option crucial for autonomy the sort of choice situation possible only against the background of a market economy? Again, one's answer to this will require some description of and moral commitment for or against a market economy. Raz actually claims that the free market is "a normative social institution" that is a "collective good."[13] In doing so he again trespasses into the theory of institutions, but without offering arguments for or against the claim that this institution is a collective good. Such arguments would be necessary to complete the case that market-generated options are essential to genuine autonomy. Consider also the condition of independence, which requires absence of coercion or manipulation. Both of these concepts are ideologically nonneutral. Deciding whether a person has been coerced or manipulated will require reflective understanding and evaluation of the workings of major social institutions.

Raz's hypothetical examples are undoubtedly useful for certain illustrative purposes. But the much harder cases that would need to be dealt with by political morality would require subtler discussion of what sorts of institutional relations involve weakening (or loss) or strengthening (or gain) in personal autonomy. We would need subtlety, variety of examples, and realism. Is an ordinary citizen-worker under contemporary capitalism or state socialism comparable to the Man in the Pit or the Hounded Woman? If so, why? If not, why not? Answering these or better questions would require a philosophy of institutions, including not just description but also expression of moral attitudes and justification of the attitudes.

IV

Raz thinks that tolerance as a moral virtue should be valued highly in any society that values autonomy.[14] This thought is plausible. However, Raz is vulnerable to two kinds of criticism. First, there are flaws in his account of tolerance. Second, Raz's emphasis on tolerance, as distinguished from other virtues vital for autonomy, is bound to be one-sided and inadequately supported without a discussion of the morality of institutions. These criticisms are elaborated below.

Raz writes of tolerance as a virtue and of the duty of toleration, but a virtue perspective is primary for him. Raz brings up the topic of tolerance in the context of his acceptance of moral pluralism.[15] This is the view that there are various forms and styles of life that involve different virtues and are incompatible. The attractive picture one derives from Raz's book is roughly this: An autonomy-supporting society will offer opportunities for choice among many distinct, even incompatible, options that have genuine but distinct, even incompatible, sorts of value. These choices include choices of lifestyle with concomitant virtues. One problem in such an environment is that it will be tempting for individuals to be intolerant of those who lead different lifestyles. Some of these lifestyles will be such that A will have genuine virtues (understood as such by A) that lead A to be inclined (a valuable inclination) to be intolerant of B, who also has genuine but rival virtues. "Toleration is a distinctive moral virtue only if it curbs desires, inclinations and convictions which are thought by the tolerant person to be in themselves desirable. Typically a person is tolerant if and only if he suppresses a desire to cause to another a harm or hurt which he thinks the other deserves."[16] Competitive pluralistic moralities are those allowing for virtues that involve intolerance of other virtues. On Raz's view, a society that furthers autonomy will need to put special emphasis on the virtue of tolerance, understood very crudely as the tendency to suppress hostile behavior toward persons who exemplify distinct, even incompatible virtues from one's own. Raz writes: "Toleration, then, is the curbing of an activity likely to be unwelcome to its recipient or of an inclination so to act which is in itself morally valuable and which is based on a dislike or an antagonism towards that person or a feature of his life, reflecting a judgment that these represent limitations or deficiencies in him, in order to let that person have his way or in order for him to gain or keep some advantage."[17]

Note that Raz writes in one passage of a desire the tolerant person thinks is morally valuable and in another passage of an inclination actually morally valuable and reflecting what the tolerant person thinks. These are very different views. Call the passages in which each view is expressed the "remark" and the "definition," respectively.

One weakness in Raz's concept of tolerance is that according to the remark on or the definition of tolerance, cases are not counted as toleration, strictly speaking, when A curbs an inclination in himself that A regards as bad or seriously questionable. This is surely odd, on ordinary usage. Ordinarily, A would be said to be tolerant if he struggles with and overcomes some unjustified dislike of a class of persons grounded mainly on the perception that they are different from A. A settled habit of overcoming dislikes based mainly on mere differences would be one manifestation of the virtue of tolerance.

This point should be linked with the criticism of Raz's omission of the theory of institutions. It is easy to imagine (indeed there are) institutional circumstances in which the sort of tolerance neglected by Raz would be an important virtue. Imagine an ethnically and racially diverse country. It has open immigration policies. It has a legal framework shaped partially by principles of nondiscrimination in the workplace, public schools, and housing. In these institutional circumstances, it is obvious that the encouragement of intergroup contact will require concern for tolerance of the kind neglected by Raz. The point might also have been noticed by Raz in John Stuart Mill's warnings about the desire for uniformity, warnings that assume a rather different institutional context.[18]

It is not merely that Raz's account neglects some subtleties of how we talk about tolerance but that background institutions will be an important determinant of which exercises of tolerance matter morally. This suggests that the value of an account of tolerance can be assessed only if we think in detail about what our actual institutions are, what they ought to be, and what difficulties the institutions generate. This claim can also be illustrated by considering another weakness in Raz's account.

Raz emphasizes as expressive of intolerance acts likely to be unwelcome to B, the potential victim of intolerant behavior. But it seems it could be tolerant to refrain from (and intolerant to engage in) behavior of a different sort, which Raz's account leaves out. Suppose that A is a powerful man of wealth or political influence who dislikes B's supposedly disruptive (but legally and morally justifiable) populist politics. B happens to be amenable to inducements to give up her politics. A knows that he could distract B from B's political activity by offering B money or attractive opportunities to do something else. B may welcome the money or other opportunities. Most people do. Yet A is intolerant of what B does if A succeeds in this scheme.

Raz says that there are noncoercive ways to be intolerant and that tolerance or intolerance depends on one's reasons, but he apparently does not see the implication for his account. Moreover, there is a general point behind this more particular and local criticism. In our Western liberal society many forms of social control are not only not coercive but not even likely to be unwelcome to the person controlled. Some of the major threats to autonomy, such as skillfully manipulative advertising or government propaganda, fall into this category. These practices may successfully implement intolerant attitudes the controllers have or exploit. A rather egoistic, consumption-oriented lifestyle and conformist, uncritically obedient political behavior are fostered by many of our institutions. Yet intolerant efforts to eliminate alternatives to such habits may use techniques to persuade, soothe, flatter, or bribe, rather than techniques likely to be unwelcome to the objects of manipulation. These are contemporary "institutional" reasons for emphasizing the point about the possible range of intolerant behavior. Raz has, however, deprived himself of the resource of a study of institutions that might challenge his picture of tolerance.

It might be objected to my point about welcome but intolerant behavior that it requires an implausibly extended use of *intolerant*. To this an appropriate reply could be as follows: First, intolerance can be conceived roughly as a matter of the intolerant person (A) acting on reasons that make A determined to eradicate B's acts or lifestyles to which A is hostile, determined even if this interferes with the autonomy of B and even if A wishes to avoid B's resistance or hostility. There seems nothing linguistically strained about calling some noncoercive instances of this intolerance. Second, suppose that one chooses another word (not *intolerance*) to describe the behavior and character trait. One could then make an argument that Raz's discussion of *tolerance* involves neglect of a vice (call it what you will). That vice detracts from respect for autonomy and should attract our attention for that reason.

The immediately preceding point leads us to a general problem about Raz's discussion of tolerance and autonomy, not a problem about his account of tolerance but why tolerance should be so central to one's account of an autonomy-supporting society. What reasons are there for focusing on the virtue of tolerance and not worrying about other virtues that may be equally crucial for autonomy? This request for reasons is a request for institutional reasons. Once again, we need a critical discussion of institutions in order to address a problem.

This is a general point about any moral philosophy that focuses on any virtue or set of virtues. Why those virtues? The answer (at least an important part) must always be in terms of some presupposed institutional background. There must be some institutional reasons why those sorts of virtues supposedly matter most. For example, some martial forms of courage will matter in a warlike society. The virtue of personal generosity, spending voluntarily on projects beneficial to the public, will matter in a society in which there is insufficient public provision for such projects and significant wealth in private hands. And so on. Why does such and such a virtue (e.g., tolerance) matter? Part of the answer must be that we have such and such institutions and such and such reasons for and against the institutions. The last clause is important. It is one thing to praise a virtue as crucial in the context of institutions deemed inadequate, another to praise a virtue in the context of institutions deemed sound. It must be made clear why that virtue is to be praised. Making this clear requires explaining one's views about the adequacy of the presupposed background institutions. The problem of providing a critical account of the institutional background of virtues is a difficulty for Raz, as it was for Aristotle.

Modern liberal pluralist societies generate a tendency toward excessive or inappropriate "tolerance" and intolerance.[19] This is a point about institutions, of course. Such "tolerance" is a vice rather than a virtue. Whatever term we use, it is a failure to develop and assert one's personal autonomy. Modern liberal pluralist societies encourage (in their less-attractive operations) acquiescence in evil behavior that the "tolerant" person feels it inappropriate to act against because such action is perceived as intolerant. It is common for individuals in modern liberal societies to have nihilistic self-doubts about their capacity to judge whether someone is acting or living wrongly. Worst, in modern liberal pluralistic societies it is common for the "tolerant" to manifest unreflective acceptance of the rules of the basic social framework. This framework is often defended as institutionalizing tolerance of variety in lifestyles even as it favors the interests and options of the wealthy and powerful. Any of these three traits (acquiescence, self-doubt, unreflective acceptance) might be called aspects of genuine tolerance and esteemed as part of virtue or disesteemed as "tolerance" and disesteemed as vice. Which way to go is mainly a matter of one's moral assessment of the tendencies of the institutional background.

I am inclined to see these as vices that deserve attention as such. Why does Raz not agree? To say why, he would need to delve into the theory of institutions. The identification and criticism of what have been called vices matters very much for autonomy. Which examples of virtues and vices one selects for attention will depend on an underlying morally motivated view about institutions. By omitting this, Raz has omitted something essential to evaluating his position about the importance as well as the definition and use of the concept of tolerance. A better approach would concede that the liberal political tradition that emphasizes tolerance and pluralism is often blind to the other traits mentioned and thereby lacks a full understanding of what matters for the encouragement of autonomy.

V

Next I consider selectively some major moral principles and other moral generalizations about autonomy that Raz offers as part of his political morality. This section will be confined to a number of interconnected topics chosen because they seem very basic and because of their implications for institutional issues. In general, Raz professes to offer an autonomy-based doctrine of political freedom. By this he seems to mean, roughly, that both the moral value of personal freedom and the political action that promotes personal freedom can be defended by showing the connection of such freedom with the autonomous life. In what follows the focus will be on autonomy and not on Raz's views about the relation between freedom and autonomy.[20]

First, Raz gives rather short shrift to explaining and justifying the value of autonomy. His argument also seems tortuous and elusive on this fundamental topic.[21] He seems to argue that one's well-being in an autonomy-enhancing culture depends on leading what is basically an autonomous life. If this is the right interpretation, the value of autonomy depends on the social forms of those societies that incorporate concern for the conditions of autonomy. Raz unfortunately seems to assume, without argument or consideration of alternative views, that many social changes in Western societies are obviously changes that favor assigning a higher value to autonomy. He gives as examples changes in attitudes about marriage and work, changes in which individual choice of partner or job is viewed as increasingly important. But Raz's argument equivocates. At times it seems to say that the standards of well-being that incorporate a high regard for autonomy can be justified by appeal to the social forms of many modernized or modernizing societies. At other times it seems to be that goods necessary if one is to prosper can be obtained only by being autonomous if one lives in an autonomy-valuing culture.

The defect of the argument on the first interpretation is that it provides inadequate support for the claim that our modern liberal cultures really do value autonomy and are generally competent to understand what it is and why it is valuable. Of course, providing adequate support would require contributing to the theory of institutions. One defect of the argument on the second interpretation is that more empirical evidence would be necessary to support an empirical thesis that autonomy is necessary for prospering. Another is that the most that such an argument could establish would be the instrumental value of autonomy for the prospering individuals, a disappointingly limited result.

Though Raz provides only murky arguments for the value of autonomy, it is plausible to maintain as he does that autonomy is a

valuable ingredient in well-being. I will consider some further generalizations and principles about autonomy, assuming that it is valuable both
intrinsically and instrumentally.

Raz refers to "the duty of respect for autonomy."[22] It is not clear
exactly what the relation is between the duty of respect for autonomy
and "the principles of autonomy . . . the principle requiring people to
secure the conditions of autonomy for all people."[23] Perhaps the claim
that one has the duty is thought derivable from the principle of
autonomy. Raz points out (correctly in my opinion) that one's duties are
not only not to coerce or manipulate but to provide help in developing
the inner capacities for autonomy and to create an appropriate range of
(presumably objective, situational) options for persons to choose among.

The major omission noticeable at this point is that Raz says nothing
useful about distributive questions concerning the conditions of
autonomy. His "principle of autonomy" says that we have a duty to
secure conditions of autonomy for all people. What if a social policy we
might support does something to improve prospects for autonomy for all
but much more for some? What about the relative distribution of
conditions for autonomy in the population governed by a political system
and those outside that population? These would be problems, whether
autonomy was a matter of degree or not. But especially since autonomy
is a matter of degree, we shall often face hard choices in which prospects
for some persons' greater gains in autonomy would have to be balanced
against prospects for lesser gains in autonomy for others. Consider
educational funding policies by which we might fund different mixes of
school and mass-media programs. Some such policies might arguably
increase the autonomy of all citizens to some degree. But different
funding policies within this category would produce different distribu-
tions in prospects for varying increases in autonomy. Raz's references to
the duty of respect for autonomy and the principle of autonomy offer no
relevant guidance.

Elsewhere there is a negative discussion of one class of distributive
theories, egalitarianism.[24] Raz, however, does not apply this discussion
specifically to autonomy. And Raz does not explain or support any
worked-out nonegalitarian distributive principles. Yet such principles
would surely be necessary in the political morality Raz regards as distinct
from the theory of institutions.[25] The best way to state and test such
principles would require extensive reference to the theory of institutions—a discussion from a moral point of view of the good and bad
points of various institutional possibilities together with an account of
what principles would be embraced as a predominant view under those
institutions.

Raz sees no value in providing people with options that are bad.[26]

This generalization could be regarded as an extension of his principle of autonomy. Raz says that we cannot make someone autonomous but that we can provide the conditions for autonomy and should do so for all. In doing this, as the principle of autonomy requires, we should provide people with the conditions for an autonomy that could be valuable (presumably in its exercise). There is nothing valuable about an autonomously chosen bad life for Raz. While these views are plausible, they are excessively abstract and sketchy, as well as somewhat threatening as political philosophy. What are the standards for judging which exercises of autonomy are good? Raz does not say.

Why should we not fear what might be done by a government that announces a desire to improve the conditions of autonomy for all? Suppose it also insists that it will provide only the conditions for an autonomy that is valuable in its exercise while refusing to say what the standards of value will be or who will decide this question. This will increase our anxiety. Raz has written of the ideal of autonomy as the ideal of free and conscious self-creation. Yet nothing in Raz's approach rules out oppressive political manipulation of individuals with the justification that society is encouraging the autonomous choice of good options.

These worries are generated by Raz's willingness to say that autonomy is valuable only if exercised in good choices. We should demand an institutional interpretation and illustration of this, a description and defense of the institutional structures by which "good choices" would be identified while individual autonomy would be protected against political oppression.

Raz's reference to a good independent of autonomy also raises questions about the extent to which his position is autonomy-based. These questions would have arisen anyhow, given his endorsement of value pluralism.

The best hope mentioned by Raz for some restriction on abuses of state activism would be his reinterpreted *harm* principle. Let us turn to Raz's discussion of this. Raz places himself in the tradition of John Stuart Mill, in the sense that Raz considers himself a liberal, one supposes in the sense that Raz wishes to set limits on state action with the harm principle. Raz, however, abandons Mill's antipaternalism, so we are left with a principle that says it is permissible for the state to act coercively only to prevent harm, whether to self or others.[27]

It is a further interesting feature of Raz's position that he interprets harm as damage to autonomy. The harm principle is "defensible in the light of the principle of autonomy" on his view. The details of the defense are never worked out. It is nonetheless clear that Raz accepts the harm principle, even though he writes of the necessity to go "beyond" it. State coercion interferes with autonomy, so it cannot be justifiable unless the coercion encourages autonomy by preventing harm. It is in Raz's view a necessary (not a sufficient) condition for justifiable state coercion that it promotes autonomy by preventing harm, where harm is construed as damage to well-being. The reason why harm prevention can sometimes justify coercion for Raz is that harm interferes with autonomy.[28]

I am sympathetic to abandoning Mill's antipaternalism. Cases of justifiable state paternalism (in particular), state control of persons for their own good, are so numerous that antipaternalism is not a credible proposal for public policy. A recent sophisticated liberal, Joel Feinberg, preserves some of the attitudes of Mill's antipaternalism but allows many policies Mill would have rejected.[29] There is no special problem for an autonomy-based theory in admitting a substantial measure of paternalism, including state paternalism. As Gerald Dworkin implied years ago, a rather substantial measure of paternalism could be justified on the grounds that it helps preserve or extend autonomy.[30]

The main problem about Raz's position on the harm principle is not that he accepts paternalism but that the principle no longer does much to restrict state coercion. Nor does it make clear enough the nature of the limits it sets on state coercion. Or rather, the limits on state coercion and manipulation are not made clear. Raz perceptively remarks that either coercion or manipulation can limit autonomy.[31] The main problem is that much objectionable state coercion or manipulation could arguably be defended on grounds that such coercion or manipulation is necessary to prevent harm as interference with autonomy. Also, in most cases the issue will become one of balancing gains and losses in autonomy, and Raz neglects the principled ways such balancing might be decided. My main objection is that at this level of generality, the harm principle provides little or no protection against objectionable acts of state coercion or manipulation.

One way to make clearer what might be protected by the harm principle would be to provide an institutional interpretation of the principle. That is, one needs to say what institutional arrangements and practices one has in mind in saying that an individual has a suitable level of autonomy or that an individual's autonomy would be illegitimately affected if the state were to support a particular coercive policy. Even legitimate policies often negatively affect the autonomy of some persons, and nonlegitimate policies might be defended as preventing someone's loss of autonomy. Raz lacks an institutional interpretation and defense of what an individual should be able to expect about the appropriate sort of autonomy the state will be required not to neglect or undermine. We cannot possibly get what is needed from an account of autonomy composed of the Razian definition, conditions, examples, discussion of tolerance, and moral generalizations such as the principle of autonomy and the reinterpreted harm principle.

VI

In closing, it is worth noting that there is a conflict between two features of Raz's book. (1) He purports to reject (humanistic) individualism, "the doctrine that only states of individual human beings, or aspects of their lives, can be intrinsically good or valuable."[32] He affirms the existence of collective goods. These include the existence of some communities (including institutionalized practices). Reference to such communities (e.g., religious or economic communities), he claims, clarifies, among other things, the role and justification of fundamental rights.[33] (2) He purports to be able (for the most part) to avoid the "theory of institutions" in this book that he conceives of as an essay in "political morality."

My criticism of Raz's bracketing of the theory of institutions might also be read as a sympathetic extension of some of the anti-individualist aspects of his position. But it must be emphasized that such an extension requires a thoroughgoing change in strategy. The theory of institutions would better be understood as more fundamental than political morality, the former providing arguments for the principles and other claims of the latter, even as the two are conceived as inseparable. I do not aim to demonstrate the thesis that the theory of institutions is more fundamental than political morality, though I have included evidence that some of Raz's arguments tend to confirm the thesis. What I do claim to show is the damage done to Raz's account of autonomy by the omission of a theory of institutions.[34]

NOTES

1. Joseph Raz, *The Morality of Freedom* (Oxford: Oxford University Press, 1986), p. 1; see especially part 5, chaps. 14 and 15, for the bulk of Raz's account of autonomy.

2. Raz, *Morality*, p. 3.

3. See note 5 for a reference to a part of Raz's argument in which he provides a justification fitting the pattern described. See also Raz's section on the value of autonomy, referred to in note 21 below. On one interpretation of that section, Raz's argument for the value of autonomy is a justification fitting the pattern described.

4. See, for example, *Morality*, p. 428.

5. See *Morality*, pp. 250–63, especially p. 257.

6. Compare the definition of *institution* in John Rawls, *A Theory of Justice* (Cambridge, Mass.: Harvard University Press, 1971), p. 55; the concepts of a "practice" and

an "institution" in Alasdair MacIntyre, *After Virtue* (Notre Dame, Ind.: University of Notre Dame Press, 1981), especially pp. 175–77, 181, 206; the concept of an "institution" in Lawrence Haworth, *Autonomy—An Essay in Philosophical Psychology and Ethics* (New Haven and London: Yale University Press, 1986), especially p. 110. These concepts are not identical with one another or with the definition in this essay, but probably any of the other accounts would serve the purposes of this essay.

7. *Morality*, p. 370.

8. *Morality*, p. 370, note 2.

9. *Morality*, p. 154.

10. *Morality*, pp. 372–73.

11. See *Morality*, pp. 373–74, and also the "rather artificial and extreme example" given on p. 379.

12. *Morality*, p. 375.

13. *Morality*, pp. 252–53.

14. See *Morality*, "Pluralism and Intolerance," pp. 401–7.

15. See *Morality*, "Value Pluralism," pp. 395–99, and "Pluralism and Intolerance," pp. 401–7.

16. *Morality*, pp. 401–2.

17. *Morality*, p. 402.

18. See *On Liberty*, especially chap. 3, on individuality.

19. See Herbert Marcuse, "Repressive Tolerance," in Robert P. Wolff, Barrington Moore, Jr., and Herbert Marcuse, *A Critique of Pure Tolerance* (Boston: Beacon Press, 1965). Although my position is rather different from that of Marcuse, it is worth comparing the two.

20. For some of Raz's views about the relation between freedom and autonomy, see especially *Morality*, chap. 15.

21. See *Morality*, "The Value of Autonomy," pp. 390–95.

22. *Morality*, p. 407.

23. *Morality*, p. 408.

24. See *Morality*, chap. 9, "Equality," pp. 217–44, especially sec. 8, "The Rejection of Egalitarianism," pp. 240–44.

25. No doubt Raz omits distributive principles because he thinks that the distinctive political contribution of liberalism has not concerned justice, and this is a book about liberalism. See *Morality*, p. 2. But such considerations about distinctiveness do not address genuine problems for liberals or anyone else who values autonomy about the distribution of the conditions of autonomy.

26. *Morality*, pp. 380, 411–12.

27. *Morality*, pp. 412–13.

28. See *Morality*, "Autonomy and the Harm Principle," pp. 412–20, especially p. 419.

29. Joel Feinberg, *Harm to Self* (New York and Oxford: Oxford University Press, 1986) for a recent discussion of liberalism, paternalism, autonomy, and related concepts.

30. Gerald Dworkin, "Paternalism," in *Morality and the Law,* ed. Richard A. Wasserstrom (Belmont, Calif.: Wadsworth, 1971).

31. *Morality*, pp. 420–21.

32. *Morality*, p. 18.

33. *Morality*, pp. 250–55.

34. A useful recent volume on the works of Raz, including discussions of *The Morality of Freedom,* is 62 *Southern California Law Review* Nos. 3, 4 (March–May 1989). Some helpful recent book reviews are those by Roger Shiner, *Philosophy* 63(January 1988), pp. 119–22; Gerald Dworkin, *Ethics* 98(4)(July 1988), pp. 850–52; and John Martin Fischer, *Philosophical Review* 98(2)(April 1989), pp. 254–57. See also the critical notice by W. J. Waluchow, *Canadian Journal of Philosophy* 19(3)(September 1989), pp. 477–90.

5

Sharing Responsibility:
The Logic of *We* and *We, Qua . . .*

J. K. SWINDLER

I

Ipropose to explore some aspects of the language and logic of collective agency. I assume that no group of people is a person; hence in some way every collective action can be understood as constituted by the actions of members of the collective. It is also clear that for many ordinary purposes, though not for all, we do not bother producing an appropriate analysis. So our language often suggests that we take groups as irreducible agents. The commonest and logically the most primitive form of attribution of actions to groups occurs with use of the first-person-plural subject *we*. My focus is on the first rather than the second or third person because I am interested in genuine actions and I am Kantian (perhaps Hegelian) enough to think that the self-consciousness, which is a necessary condition of genuine agency, is, in the appropriate sense, expressed only by that grammatical form.

In the literature there are three possible positions we need to examine: John Ladd's, that organized collectives are not persons, so have no moral properties; Peter French's, that organized collectives are persons possessing moral properties; and the reductivist alternative of David Copp and perhaps Larry May, which holds that organized collectives are personlike and that their properties are logically and perhaps causally reducible to those of their constituents.

My view is that French and Ladd nurture their respective views with only a relatively narrow range of English locutions and that they are both misled by ignoring or not emphasizing others. They generally attend only to third-person constructions that ascribe collective agency to groups of which one is not a member. French is led by the fact that we often use proper names for conglomerates, like Exxon or the PLO, and the fact that we often attribute moral (as well as legal) properties to conglomerates—"Exxon decides to . . ." or "The PLO attacked . . ."—into holding that conglomerates are moral individuals. Ladd, on the other hand, is led by the fact that we normally distribute moral attributions within associations—"Exxon cheated me; *they* billed me twice" or "The PLO denounced terrorism; Arafat said the magic words"—into holding that associations have no moral properties and that they are not individuals. What I want to suggest is that we can preserve all aspects of the relevant locutions by maintaining with French that groups can have moral properties, but with Ladd that they are not individuals. The key is to understand the moral ascriptions reductively.

II

If we can make out a reasonably clear case for a moderate reductionism, we will be able to see that irreducibly holistic ascription of actions to groups is not only needless reification but is simply a kind of category mistake, the ascription to collectives of properties and relations only logically ascribable to noncollectives, individual agents capable of awareness of their own agency.

Out of charity we should note that this particular kind of category mistake is understandable, for it seems grounded in an involuntary and normal activity of the mind—synthesis of objects from aggregates of objects, forests from trees, figures from lines, numbers from units, machines from parts, paintings from scraps of paint; in general, wholes from parts. Often ordinary language can be depended upon to tell us what predicates apply to the parts and what to the whole, but there are limits. If we rebuild a car part by part, ordinary English gives us no clue about when we have a new car. Nor, if we recharacterize an object or species property by property, is there a univocal ordinary language guide that informs us when we no longer have Socrates but a new person, no longer drosophila but a new species of fly. Sometimes, though, it is quite clear how many parts of members, and in what order, are necessary and sufficient for a certain kind of whole. The best examples are in team sports or military organizations where clear-cut rules lay down necessary and sufficient conditions of identity for such collectives. Good natural examples are supplied by descriptions of chemical composition.

Since the identities of many collectives, like nations and corporations, are flexible enough to leave us comfortable with applying the same names to them through substantial changes not only in their members but in their goals and structure, the analogy Ladd draws between formal organizations and machines can be quite misleading. An organization's internal decision structure is much more like a blueprint for a machine than an individual machine; a corporate office is a kind of universal and as such does not entail any particular action by any particular officer. Moreover, unlike any possible machine, the constituents of corporations are themselves moral agents, hence capable of revising or ignoring, as well as implementing, any aim, plan, or structure of the organization.

It is important to see that collectives, even large ones, can be organized in many essentially different ways, some rigid, some not, and that group structure can change dramatically without disturbing the identity of the group. The upshot is that group identity is largely a conventional matter and that it is largely irrelevant to the ascription of moral and other complex relational properties to groups. Or at most, having a rigid division of labor makes precise division of accountability possible internally, but even without it, externally one can still legitimately ascribe moral responsibility. But more importantly, no organizational structure is necessary for a group member to ascribe collective agency and responsibility using the first-person plural. Even quite unorganized and spontaneous mobs, like those present in the Overtown section of Miami during the recent riots, can normally and unobjectionably be morally characterized by their members and by observers.

French has made much holistic ado about the use of proper names to denote corporations. Supposedly following Kripke, he construes them as rigid designators and concludes that the corporations they denote are individuals. I doubt that even Kripke would applaud this use of his theory. Here I would like to direct attention to what seems to me the more basic logical and grammatical issue, namely the conditions of use for the word *we* and the categorically acceptable properties of the referents of *we*. The reason that the conditions of use for *we* are more basic than talk about names of groups is, as Quine has maintained, that pronouns are logically more basic than names and that, as I suggested, for the purpose of tracking accountability of actions, what is really at stake is *self*-ascription of moral properties.

The first point I want to make about the logic of *we* is that one may correctly reason as follows: (1) I have property P; (2) you have property P; therefore, (3) we have property P. (And vice versa, from we have P to I and you have P.) I will call this the *rule of collective instantiation*. This, I claim, is a valid rule of inference in English, and transparently so. Moreover, it holds whatever and however complex property P might be. It holds for physical, dispositional, causal, modal, intentional, moral, and institutional properties and relations. And its importance is that proper names can be substituted for any of the pronouns, *I, you,* and *we,* without any implication that the subject of the conclusion is singular and not plural.

But as with any inference rule, care is needed in using this one. If I have a cousin and you have cousin, it does not follow that we have the same cousin. If I pay my taxes and you pay yours, it follows that we pay our taxes but by no means that our taxes are the same. So in many cases the plural ascription will be of the same kind but not necessarily of the same instance.

Sometimes we want to conclude more than this simple rule will allow. If you and I are the only members of a moving company and our job today has been to move a piano upstairs, it will be true that I helped move the piano and you helped move the piano and therefore that we both helped move the piano. But if we introduce closure, a premise to the effect that no one else helped, then we can conclude not merely that we *helped* move the piano but that we *moved* the piano. Our collective action was sufficient to the task. The reverse inference is likewise interesting. "We moved the piano" does not entail that I moved the piano, only that I helped move the piano. Why? Because normally the inference should be understood to contain a suppressed premise to the effect that I can't move a piano alone. Let's call this the *two-to-tango rule,* which will say that when the property or relation ascribed to a group is not, for logical, categorical, or causal reasons, ascribable to any of its members, that property or relation may be ascribed to the members only distributively and not wholly to any one. At the very least we may say that even if no member of a group has some specific property of a group, like being able to lift two thousand pounds or being wholly responsible for the explosion of the *Challenger* space shuttle, still some member of the group has a relevant generic property, like being able to lift part of the weight or being partly responsible for the O-ring's failure.

To allay fears of compositional fallacies, we must admit, of course, that *certain* properties of individuals are not ascribable to the groups they constitute, like age and weight, and vice versa. But there is ambiguity here. If I say, "I weigh 150, and you weigh 150," I may draw two different conclusions: either "We weigh 150" or "We weigh 300." To disambiguate, it is sufficient to add a qualifier to each conclusion, thus: "We weigh 150 *each*" and "We weigh 300 *together.*"

On the other hand, moral predicates do not behave in this way. They are ascribable to groups only because they are ascribable to their members. Furthermore, the properties relevant to moral accountability, like intention, decision, desire, interest, are ascribable to groups only if their members can ascribe them to themselves. This follows from the fact, emphasized by Kant, that moral agents are essentially self-conscious since this is a necessary condition of being responsible either for not making an exception of oneself or for the consequences of one's action. In general, the properties of groups that are due merely to their being groups are irrelevant to their being persons, and the moral and mental properties of groups are not due to their being groups particularly but to their being groups of individuals with moral and mental properties.

With these qualifications in mind, we can say that it is a necessary and sufficient condition of the use of *we* that the speaker be able to correctly make the same attribution using *I* and *you*. Indeed, a group can never refer to itself with the singular pronoun. Its reference to itself is ersatz reference. It refers to itself only through its constituents' use of the first-person plural. *We* denotes its user together with someone else. *We*, like *I*, is the subject of both physical and mental predicates. The use of *we* requires that two or more individuals are subjects and subjects of the same predicates. Finally, the identity of *we*, a group, usually depends on institutional conventions categorizing the individual constituents of the group by selections of their properties. It follows that group identity is constituted by member identities, that group actions are reducible to actions of members contextually defined, and that groups have normative properties if and only if their members have those same properties, either individually or distributively. Thus, we can make sense of ascriptions or moral and other intentional predicates to groups (contra Ladd) without admitting that social groups are in any sense irreducible subjects of such predicates (contra French).

III

Besides joining forces and carrying out projects in direct union with one another, we often consider that the action of some subgroup or someone outside the group is tantamount to the action of the whole. Our breasts may swell at "We the people," but the actions begun with those words were the actions of only a few. The rest acted vicariously, if at all. Vicarious action is, in my view, no less reducible to the basic actions of individuals than direct collective action. And not surprisingly, we find grammatical and logical rules governing the first-person-plural expression of vicarious action not unlike those described for direct action.

The topic now is the use of the phrase *we, qua* . . . and its cognates. The members of the constitutional convention may literally have thought of themselves as the people, but it seems more likely that they meant and certainly they should have meant "We, *qua* agents of the people" since they were exercising powers authorized by their constituents. Since among competent agents (an exception is necessary here for action for another not capable of acting for himself) vicarious agency is constituted only by direct authorization of individual agents, we may ask whether the lines of responsibility for resulting collective action descends back down the chain of authority all the way to the constituents. And just as individual responsibility is limited by what powers the individual has in the case of direct collective action, so it is in the case of vicarious collective responsibility. *Ought* implies *can;* one is accountable only for what one can do. If a constituent would not have been able to do alone what his agent has done in his name, he is not responsible for the whole action and its consequences but only for what he could have done alone.

In terms of the rule of collective instantiation noted earlier for *we,* what this point challenges is the inference from "We act thus" to "You and I act thus." Disambiguating the premise yields either "We act thus" or "We, qua agents, act thus." "We act thus" does indeed imply that you and I, the relevant constituents, act thus. But "We, qua agents, act thus" supports no such implication. Here is the logical contrast between direct and vicarious agency. My authorization of an agent's action is sufficient only if I could have done single-handedly what my agent does. If his action exceeds my powers, my authorization is insufficient and my responsibility only partial. Here we have extended the two-to-tango rule into the context of vicarious agency. Collective vicarious agency follows the rule no less than direct collective agency.

Some examples will help make these points clearer. Consider the contrast between my lawyer filing a court action in my name and my congressman voting for a bill in the name of his constituents. Legally it is in my power to get along without the lawyer, but it is not in my power to vote for a bill in the House. There is vicarious agency in both cases, but my responsibility is reduced in the latter case because what is done in my name is not in my power. It does not disappear altogether since it is still possible for me to influence the vote.

We have, then, four cases, two direct and two vicarious. In one member of each pair, I would be able to carry out the action that has been done collectively alone; in the other, the action requires cooperation among agents. I am suggesting that the logic of *we* and of *we, qua* . . . respects these distinctions and that lines of responsibility for collective actions can be traced accordingly.

In particular, where a collective action exceeds the powers of one of its members, that agent's responsibility is reduced. It is not, however, the case that responsibility is reduced just because the action is done collectively. For the agent's willingness to cooperate is evidence that even alone he would have sought the same end. I conclude that it is both a necessary and sufficient condition of reduced responsibility for collective action that the action exceed the powers of the individual agent. Of course this is to be understood contextually, so that the agent's powers should be understood as those he actually possesses, not ones he could possess under different circumstances.

The interesting upshot of these lines of argument is that part of the evasion of individual responsibility in contexts of collective action that has motivated holism can be managed by a moderate reductionism without sacrificing either the intuitively plausible view that collectives act only through their members or the clear necessity to admit that there are collective actions.

II

Marxism

6

Michel Foucault, Analytical Marxism, and Functional Explanation

STEVEN JAY GOLD

Any brief inquiry into the tensions between Marx and Foucault must, of necessity, take a narrow focus. In this chapter I propose evaluating the reservations Michel Foucault expressed about historical materialism in his influential set of lectures and interviews known as *Power/Knowledge*.[1] While the three objections I have uncovered may not be representative of the general contradictions between the vast discourse known as "Marxism" and the grand "Genealogies" left to us by Michel Foucault, they do, I believe, represent three of the major objections to historical materialism put forward by Foucault and many other poststructuralist writers.

Each objection presented here deals with the issue of functional explanation—a mode of explanation that Foucault endorsed and employed in spite of the ridicule and disdain brought out by those who conflate it with the dubious sociological tradition of structural functionalism. To be more specific, Foucault was wary of the mode of production analysis in historical materialism because it entails, he suggests, three tendencies:

1. Crude functionalism, the tendency to assume that merely pointing to the benefits that a social phenomenon has for the mode of production, is an adequate explanation of that phenomenon.

2. Instrumentalism, the tendency to assume that all Marxian functional claims can be elaborated in terms of the dominant class's

direct exercise of power.

3. The functional subordination of politics to economics; in historical materialism this entails a tendency to ignore crucial nonproductive institutional developments because every social phenomenon must be explained in direct relation to the economy and an insistence that all microcontextual power relations must be interpreted in terms of the global relations of power.

Responses to each of these claims can be found in one form or another among contemporary Marxist thinkers who have come to be called analytical Marxists. In the first section of this chapter I will refer to G. A. Cohen's defense of functional Marxism to demonstrate that, contra Foucault, crude functionalism is not a necessary element of Marxian social theory. In the second section, part of Jon Elster's working out of Marx's understanding of game theory will be used to show how Marx saw the need for an independent state to control the excesses of the bourgeoisie. This will lead us to the conclusion that against Foucault's second objection, Marx did not see power as the exclusive possession of the dominant class. And in the last section, after dismissing the first half of the third objection on logical grounds, I will make use of Andy Levine's formulation of the scope of historical materialist explanations to show that the functional subordination of politics to economics in Marxism does not entail cashing out all microcontextual power relations in terms of the global patterns of domination.

I

One of Foucault's main reasons for rejecting historical materialism lies with the charge of what I will call crude functionalism. Crude functional analysis in Marxism entails the assumption that citing the beneficial consequences of the *explanandum* for the development and maintenance of the mode of production is adequate to explain the phenomenon. This view neglects the possibility that the benefits may arise accidentally, that they may not be accidental but nonexplanatory, or that there may be a third variable that accounts for both the *explanandum* and the benefit.[2]

Referring to attempts to explain the exclusion of the insane and the repression of infantile sexuality by reference to the needs of the dominant mode of production, Foucault illustrated the absurdity of the brand of crude functional explanation he claimed to be common among Marxist thinkers. Foucault explicitly rejected Wilhelm Reich's explanation of the repression of infantile sexuality, namely that it was banned and excluded since the body had essentially become a force of production and all forms of its expenditure that did not lend themselves to constituting the productive forces were repressed.[3]

Leaving aside the veracity of Foucault's interpretation of Reich, the crude functionalism exemplified here certainly fails to explain the phenomenon of the repression of infantile sexuality as, like all explanations of this type, it fails to account for plausible alternatives. Other responses to infantile sexuality—for example, Foucault suggested sexual precociousness—may have provided greater utility for a needed expansion of the work force. Why, Foucault asked, should repression in particular occur?

Foucault was not the first philosopher to make this claim about crude functionalism. C. G. Hempel criticized structural functionalism for the same reason, namely, failing to take into account what Hempel called functional equivalents.[4] Nearly a century earlier, Nietzsche, in *Daybreak*, similarly lamented the tendency in the physical and social sciences to confuse the utility of a phenomenon with its causal explanation.[5] More recently, Jon Elster has made much of how Marxism has suffered from crude functional explanation.[6]

But is crude functionalism a necessary element of historical materialism? I think not. Historical materialism is an optimizing theory like those used in the biological sciences. As such, G. A. Cohen is right to insist that Marx's central historical premises can be understood only in functional terms.[7] And if Cohen has shown anything in his reconstruction of Marx's theory, it is that historical materialism does not entail crude functionalism.

On Cohen's view of Marx, functional explanations inform our understanding of social phenomena by reference to the explanandum's beneficial consequences for the maintenance of the mode of production optimal for developing the productive forces. Cohen is well aware of the claim that to identify a function that something serves is not necessarily to explain why that phenomenon occurred. He argues that this doesn't show that functional explanations are not explanatory or useful for Marxism, only that acceptable functional explanations necessitate a genetic theory, that is, some mechanism, in his terms, *elaborating theory*.

Cohen points out numerous ways a Marxian functional explanation can be confirmed genetically, and I will not bother to spell them all out here. He discusses purposive elaborations in terms of industrial decision makers; Darwinian elaborations in terms of competition, chance variation, scarcity, and natural selection; Lamarckian elaborations; and others. These types of explanatory mechanisms and others may be found, he suggests, throughout Marx's complex historical narratives and in his theoretical works on economics.

For example, Marx makes the functional claim that the state acts on the collective interest of the bourgeoisie by maintaining the system that guarantees their domination. In my article "Towards a Marxist Theory of the State" I have identified in Marx's historical writings numerous types of elaborating reasons for this functional claim.[8] From *instrumentalism*, where the bourgeoisie occupy strategic locations in the state apparatus or indirectly affect state action through economic pressure, to *structuralist* conceptions, where the state, given its insertion in capitalist production relations, must ensure a healthy accumulation process to maximize tax revenues, to *class balance* conceptions, where the state must balance between competing class interests to maximize autonomy, I have tried to show how Marx attempted to elaborate on his general functional theory of politics. Marx was never satisfied with crude functional explanations.

It should be noted that in his famous debates on the subject with Jon Elster, Cohen does suggest that functional explanations can be confirmed even in advance of some mechanism setting out how the dispositional property figures into the explanation. Elster, on the other hand, rejects Cohen's view that in advance of *any* mechanism we can still see the functional relationship as explanatory. But I think that Cohen's claim here is one for general historical research. Functional explanations in this context have validity, Cohen says, in that they point research in the right direction and are tentatively acceptable, given certain provocative correlations, pending further explanation. Nowhere does he suggest that functional explanations are entirely adequate without an acceptable exposition of the underlying mechanism.

II

A further reason Foucault gave for suppressing the mode-of-production analysis entails the rejection of a particular kind of elaborating theory, namely instrumentalism. Traditionally, when the Marxist was asked why the state acts on the collective interest of the bourgeoisie (the functional claim), the simple elaborating answer was that the state is an instrument of the bourgeoisie, in its control; that is, the bourgeoisie has power. This Foucault clearly rejects.[9] Power, he tells us, is not to be seen as the exclusive possession of one person or one class to be used against another person or class.

The essence of the claim lies in Foucault's rejection of a view of power that sees things conspiratorially; class domination does not *simply* proceed through one class's expressed wishes or through their representatives. This paranoia, to be sure, can be seen as preoccupying many

Marxists of this century. However, it is hardly intrinsic to historical materialism.

Instrumentalism partially elaborates Marx's functional claim about the state. The bourgeoisie often does control state action directly or indirectly. But given the nature of capitalist competition, the bourgeoisie, as a collective agent, is simply incapable of the organized action necessary for maintaining capitalist production relations through the state.

Jon Elster, for one, has made much of Marx's anticipation of game-theory devices such as the prisoner's dilemma and the free-rider problem to show how Marx understood the dynamic of capitalist production. He cites texts from Marx in which it becomes clear that "capital cares nothing for the length and life of labour-power. All that concerns it is simply and solely the maximum of labour power, that can be rendered fluent in a working day."[10] Elster effectively sets out Marx's understanding of bourgeois rationality—the hope that the crash that is inevitable in every "stock-jobbing swindle" will fall on the head of his neighbor only after he "safely stashes away his shower of gold."[11] The inevitable conclusion that *"Après moi le déluge!"* are the watchwords of every capitalist and of every capitalist nation,"[12] is expressed most succinctly in a passage Elster cites from the *1861–3 Critique:*

> But Capitalist A may be able to grow rich on the policy that this "killing is no murder," while Capitalist B, or the generation of Capitalists B, may have to foot the bill. For the individual capitalist is in constant rebellion against the general interests of the capitalist class as a whole.[13]

The bourgeoisie, Marx suggests, are a latent group whose individual interests are inescapably at odds with their collective needs.[14]

The functional claim about the state cannot then be supported simply via purposive behavior of members of the dominant class. That individual capitalists would, absent an external check, destroy out of competitive necessity the very thing that their position depended upon— wage-labor—entailed, Marx saw, an independent state. Elster is keen to point out that Marx said time and again that the state is forced to act "despite the bitter opposition of the capitalist class."[15] Thus, Marx says the state

> is nothing more than the reciprocal insurance of the bourgeoisie against both its own members and the exploited class, an insurance which must become increasingly expensive and apparently increasingly independent as against bourgeois society, because the subjection of the exploited class becomes increasingly difficult.[16]

Marx knew that the bourgeoisie needed an independent state apparatus to curb the excesses of a dominant class that was made up of narrowly rational individuals. Hence, state power cannot be reduced to the will of capitalists or to the wishes of the bourgeoisie in general.

The implications of a rejection of instrumentalism for Marx's understanding of power are too numerous to set out here. However, it is important to point out that for Marx, the wheels of power in general operate not through purposive activity of the dominant class but by the logic of the capitalist mode of production itself. In a passage from *Capital* cited above where the tendency of the bourgeoisie to burn out labor power was discussed, Marx says:

> But looking at things as a whole, all this does not, indeed, depend on the free will of the individual capitalist. Free competition brings out the inherent laws of capitalist production, in the shape of external coercive laws having power over every individual capitalist.[17]

The capitalist is just as much bound by the "inexorable laws of capital" as the worker. Hence, to suggest that Marx saw power as the exclusive possession of the bourgeoisie is simply false.

III

Foucault flatly rejected the economic understanding of power he claimed to be implicit in both liberal and Marxian social theory. In the liberal position Foucault dismissed the assumption that power is a possession that can be alienated like a commodity through a legal power-establishing act. What Foucault rejected in Marxism here—and this was his third reason for discarding historical materialism—is what he called the functional subordination of politics to the economy found in "the Marxist conception, or at any rate a certain conception currently held to be Marxist." Though once again he seemed to suggest that the problem began with "Marxists" rather than historical materialism per se, Foucault went on to reject explicitly the essential notion that superstructural institutions rise and fall insofar as they help to stabilize and develop the economic structure of a given mode of production.[18]

On Foucault's understanding of this functional subordination of politics to economics, two things are said to follow. First, Foucault insisted that since on the Marxian view power must be reduced to economics, there is a tendency in Marxism to ignore crucial institutional power relations that don't directly affect the economy. Second, the functional subordination of politics to economics, Foucault claimed, means that all microcontextual power relations must be understood in the terms of global strategies of power. The former claim, I will argue, conflates the functional role of the superstructure with each individual element of it; the latter claim simply misunderstands the level at which historical materialism, as a theory of historical change, operates.

Foucault told us that his areas of study—psychiatric internment, the mental normalization of individuals, and penal institutions—had little if any direct importance to the economy.[19] However, it was obvious that these practices are essential to the "general functioning of the wheels of power." Hence, the Marxist subordination of power to the economy has produced, Foucault told us, a tendency to regard these practices as marginal and insignificant. This is why, Foucault believed, "a certain kind of Marxism" constituted an objective obstacle to understanding power.

While "a certain kind of Marxism" may have presented such an obstacle, I believe that Foucault was wrong to insist that this functional subordination of power to the economy in historical materialism entails neglecting fundamental power relations that have no direct bearing on the economy. I would suggest that what Foucault has done here is commit what has often been called the fallacy of division. The fallacy of division obtains when one attempts to argue from the premise that something is true of some whole to the conclusion that the same is true of the parts of that whole. For Marx, the superstructure as a whole serves to maintain and develop class divisions and the general economic structure. When that "real foundation" upon which it arises becomes fettered by that form of superstructure, these institutions adapt, fade, or collapse altogether. It need not be the case that every individual element of the superstructure directly serves the economy, though many, or probably most, do. Rather, the superstructure *as a whole* maintains production relations, and individual elements of it must act together to do so.

On Marx's view, one way that individual political and social institutions may have a marginal direct impact on the economy and yet still serve to maintain class relations lies in their ability to support the power relations intrinsic to the superstructure. Foucault, in explaining why he rejects the functional subordination of politics to the economy, actually provides an excellent example of this. He claims not to refer to productive labor often as he happens to be dealing with people situated outside the circuits of such labor, specifically the insane, prisoners, and children. Labor for them, Foucault told us, has a value that is chiefly disciplinary; it has no productive benefit for the economy. This *dressage*, however, provides the training, normalization, and correction necessary for the expedient use of political power and an efficient working class. What we have then is labor that is not productive—not *directly* relevant to the economy in that no surplus value is derived from it. And yet, such *dressage* does serve to maintain political power as well as condition and create an individual who engages in productive labor more efficiently. Hence, these institutional practices help maintain the "wheels of power" so that superstructural institutions reinforce and develop production relations. So while many Marxists may have ignored these "nonproductive" institutions, there is nothing in Marxian social theory that necessitates this mistake.

The second result of the functional subordination of power to economics, according to Foucault, lies in the claim that all microcontextual power relations must be understood in terms of global patterns of domination. With this, notable philosophers such as Charles Taylor agree.[20] By taking macrocontextual relations as explanatorally basic, historical materialism, Foucault told us, is committed to explaining the way people square off in the microcontexts of family, religious organizations, and so on in terms of class relations. The claim here then means that the origins and operations of microcontextual power relations must be explained in terms of how they meet the requirements of a rising bourgeoisie. But on Foucault's account, microcontextual power relations are relatively autonomous from global forces, and the task lies in seeing how these relations developed *on their own* and gradually became colonized by the global mechanisms that exist in a society in which the bourgeoisie was becoming hegemonic.

It seems to me that Foucault here has simply misunderstood the level at which historical materialism as a theory of historical change is geared. In *The End of the State,* Andy Levine tells us that "historical materialism is not . . . a general sociology: a set of trans-historical sociological laws."[21] Historical materialism individuates historical epochs into discrete modes of production that are natural divisions. As a macrotheory, it attempts to analyze the nature of each mode of production and to expose the structure and dynamic of the transformations between these modes. Historical materialism is, as Levine puts it, "a theory of trends and transformations."[22] As a macrotheory, historical materialism deals with large-scale tendencies and has little if anything to say about operations within the microlevel of human experience. There may well be sociological laws, Levine tells us, that explain particular events or the evolution of capillary power relations that are independent of the claims made by historical materialism.

Marx's theory of history, then, contra Foucault and Taylor, is silent about the nature and mechanisms for change of microcontextual power relations. Rather, like Foucault, Marx saw these capillary modes of power as independent, or at least relatively autonomous, of the global context. The key, they agree, is to come to understand how these relatively autonomous power relations came to represent the interests of a rising bourgeoisie.

Foucault's explicit reasons, then, for rejecting the mode-of-production analysis in historical materialism fail. While I cannot make the claim out in detail here, I would suggest that Foucault accepts functional explanation in a Marxian format with the task in mind of developing a method for providing a complementary microfoundational explanation. Gearing his inquiry, or genealogy, at the level of interaction between micro- and macrocontextual power relations and attempting to see how this nexus comes to represent the interests of the dominant class, Foucault is in harmony with the mode-of-production analysis that is fundamental to historical materialism.

To be sure, Foucault's elaborate genealogies are but one method for providing microfoundations to Marxian functional claims. Game-theory and rational-choice models are also enlightening to this end, if not in themselves exhaustive as their proponents claim. Either way, functional explanation is a necessary and useful tool in historical studies. Looking at the big picture, we can see how certain historical phenomena came to represent different class interests. The challenge Foucault has set for us is to explain in historical detail just how the history of a particular microcontextual power relation came to be incorporated into the grand historical scheme. And this, as far as I can tell, remains well within the Marxian project.[23]

NOTES

1. Michel Foucault, *Power/Knowledge* (New York: Pantheon, 1977), p. 53.

2. Jon Elster, "Further Thoughts on Marxism, Functionalism, and Game Theory," in *Analytical Marxism,* ed. John Roemer (Cambridge: Cambridge University Press, 1986), p. 203.

3. *Power/Knowledge,* p. 100.

4. C. G. Hempel, "The Logic of Functional Analysis," in *Symposium on Sociological Theory,* ed. Llewellyn Gross (Evanston, Ill.: Row, Peterson, 1959).

5. In an aphorism entitled "False conclusions from utility" Nietzsche says, "When one has demonstrated that a thing is of the highest utility, one has however thereby taken not one step towards explaining its origin: that is to say, one can never employ utility to make it comprehensible that a thing must necessarily exist. But it is the contrary judgement that has hitherto prevailed—and even in the domain of the most rigorous science." *Daybreak,* trans. R. J. Hollingdale (Cambridge: Cambridge University Press, 1982), p. 37.

6. See *Explaining Technical Change,* (Cambridge: Cambridge University Press, 1983), ch. 2.; "Marxism, Functionalism and Game Theory," *Theory and Society* 11(1982), pp. 453–82; "Further Thoughts on Marxism, Functionalism and Game Theory," in *Analytical Marxism,* ed. John Roemer (Cambridge: Cambridge University Press, 1986).

7. G. A. Cohen, *Karl Marx's Theory of History: A Defense,* (Oxford: Oxford University

Press, 1978); "Functional Explanation, Consequence Explanation and Marxism," *Inquiry* 25(1982), pp. 27–56; reply to Elster, "Marxism, Functionalism and Game Theory," *Theory and Society* 11 (1982), pp. 483-96. I am not attempting a full-scale defense of functional explanation. The debate between Cohen's functional interpretation of historical materialism and Jon Elster's insistence on methodological individualism is well known. I would like to point out here only that Elster moves in the course of the debates from the rigid position that functional explanation has no place in the social sciences to a considerably weaker position. He says, "As I presently see the proposal, it is vulnerable to strong pragmatic objections, but on the level of principle it is hard to fault it." However, about these "pragmatic objections," he admits that "in principle, however, these objections could be overcome." ("Further Thoughts on Marxism, Functionalism and Game Theory," in Roemer, note 6, p. 204). Though Elster still maintains that functional explanation is a second-best mode of explanation when compared to those of the causal variety, he clearly gives up his goal of refuting functional explanation per se.

    8. Steven Jay Gold, "Towards a Marxist Theory of the State," *Philosophy Research Archives* 14(April 1989).

    9. *Power/Knowledge,* p. 98.

    10. From *Capital I,* cited in Jon Elster, *Making Sense of Marx,* (Cambridge: Cambridge University Press, 1985), p. 188.

    11. Ibid., p. 187.

    12. Ibid., p. 187.

    13. Ibid., p. 189.

    14. On latent group action, see Mancur Olson, *The Logic of Collective Action* (Cambridge: Harvard University Press, 1965). pp. 48–52.

    15. Karl Marx, *1861–3 Critique,* cited in Elster, *Making Sense.*

    16. Marx's review of E. de Girardin's "Le Socialisme et l'Impôt," in *Collected Works,* vol. 10 (New York: International Publishers, 1978), p. 333.

    17. Karl Marx, *Capital I,* Elster, *Making Sense,* p. 187.

    18. *Power/Knowledge,* pp. 88–89.

    19. Ibid., p. 116.

    20. Charles Taylor, "Foucault on Freedom and Truth," in David Hoy, *Foucault: A Critical Reader* (New York: Blackwell, 1986), p. 85.

    21. Andy Levine, *The End of the State* (London: Verso, 1987), p. 98.

    22. Ibid.

    23. The author would like to thank Tony Smith, John Elliott, and the members of the NEH summer seminar on Marx for their helpful comments.

7

Lukacs:
Theory and Praxis

JOSEPH BIEN

What Lukacs claims to have given in *History and Class Consciousness* is only an "interpretation" of the method employed by Marx.[1] On the one hand, Lukacs does not want to revert to pure theory; as a Marxist, he cannot. Yet on the other hand, as a Marxist, he cannot opt for pure action, for practice without theory. The claim that a fact is a fact only relative to a theory implies the claim that a theory is somehow to be justified on its own. The theory cannot be legitimated by the facts, for the facts attain their objectivity only within the context of the theory. A justification of the theory by the facts would be a *petitio principii:* the facts legitimate the theory, and the theory legitimates the facts. The demand for self-justifying theory emerges in Lukacs's definition of orthodox Marxism. If all Marx's factual claims were disproved, orthodox Marxism would still be unaffected, for orthodox Marxism "is not the 'belief' in this or that thesis, nor the exegesis of a sacred book. On the contrary orthodoxy refers exclusively to method."[2] But if the facts do not justify the method, what does? The justification must be theoretical.[3] It might seem, however, that Lukacs has misunderstood the Marxian method from the outset. Is not Lukacs falling back into idealism, the primacy of the idea over being, and does not Marx explicitly maintain the opposite? Lukacs claims not to have done so and heartily endorses Marx's anti-idealism. How, though, can a relative theory claim truth? The understanding of Lukacs's answer takes us into the heart of his enterprise, the notions of theory and history.

There are two thrusts to Lukacs's theory: a theory of history and society, and a theory of social knowledge. The latter strikes a transcendental note; it seeks the grounds of the possibility—or better, the validating principles—of social and historical knowledge. The ground adduced is a "logical" ground; it proffers an account of what it provided in truth[4] rather than a typology of true judgments, a criteriology.[5] This account of knowledge completes the theory of society. After the delineation of the nature of society and history,[6] we are given an account of the account, a justification of the claims made in the ontology. The theory of knowledge provides the justification that the claims made about society and history are true—that one has grasped the "object" as it is in itself.

Lukacs would have denied a characterization of his thought as transcendental because of its connotations as a philosophy of subjectivity.[7] The reason for this was simple: All the so-called transcendental philosophies had adduced the theoretical subject as the ground of knowledge. In some of his pre-*History and Class Consciousness* writings even Lukacs spoke of subjectivity as the ground of knowledge.[8]

As Hegel showed in the *Logic,* quantity in its abstract, undeveloped form is indifferent to quality. Class consciousness grasped quantitatively is seen in a mode indifferent to its content, its qualitative character. Class consciousness is not, however, some neutral "form" into which any content can be placed. The proletariat's thought is determined by its place within the system of production. Hence, according to Marxist analysis, the proletariat's thought will not be fortuitous but will reflect in some way the prevailing economic conditions. Insofar as consciousness can always be traced back in principle to its material conditions, class consciousness cannot be an empty vessel for any content. Instead, the consideration of it in regard to the concrete totality transcends "pure description and yields the category of objective possibility."[9] The actual state of mind of individual members of a certain class cannot be automatically equated with their proper class consciousness. Lukacs sums this up by saying, "Now class consciousness consists in fact of the appropriate and rational reactions 'imputed' [*zugerechnet*] to a particular typical position in the process of production."[10] Class consciousness, then, as a principle, is a potential consciousness, an "objective possibility." It is not a potentiality in the sense of an entelechy, a final cause prompting the seed to grow into a tree. It is that consciousness that one would have if one had a clear grasp of the nature of his situation. The young Marx adequately metaphorized such a conception by referring to the proletariat's class consciousness as "the secret of its own existence."[11] The young Marx does, however, sometimes speak of it in a manner suggesting entelechy—for example, when he claims, "It is not a question of what this or that proletarian or even the whole proletariat momentarily imagines to be the aim. It is a question of what it consequently is historically compelled to do."[12] Nevertheless, class consciousness in Lukacs's sense only delineates the possible actions of the class that can have possible historical significance. It is important to note this one overriding feature of this theory of class consciousness: It is what men *would do* if they adequately grasped their situation. The nature of the grasp is still to be delineated.

Class consciousness is a peculiar type of concept. It is the "sense . . . of the historical role of the class."[13] The other principles thus far discussed hold for any social formation. Class consciousness, however, is not necessarily instantiated. It is, as said, an objective possibility. It is a possibility only within class society; the classless society will have nothing like it. The possibility can be brought about only through the "conscious will of the proletariat."[14] It does not necessarily have to come about, but at a given point in history the possibility or impossibility of its coming about is demonstrated by Marxism. There are alternatives open, and the class must make a decision.[15] A class can take power when "its interests and consciousness enable it to organize the whole of society in accordance with those interests";[16] in short, it can take power when it is objectively possible.

Class consciousness is the means by which history is theoretically handled. History has a "sense" that is revealed in class consciousness; class consciousness is the historical principle of Lukacs's system, necessary to push history to its possible goals. It is what people ought to do, not necessarily what they actually do. In this respect it often stands in opposition to the false beliefs people of a given class sometimes hold. False consciousness is the actual consciousness of individuals who do not perceive their real interests, who do not see what they ought to do.

Class consciousness plays a double role in Lukacs's thought. It is, first, a category of historical analysis—the notion of objective possibility. Second, it is in the class of the proletariat an "ought," a demand that men act in certain ways so that history may achieve its sense. It demands that imputed class consciousness be made identical with actual consciousness.

The importance of class consciousness in the case of the proletariat lies in the fact that the proletariat is the potentially universal class, the one class that does not necessarily have to adopt a point of view that is only relative. The proletariat can adopt the standpoint of totality. As capable of grasping the totality, the proletariat is a "universal class," not just another partial interest.

This notion, the universal class, is a problematic note in Marxist thought. Obviously, for any semiorthodox Marxist, the proletariat has to possess some kind of universality. The justification of the proletarian revolution lies in the claim that the proletariat holds within it the interests of humanity as a whole. In what, though, does its universality consist? The term *universal class* originally was Hegel's. In paragraph 303 and paragraph 205 of the *Philosophy of Right*, Hegel speaks of the bureaucracy as a "universal class" having "the universal as the end of its essential activity."[17] These are bureaucrats who, having no stake in any particular class, can act in the interests of all classes. This ability to legislate for the good of all of society and not just any particular part constitutes their universality.[18]

Marx claims that Hegel's notion is based upon a misunderstanding of the nature of the state. The state is not a structure, Marx argues, acting in the interests of all society but a particular apparatus by which one class dominates all of society. The state always acts in the interests of one class, not in the interests of all classes. A truly universal class would be a class to which all men belonged; it would cease to be a class.[19] Marx's notion of the universality of the proletarian class, then, takes two forms. First, there is his early conception where the proletariat is universal "because of its universal suffering and claiming no particular right because no particular wrong but unqualified wrong is perpetrated on it."[20] Private property is alienating, and since private property is the result of alienated labor, the abolishing of alienated labor is the freeing of all mankind.[21] In the older Marx the proletariat is universal because it is the one class that cannot produce another class to exploit. It has this characteristic because of its specific place in the process of production: The proletariat produces all the wealth but gets back only that fraction of it necessary to reproduce itself. The proletariat is exploited and produces surplus value. Since the proletariat is the basis of all societal wealth, the proletarian revolution necessarily means the end of economic exploitation.[22] Lukacs's conception of the proletariat's universality is a mixture of the ideas of the young Marx and the old Marx.

When the imputed class consciousness of the proletariat becomes identical with its actual consciousness, the subject of history—the class that makes history—becomes identical with the object of history. The proletariat becomes the unity of subject and object in history, which Lukacs claims is Hegel's absolute "endowed with concrete historical shape."[23] It is the final standpoint of the dialectic, the point from which truth is possible. In Hegel the terminal category, the absolute, is the final unity of thought and being, the stance where there is no more opposition, where all the moments are gathered into their final context, the whole. Specifically, it is, in the *Logic*, thought explicit to itself, the "idea thinking itself,"[24] thought comprehending itself as comprehending its other. In terms of Hegel's dialectic, it is thought realizing itself as identical with its other (being) yet different from it. The proletariat is the absolute as that class comprehending the whole in comprehending itself. It is identical with, yet different from, the concrete totality.

Lukacs says that the subject of history is the class,[25] and the individual always appears on the object side.[26] Each ruling class rules in the name of the whole, organizing society around its particular interests, trying to make itself the subjectivity of society. However, because none of the classes really represents the interests of all society, none can know the totality by knowing itself. Only the proletariat can do this. Each class is the subject of history during its era of dominance.

Each class, however, is to be seen as a partial totality. Were it not a partial totality, it could not even partially make history.[27] The class is a partial totality because it is a dialectical unity, an identity in difference. The moments of the totality (i.e., the individuals of the class) are each independent and self-subsistent while maintaining their peculiar immediacy only through their mediations with others. The class as a partial totality can know the "whole" totality only if its point of view coincides with the point of view of society as a whole. Nonproletarian classes, although themselves partial totalities, cannot achieve the "true" grasp of the whole. A split always remains for them between the subject, the maker of history, and the object, what is being made. What are made are the intersubjective forms, the objectifications of man's existence; in short, the norms by which individuals act and think. A class that is not representative of the totality cannot realize these forms as totally intersubjective; it can see them only as objectivities and try to impose them upon society at large.

Because each class has its own point of view, it is impossible, so it seems, for any class to attain a true intersubjectivity, an authentic "we-subject." Because nonproletarian classes cannot reach the principle of those forms—the concrete totality—they see history in a fantastic, transcendent form; it appears to them to follow laws akin to natural laws, divorced from human activity. There is a split for them between the subject and the object on two levels. First, nonproletarian classes cannot grasp the whole because they are a partial interest. Second, they cannot grasp themselves because they cannot grasp the whole.[28]

The problematic note here is the "grasp" of the whole. Lukacs inveighs against all purely contemplative theory. His notion of class consciousness as presented so far seems, however, to fall prey to just that objection. The coming to be of concrete class consciousness is a rising to awareness, a knowledge that such and such is the case—or so it seems. But if the theory is to be a spur to action, the class-conscious worker must not remain contemplative. Lukacs tries to avoid regressing into contemplation by invoking a classical distinction between the theoretical and the practical, of contemplation and action. Theory, or contemplation, is the transference of what is external to thought into a form congenial to thought; it grasps the world as it is through concepts. Action, praxis, on the other hand, tries to make the world what it ought to be rather than grasping it as it is. Both theory and praxis are manifestations of rationality, but praxis establishes a more reasonable world then theory, which accepts the world as it is in all its unreason.[29]

Lukacs furthers the classical claim and holds that praxis, like theory, is an instrument of critique. Both are manifestations of rationality.[30] Theory has a rationale peculiar to itself. The question is, does praxis have the same rationale as theory, or does it have one of its own? Praxis, for Lukacs, must display a rationality similar to theory; otherwise, praxis would not be critique. The efficacy of praxis as critique is that its critique, as opposed to that offered by contemplation, actually goes to the root of that which it critiques. Theoretical critique seeks to uncover the basic conditions (the "categorical" features) and the limitations of the critiqued. All that theoretical critique can do is observe and contemplate what it finds, but mere contemplative knowing does not change the object. Praxis obtains its power through the fact that it and only it can change the "root," the organization of society. Praxis "comprehends" things because it is a rational endeavor that grasps the basic conditions of things and moreover brings these things into closer conformity with reason. Since only a totality can perform this, only a class can achieve an adequate praxis. Because only the class can change the roots of society through praxis, only the class, a partial totality, can penetrate the totality. The proletariat comprehends itself by acting on the basic conditions that structure it, namely, the conditions of capitalist society. Its "secret" is the dissolution of all classes, and it grasps this secret not through a mere recognition of it—that would be contemplation—but through an actual change of society through proletarian action. Praxis replaces theory; theory "spills over" into praxis.[31]

Lukacs, however, does not call for a full-scale rejection of theory in favor of praxis. Quite the contrary: Lukacs always stresses the absolute need for theory. Theory's function is the raising to consciousness of the basic features of social reality. In this way theory assists in changing reality. The function of the categories of mediation in theory is that "with their aid those immanent meanings that necessarily inhere in the objects of bourgeois society . . . now become objectively effective and can therefore enter the consciousness of the proletariat."[32] The proletarian achieves a grasp of his place in society when he or she becomes "aware."[33] And this "knowledge is practical. That is, this knowledge brings about an objective structural change in the object of knowledge."[34]

It is only after theory has grasped the logic of a situation that praxis becomes effective. Theory is the grasp of the basic objectified forms that shape human existence. These forms are not eternal verities; they are specific to their historical locales. Theory, by grasping them according to the relation they have to one another in society provides for knowledge of the society and knowledge of it as merely a stage in history, not as a form of society that is universally valid. "Praxis cannot be divorced from knowledge. A praxis which envisages a genuine transformation of these forms can only start to be effective if it intends to think out the process immanent in these forms to its logical conclusion, to become conscious of it and to make it conscious."[35] The theoretical grasp of society is necessary for an adequate praxis. Praxis cannot validate itself purely on the basis of its own rationale. It requires class consciousness, which requires theory. Theory grasps the world as it is, and on the basis of what the world is, praxis can make the world what it ought to be.[36]

Class consciousness is the mediating factor between theory and praxis. Historical movement is seen to be a movement of class praxis: "History is the history of the unceasing overthrow of the objective forms that shape the life of man."[37] This overthrow, of course, is through action. Class consciousness is necessary to guide praxis. In particular, proletarian class consciousness is necessary to guide proletarian praxis, for proletarian praxis is legitimate—that is, properly proletarian, in accord with the class consciousness of the proletariat—if it acts by the secret of the proletariat's existence. The transformation of philosophy (theory) into praxis is possible for Lukacs because of the mediating influence of class consciousness.

Theory provokes awareness of what was previously only immediate. Once this awareness has come about, praxis necessarily results. The proletariat could not remain contemplative after achieving its imputed class consciousness. Its class consciousness is the grasp of itself as the dissolution of class society. It cannot dissolve class society by thinking about it; hence, it must act. The proletariat comprehends itself fully through praxis, but it becomes aware of itself through theory.

Lukacs claims praxis is the completion of the task of philosophy, the establishment of reason. But Lukacs does not see this praxis as the proof of philosophy, or theory. Lukacs here parts with young Marx. For young Marx, the theory is "untrue" until united with the world. The second thesis on Feuerbach claims: "The question whether objective truth can be attributed to human thinking is not a question of theory but is a practical question. Man must prove the truth, i.e., the reality and power, the this-sideness of his thinking in praxis. The dispute over the reality of non-reality of thinking that is isolated from praxis is a purely scholastic question."[38] The proof of the theory lies in the action preformed. For young Marx, praxis is the union of philosophy (reason) and the world.

The Hegelian system, the perfect embodiment of reason, is nevertheless unreasonable because it ignores the unreasonable world.[39] The dialectic that resolves opposites finds its culmination in proletarian praxis. Faced with two opposites, reasonable philosophy and the unreasonable world, Marx seeks a third thing that would be higher than these two (since it would include them as constituent moments of itself and yet would be irreducible to one or the other) but would be neither pure philosophy nor pure action. If the third were another philosophy, then the opposition would remain. If it were pure action, one would merely repeat the existing unreason of the world. There would be only practice, not praxis.[40] It must be praxis, or action that is worldly and carries philosophy, rationality, to completion. Praxis builds the reasonable world and hence proves the rationality of theory.

For Lukacs, a theory may be true but ineffective.[41] The relation of theory to praxis is not that of theorem-proof; theory is a heuristic lead for praxis. It awakens class consciousness and articulates the goals of praxis. Once awakened, the worker cannot fail to act. Theory preserves the final goal; it holds it in sight even though the actual consciousness of men may stray from this goal. Theory is necessary to preserve the authenticity of class consciousness, for imputed class consciousness can stand in direct opposition to the workers' perceived interests. The immediate interests of the proletariat can be in opposition to their secret, to their true interests—their historical mission. The confusion of final goal and immediate interest, Lukacs claims, is the root cause of opportunism. Instead, both final goal and immediate interests should be seen as moments of the historical totality. Their relationship to each other must be understood dialectically; that is, each is what it is only in its reference to the other.

NOTES

1. Georg Lukacs, *History and Class Consciousness,* trans. R. Livingstone (London: Merlin Press, 1971), p. xiii.

2. Ibid., p. 1.

3. Indeed, after the revolution that the theory is to help provoke, the theory undergoes a "change in function." Formerly an ideological weapon, it becomes a scientific method of research. See Lukacs, *History,* pp. 223–25.

4. This is, for Lukacs, "attained intersubjectivity," the we-subject.

5. This is the case with Descartes, where we are given the *types* of judgments we can "know" to be true.

6. Later, Lukacs frankly admits that this delineation is an ontology. See Georg Lukacs, *Gesprache mit Georg Lukacs* (Reinbeck bei Hamburg: Rowohlt, 1967).

7. Hegel, who also qualifies as a transcendental thinker, thought of transcendental

philosophy this way; his models were the transcendental philosophies of Kant, Fichte, and Schelling. In his last work, Husserl went so far as to claim that the transcendental problematic consists solely in the showing how objectivity is produced from subjectivity. *The Crisis of European Sciences and Transcendental Phenomenology*, trans. David Carr (Evanston, Ill.: Northwestern University Press, 1970), pp. 97–98.

8. See Georg Lukacs, "Das Problem geistiger Fuhrung und die 'geistigen Arbeiter,' " *Werke*, Band 2 (Neuweid und Berlin: Luchterhand Verlag, 1968), p. 57n.

9. Lukacs, *History*, p. 51.

10. Ibid.

11. Karl Marx, *Writings of the Young Marx on Philosophy*, trans. L. D. Easton and K. Guddat (New York: Doubleday, 1967), p. 263.

12. Ibid., p. 368.

13. Lukacs, *History*, p. 72.

14. Ibid., p. 70.

15. Indeed Lukacs speaks in his later work of man as an "antwortendes Wesen," an answering or responding being, who must choose between alternatives. See *Gesprache*, pp. 103–8.

16. Lukacs, *History*, p. 52.

17. G. W. F. Hegel, *Philosophy of Right*, trans. T. M. Knox (London: Oxford University Press, 1952), p. 198.

18. See Joseph Bien. "Je li partija filozofijski problem," *Kulturni Radnik* 38(2)(1985). Also of note are Revai's review of *Geshichte und Klassenbewusstein*, in *Archiv für die Geschichte des Sozialismus und der Arbeiterbenegung* (Leipzig: C. L. Herschfeld Verlag, 1925), and Merleau-Ponty's *Adventures of the Dialectic*, trans. J. Bien (Evanston, Ill.: Northwestern University Press, 1973).

19. *Young Marx*, p. 263.

20. Ibid.

21. Ibid., p. 299.

22. This discussion is too brief to do full justice to the complexities of young Marx's and old Marx's notions.

23. Lukacs, *History*, p. 188.

24. G. W. F. Hegel, *The Logic of Hegel*, trans. W. Wallace (London: Oxford University Press, 1873), p. 236.

25. Lukacs, *History*, p. 165.

26. Ibid.

27. Ibid., p. 28.

28. Henri Lefebvre has objected to this whole presentation with the simple statement that "no such historical consciousness is to be found in the working class anywhere in the world today—in no real individual, in no real group. It is a purely speculative construction on the part of a philosopher unacquainted with the working class. Thus it is subject to the general criticism which distinguishes between spontaneous (uncertain, primitive) consciousness and political consciousness (resulting from the fusion in action between the conceptual knowledge of scientists and scholars—i.e., intellectuals—and the spontaneous consciousness)." Lefebvre, *Sociology of Marx*, trans. Norman Guterman (New York: Vintage, 1969), p. 36.

29. Hegel argues for a similar notion of praxis in the last section of the *Science of Logic*, "The Idea," but Hegel argues that such a notion is feasible only under the aegis of an overarching notion of reason, which is supplied by the "Absolute Idea," or thought explicit to itself as identical with itself in grasping its other. Lukacs, however, does not explicitly argue for this higher notion.

30. Rationality is not to be confused with reasonableness. Evil has a rationale but is not reasonable.

31. Lukacs's notion of praxis is not, however, to be identified with class consciousness, as Merleau-Ponty does in his interpretation of Lukacs. Merleau-Ponty claims, "Class consciousness is not, in the proletariat, a state of mind or knowledge. Nor is it a theoretician's conception. It is praxis, i.e., less than a subject and more than an object." *Adventures of the Dialectic*, p. 47. Class consciousness structures praxis but is not identical with it. Praxis is action; class consciousness is a guide to action. Parkinson's characterization of Lukacs's notion comes closer but is still inadequate: "In other words, the subject does not merely reflect its object in a passive way, but it also acts on it, and this action is what Lukacs calls praxis, practice." Parkinson, *Georg Lukacs* (New York: Vintage, 1970), p. 11. No mere action upon the object is necessarily praxis. Action that reverts to the status quo or which acts on nonessential features cannot be called praxis. Praxis is critique; it is "practical-critical activity." *History*, p. 20. Parkinson's error lies in his confusion between praxis and practice. He obviously thinks the two are the same, but they are not. Praxis is to be distinguished from practice. Practice is more akin to "habit," the carrying out of a set plan. Practice has no inherent rationality; it merely tries to conform to a pattern. It does not try to remake the world according to some norm. Praxis is "practical" only in the sense that it is related to "doing" something; a question of praxis is a "practical" question.

32. Lukacs, *History*, p. 163.

33. Ibid., p. 168.

34. Ibid., p. 169.

35. Ibid., p. 177.

36. Josef Revai rightly pointed out in his review of the book that Lukacs's central question—"Can the dialectic be other than revolutionary?"—is determined by Lukacs's interpretation of Marx's eleventh thesis on Feuerbach ("The philosophers have only interpreted the world; the point, however, is to change it"). Revai claims this constitutes, in Lukacs's reading, "the essence and starting point [*Ausgangspunkt*] of Marxism. And indeed the point is for 'philosophy.' The problem of changing the world must not be understood as perhaps an application of natural science, of technology, a 'changing' of nature in the sense of 'dominating' it, but the practical movement must be given in theory itself, in its relation to its object." *Archiv*, pp. 13–14.

37. Lukacs, *History*, p. 186.

38. *Young Marx*, p. 400.

39. Ibid., pp. 52, 61–62.

40. Ibid., pp. 62–64.

41. Lukacs, *History*, pp. 173–74.

8

Marx, Nietzsche,
and the Voices of Democracy

FRED EVANS

Ohe can characterize the history of modern Western societies as the continual betrayal of democracy in its own name. Once the people have overthrown an oppressive regime, they replace their original demands for freedom and equality with a redefinition of democracy in terms of formal procedures for political succession, a set of abstract rights, and a hierarchical system of production. Although Marx has explained this development explicitly in terms of historical materialism and control of the means of production, and Nietzsche implicitly in terms of Western nihilism, I believe that their explanations separate two dimensions of society that a full account of democracy and its continual betrayal must keep together. I will therefore begin with a description of societies, or "linguistic communities," in terms of their synchronic and diachronic dimensions and then show how this structure allows us to portray democracy in a way that counters the tendency to subvert its original appeal to freedom and equality and also incorporates important elements of the viewpoints of Marx and Nietzsche and their critiques of liberalism.

Linguistic Communities and the "Creative Tension of Voices"

Because of its association with freedom of speech and political debate, the notion of democracy suggests that voices are the fundamental constituents of the linguistic community as well as a means for determining the community's political affairs. This suggestion achieves further support when we consider that the identity of each of us is bound up with the pronouncements that we make about the things around us. Our desires, thoughts, intentions, and bodily actions are inseparable from the objects toward which they are directed, and these objects are available to us only through the social discourse that assigns to each its name, value, and place within the network of practices and objects of interest to the community. Because of this intimate relationship between our identity and our discourse, *voice* seems the proper term to designate what we are, to designate the juncture of our bodies and our verbal practices.[1]

This characterization of ourselves as voices also captures the way we are related to one another as members of the linguistic community. Just as a language is the system of differences that paradoxically connects all of its terms—a unity that is founded and perpetuated through difference rather than the hegemony of a single word or grammatical pattern—so the voice of each member of the linguistic community is established by its difference from the voices of the rest of the community.

If we refer to this system of differences as a creative tension of voices, we must admit that it remains merely a formal characterization of the linguistic community unless the members of the community *hear*, in some poignant sense of the word, what one another say. To hear another voice—as opposed to reducing it to the status of an object to be manipulated, controlled, or taken for granted—is to open ourselves to the possibility of revising our pronouncements or discursive practices, to risk our identity, and to allow a tension between our words and those of another, so that the use of a term never congeals into a univocal meaning. If we no longer affirm the differences that provide the basis of the community, if we no longer *hear* one another in the full sense of the term, the community either solidifies into a set of rules or routines, the antithesis of voice, or dissolves into a mere plurality of relatively isolated speakers. The life of the community is therefore founded upon the creative tension that exists among the voices of its members.[2]

Although he does not use the term, the notion of a creative tension of voices is most poignantly expressed and elaborated in the work of the Soviet linguist, literary critic, and philosopher Mikhail Bakhtin. In his *Problems of Dostoyevski's Poetics*,[3] for example, Bakhtin argues that the characters in Dostoyevski's novels always take on a life of their own, one that goes beyond the stance of Dostoyevski and the representative of his voice in the text, so that Dostoyevski's novels are genuine dialogues without closure. In Tolstoy's novels, by contrast, the "authorial voice" dominates the text, and thus creative tension is sacrificed for the emergence of the great idea. More generally, Bakhtin holds that the voices embodied in a text, like those in society, are thoroughly social because each voice, and the structure of language itself, represents "a struggle among socio-linguistic points of view" and not merely "an intra-language struggle between individual wills or logical contradictions."[4] Not only does Bakhtin hold that the linguistic community and language are dialogical in structure, but he also seems to imply that a second and valorized sense of dialogue is the ideal norm of societies, a creative dialogue as opposed to the hierarchical form of interchange that we refer to as a monologue.[5]

In a similar vein, the American sociologist and cultural critic Richard Sennett argues that the "disorder" of cities—the preghetto jumble of social, ethnic, and racial groups—represents the ideal ground for the development of personalities that can both cope with and celebrate diversity. In his *The Fall of Public Man*, Sennett illustrates this mix of voices through a description of the coffeehouses in Paris and London during the late seventeenth and early eighteenth centuries. According to Sennett, the participants of coffeehouse conversation suspended the usual distinctions of social rank:

> As information centers, the coffeehouses naturally were places in which speech flourished. When a man entered the door, he went first to the bar, paid a penny, was told, if he had not been to the place before, what the rules of the house were (e.g., no spitting on such and such a wall, no fighting near the window, etc.), and then sat down to enjoy himself. That in turn was a matter of talking to other people, and the talk was governed by a cardinal rule: in order for information to be as full as possible, distinctions of rank were temporarily suspended; anyone sitting in the coffeehouse had a right to talk to anyone else, to enter into any conversation, whether he knew the other people or not, whether he was bidden to speak or not. It was bad form even to touch on the social origins of other persons when talking to them in the coffeehouse, because the free flow of talk might then be impeded.[6]

Unfortunately, the coffeehouses discriminated on the basis of gender and race, and once back on the street or in other arenas of power, class status immediately returned to regulate the interactions of the white male patrons of the café. In this case, then, the hearing of other voices precluded any risk of revising one's identity and concealed the political deafness at the heart of these conversations.

My experiences working in a Lao orthopedic center also suggest how the creative tension of voices is related to the way one hears the other person's voice. When I would use the Lao equivalent of the word for *rehabilitation* to designate the sort of care that we were providing for the amputees at the center, I would mean, primarily, the restoration of "self-sufficiency." On the basis of their cultural background, particularly their Buddhist religious beliefs and village traditions of mutual help, the Lao use of their term for *rehabilitation* placed emphasis on communal compassion rather than the establishment of self-sufficiency. When I had been in Laos long enough to put aside some of my Western prejudices (that is, long enough to hear Lao voices), their sense of the term *rehabilitation* began to reverberate within my own, to stand in tension with my use of *rehabilitation* and the other words related to it. I still meant self-sufficiency by *rehabilitation,* but now with a nuance that suggested some of the limitations of self-sufficiency as an exclusive cultural ideal—for example, the tendency to rely on bureaucratic institutions of care at the expense of personal and communal compassion. To the degree that I and my Lao counterparts allowed the ambiguity of the notion of rehabilitation to remain alive in our discussions about the orthopedic center, our dialogue was an end in itself as well as a means of formulating concrete policy. Of course, the overwhelming power of U.S. political and social institutions in Laos at the time (1969–1974) ultimately blunted the audibility of the Lao voice and limited the degree to which genuine dialogue could take place.

The dichotomy that Bakhtin and the coffeehouse and Lao examples set up between creative and hierarchical dialogue is similar to the opposition between what we may refer to as the synchronic and diachronic dimensions of the linguistic community. Not only is the synchronic, or "spacial," dimension identical with the creative tension or identity through difference that characterizes the primary relationship among the voices of the linguistic community, but its independent status is continually placed at risk in the diachronic, or "historical-temporal," movement of the community toward the social unity and direction required for production and governance. In the establishment of this diachronic unity and direction, the voice of one or another group is always raised to the level of an oracle, to the status of the "holy," the "true," or some other code word for nonrevisable or monological discourse. As elements of the discourse and historical narrative associated with the oracle are inculcated into the discursive practices of the other members of the community, the voice of the dominant group begins to speak from all the voices of the community, to come from everywhere and nowhere, and thus to suppress the other voices of the community, to diminish their audibility, through a form of linguistic co-optation.

Although such an oracle represents the diachronic or historical-temporal dimension of the community and is based at least in part on the ascendancy of one group in the community, it can maintain its power as an oracle only, paradoxically, by refusing a complete suppression of the other voices that make up the linguistic community; that is, only by permitting the synchronic dimension of the community to retain its unspoken but constant status as an essential part of the structure of the linguistic community. To ensure an acceptable level of organizational efficiency, for example, the representatives of the ruling oracle must preserve a division of labor and hence grant at least a limited degree of integrity to the other voices and discursive practices in the community. On pain of literally losing its voice, moreover, the dominant group must also maintain an opposing voice, one whose difference clearly demarcates the dominant group's identity and oracular status. In current U.S. politics, for example, the Republicans have to keep alive the image of an "evil empire" or "the liberal" to ensure that their identity is carried into office along with their bodies. Because the dominant group can never fully suppress the other voices of the community, because of this constant opposition between a synchronic base and a diachronic direction, the linguistic community is the source of both oracles and their continual overthrow, the nearest that the linguistic community can come to achieving the sovereignty of its "spatial" or synchronic dimension, of the full interplay or creative tension of the voices that compose the community.

Liberal Democracy and the Oracle of Modernity

By considering the modern period of Western civilization—the seventeenth through the nineteenth centuries—we can illustrate the tendency to produce oracles and to subordinate the synchronic to the diachronic dimension of the community. The modern period is characterized by a narrative that eulogizes humanity's technological mastery of nature and by the establishment of liberal democracy in Western Europe, England, and the United States. But we can equally well understand this period, and its continuation into the twentieth century, in terms of the progressive subordination of the cries for liberty, fraternity, and equality to the rhetoric of economic and technological development, the democratic play of voices to the modern oracle of capitalism and its later more technocratic developments.

In the early capitalist phase of this subordination of the synchronic to the diachronic dimension of the community, the creative tension among the voices of the revolutionary period is replaced by a set of formal rights and the sanctification of private property as the wheel of progress. Thus even in the earliest stages of the overthrow of the aristocracy and clergy of England and Europe, many of the spokespersons of revolution and social change emphasized that the right of private property and the leadership of the producers of wealth must constitute the basis of the new societies. These spokespersons assumed, moreover, that "owner of private property" and "producer of wealth" were synonymous. At the end of the English Civil War (1642–1646), therefore, property remained the foundation of political rights, and Ireton, the Leveller leader, argued that "liberty cannot be provided for in a general sense, if property [is to] be preserved."[7] In the philosophical tablets of John Locke, adult males tacitly consented to a "social contract" when they inherited property from their fathers, and the status of those who had nothing to inherit, the propertyless, was left unclear.[8]

The framers of the U.S. Constitution echoed these sentiments toward property when they attempted to establish bicameral houses that would ensure that the poorer majority could not curtail the interests of the propertied and wealthy. Thus John Adams exclaimed, "The rich ought to have an effectual barrier in the constitution against being robbed, plundered, and murdered, as well as the poor; and this can never be without an independent Senate."[9] Expressing the same attitude, Alexander Hamilton emphasized that a "representational" form of democracy could curtail the "confusion and instability" of a democracy vested in the "collective body of the people."[10]

As these examples illustrate, democracy may have started out in the Enlightenment as social movements seeking to secure popular power for the relatively disenfranchised groups in Western Europe, England, and North America, but it quickly became a means of permanently establishing a division between the rich and the poor, of converting this schism into a "fact of nature," and of controlling the conflict between the two. As all segments of society began to equate democracy and freedom with property rights and voting for representatives, the voice of the bourgeoisie attained the status of an oracle and heard itself repeated in all quarters of society. In the United States today, therefore, the tendency to link democracy with "free enterprise" and to think that capitalism is the most efficient means of production works in favor of maintaining the power of the corporate sector of society. In the class structure of the United States, therefore, democracy does not provide a basis for voices to be heard but guarantees that ownership of the means of production will determine which voices are permitted to have the last word.

Because democracy was progressively subordinated to the oracle of production, one should not be surprised that modern capitalist societies are increasingly textured if not usurped by a technical-managerial elite who advocate the rule of a technocratic form of rationality. As Gouldner states, the ideology of this new strata of elites "holds that productivity depends primarily on science and technology and that society's problems are solvable on a technological basis, and with the use of educationally acquired technical competence."[11]

Not only does the discourse of expert decision making increasingly dominate in the corporate, military, and governmental bureaucracies, but the growing acceptance of this ideology is mediated and reflected in the computational model of mind that holds sway in the new discipline of cognitive science and that is pervasively employed in cognitive psychology and linguistics. On this model, the mind is portrayed as a set of computerlike activities, as a "prototechnocrat," and efficiency, control, and transparency are implicitly valued over other human and social attributes. The "technocratic rationality" valorized in this view of the mind and in the ideology that supports the new technocratic elite replaces the play of voices with a set of rules that determine in advance what can count as a legitimate experience, or "input," and a permissible goal. Such a view of rationality and therefore of voice, elevates one type of reasoning and its specialists to the status of a modern oracle. This voice too begins to hear itself spoken from everywhere and nowhere as people increasingly incorporate elements of information-processing terminology into their everyday vocabularies. This voice too begins to identify itself with the diachronic dimension of the linguistic community, to hold the synchronic dimension or interplay of voices as a fading and discredited memory, and to rearticulate democracy in terms of the election of elites who will then make all substantive decisions on the basis of their technical knowledge.

Marx, Nietzsche, and the Critique of Liberal Democracy

Both Marx and Nietzsche criticize liberal democracy and, at least implicitly, the oracle of technocracy by placing them within the broader setting of Western history and civilization. But whereas Marx sees liberal democracy as part of the ideology that functions to support the hegemony of the bourgeoisie in capitalist society, Nietzsche views it as a continuation of the nihilism that has characterized Western civilization since Socrates and Plato. Whereas Marx attempts to show that liberal democracy and the capitalism it supports are part of a historical movement that will culminate in a classless society, a society in which "the free development of each is the condition for the free development of all,"[12] Nietzsche proclaims that the Western community must undergo a "transvaluation of values" before any political or social movement can escape the nihilistic codes that govern Western thinking and action, that "human history" must begin *before* any liberation movement and not after.

Marx and Nietzsche interpret the meaning of liberal democracy differently because each appeals to a different dimension of the linguistic community and does not see that both dimensions are necessary for the more promising society that they seek. By clarifying the sense in which Marx continues the attachment of Enlightenment thought to the diachronic or historical dimension of society and the sense in which Nietzsche seeks to transform the linguistic community through its synchronic dimension, we can also show how their views are incorporable into a single discourse on democracy.

Although Marx criticizes liberalism for curtailing the development of individuals in favor of concentrating the means of production in the hands of legally sanctioned owners,[13] he thinks that correction of this inequality will come about exclusively through the further unfolding of the diachronic dimension of society, through further changes in the social relations of production. Marx can make this prognosis because he places liberal democracy within the broader narrative of historical material-ism.[14] According to that narrative, history is a sequence of modes of production, each characterized by a dynamic or dialectical relation between the material forces and social relations of production. When the material forces of production have expanded to a critical point, the exploited members of the community will act to transform the social relations of production to accommodate the further growth of the material forces of production and to promote their own emancipation. Because the dominant ideal or ideology of the old mode of production functioned to maintain the hegemony of its ruling class, these will be replaced by the oracle of the new ruling class.[15]

In his historical narrative, Marx associates production not only with class struggle and change in the social relations among the members of society[16] but also, like Mill and other thinkers in the Enlightenment tradition, with the development of human capacities or the realization of "species being" and "self-activity."[17] In *The German Ideology,* therefore, Marx claims that "the appropriation of [the productive] forces is itself nothing more than the development of the individual capacities corresponding to the material instruments of production."[18]

Besides associating production with the development of human nature, Marx also holds that the emancipation of the proletariat requires that it be aware of this relationship. Thus Marx states not only that the proletariat is part of the social relations of production and as labor power part of the material forces of production but that the expansion of the material forces of production includes the proletariat's conscious-ness that it can take over control of the apparatus of production and thereby ensure the full development of its human capacities.[19] Because Marx adds that the proletariat advances this consciousness as its interest and destiny, and as that of all humanity, when it takes political power,[20] he commits himself to a teleological view of history.[21] In Marx's narrative of history, therefore, a classless society is not only a description of the direction of history but a moral injunction for its completion.

On the basis of this description, Marx's historical materialism is both a continuation and a radicalization of Enlightenment and liberal thought. It is a continuation because its adherents hold that human emancipation depends primarily on the development of the apparatus of production, the diachronic dimension of the linguistic community, and it is a radicalization because Marx shows that such emancipation requires the overthrow of liberal democracy's sanction of private property and the control of the means of production by a particular class.

Despite Marx's radicalization of the historical movement of the linguistic community, a Nietzschean would have to claim that his narrative should take into account the synchronic dimension of the linguistic community as well as the diachronic. Nietzsche does not state his critical treatment of Western nihilism in these terms, but his unrelenting genealogical critique of such notions as "identity," "unity," and "truth" amount to a repudiation of all totalizations of history in teleological terms, that is, in terms that subordinate difference and a proliferate present to identity and a unitary direction.

More specifically, Nietzsche portrays human communities as a plethora of value-creating powers, as "chaos," and employs his critical notion of *ressentiment*—existing as the mere negation of something else—to account for the tendency to create the oracles that repudiate or attempt to eliminate this chaos.[22] Although Marxism can explain the emergence of any oracle in terms of historical materialism, Nietzsche suggests that the source of oracularization itself is in the fear of chaos, of losing one's identity or voice in a sea of discursive possibilities.

To illustrate not only his notion of *ressentiment* but also how the metaphysical and axiological codes of the West continue to disseminate the ethos of the original *ressentiment,* Nietzsche asks us to imagine a stratum of knightly aristocrats who spontaneously affirm the fecundity, diversity, and uncertainty of life through their actions and a stratum of priestly aristocrats who do not possess, but envy, the qualities of the knightly aristocrats. Because the priestly aristocrats can neither accept the implicit value codes of the knightly aristocrats nor defeat these knights physically, they promulgate a value code that favors weakness over strength, a world of permanence or God over the world of change, and control over spontaneity.[23] When the knightly aristocrats reach a period of self-doubt and decline, they too adopt the value code of the priestly aristocrats, a code that is now repeated as the gospel from all the voices in the community.

Because one of these reactive values, truth, undermines all the rest and ultimately its own foundation, Nietzsche holds that members of the Western community are faced with an existence that they can see only as meaningless and are therefore placed in the position of either rejecting the entire tradition of oracles and affirming "chaos" and the plethora of value-creating forces[24] or adopting the position of the "last man," exchanging life for the narcotic of routine.[25]

In relation to the passive nihilism of the last man,[26] Nietzsche describes a situation that is similar to either late capitalism or technocracy:

> Once we possess that common economic management of the earth that will soon be inevitable, mankind will be able to find its best meaning as a machine in the service of this economy—as a tremendous clockwork, composed of ever smaller, ever more subtly "adapted" gears; as an ever-growing superfluity of all dominating and commanding elements; as a whole of tremendous force, whose individual factors represent *minimal forces, minimal values.*[27]

Within the "clockwork society" of the last man, Nietzsche states, democracy and equality of rights can amount to no more than the anonymity of the "herd"[28] and the violation of the rights of those who appear strange or creative or "higher."[29] Because Nietzsche believes that men and women cannot ultimately accept the strictures of such a clockwork society on their creative powers, he argues that they will throw off the tradition of oracles, transform all the old codes, and affirm a community that he likens to "controverting gods," "an eternal fleeing and seeking each other again of many gods, as the happy controverting of each other, conversing again with each other, and converging again of many gods."[30] Although Nietzsche does not say so, we can regard this community of "controverting gods" as one of the synonyms for the synchronic dimension of the linguistic community, the creative play of voices that is continually drowned out by the oracle that guides the historical-temporal or diachronic direction of the community.

If Nietzsche's image of "controverting gods" is accepted also as a description of a democratic community, democracy requires the spontaneous or autochthonous affirmation of the play of voices that establishes one's status as a voice. If this affirmation does not occur prior to the attempt to achieve a complete democracy, one will be led to evaluate everything in terms of the old codes and their preoccupation with the unity required for production and governance, thereby contributing to the continuation of the oracular tradition and the suppression of the interplay of voices. This Nietzschean emphasis upon an autochthonous affirmation of the creative tension of voices has three implications that we must elaborate if we are to complete our description of democracy and incorporate within it the views of Marx and Nietzsche, that is, both dimensions of the linguistic community.

Marx, Nietzsche, and the Creative Tension of Voices

The first of these implications is a readjustment of the status of the Nietzschean voice in the linguistic community. Since the synchronic dimension is inseparable from its continual transformation into the historical or temporal direction of society, its affirmation is equally an endorsement of any idealization of itself, of any oracle that calls for the demarginalization of suppressed voices. Because control of the means of production by one class still constitutes the most immediate and pervasive way voices are silenced, ignored, or rendered uniform through the ideological apparatus of the ruling class, Marx's narrative of the elimination of class structure is the most promising of all such diachronic idealizations of the creative tension of voices. Thus the Nietzschean voice must grant equal status to its Marxian counterpart.

But this affirmation of the interplay of voices is at the same time a call for the dissolution of all oracles, including the Marxist one to which it has just consented. For as long as the Marxist oracle is relevant to a society, therefore, it must continually be dissolved and reestablished by the members of the linguistic community, continually granted and divested of its oracular status. In particular, we must bear in mind three internal limitations of Marx's formal position.

The first of these limitations concerns the opposition that Marx's historical materialism sets up tacitly between the present and the future of the linguistic community. Because the Marxist narrative assigns members of the community a value in terms of the relationship between their actions and an end or meaning to be achieved in the future, the members of the community have only an instrumental standing for one another in the present. Such a narrative account of history overlooks the value that the interplay of voices, a unity established through difference, has as an end in itself and does not sanction the aspects and promises of the present that stand outside the goal postulated by the narrative. Because emancipation must then come from the letter of a doctrine rather than from what people might produce from their own desires, relationships, and critical thoughts in the immediate situation, the din of earthly voices is once again replaced by an oracle, and the synchronic dimension is dominated by the diachronic.[31]

Marx seems to have been aware of the restrictiveness of his or anyone else's narrative and sought to warn his readers of it. In *Economic and Philosophic Manuscripts of 1844,* for example, he states that communism should not be reified into the goal of human existence, that communism as the reified or formalized goal of political activity would destroy the possibility of achieving what communism is all about—"real life":

> Socialism is man's *positive self-consciousness,* no longer mediated through the annulment of religion, just as *real life* is man's positive reality, no longer mediated through the annulment of private property, through *communism.* Communism is the position as the negation of the negation, and is hence the *actual* phase necessary for the next stage of historical development in the process of human emancipation and rehabilitation. *Communism* is the necessary pattern and the dynamic principle of the immediate future, but communism as such is not the goal of human development—which goal is the structure of human society.[32]

Although it is difficult to say exactly what Marx has in mind by "real life" here, surely part of it is captured by Nietzsche's appeal to the positive sense of "chaos," the multidimensionality or fecundity of existence, which we have interpreted in terms of the "creative tension of voices." Although this appeal may itself be couched in terms of a narrative, it is nonetheless the antithesis of narrative to the degree that it does not posit an ideal that points to the future in order to evaluate where one is now, but demands only that we be more what we already are, members of the linguistic community and its interplay of voices. Affirmation must precede development, and one must "fall back into one's identity" at the same time that one seeks this identity's further career in the future.

The second limitation of Marx's historical materialism concerns Marx's claim that the development of our individual and social capacities, and hence our emancipation, is contingent upon society's control of the means of production. Although this doctrine is true, leaving it as it stands might tempt us to view the apparatus of production as more central than politics or the interplay of voices to society and thereby lead us to give the efficient operation of the means of production priority over the democratization of the workplace. In order to honor with Marx one of the greatest testimonies to participatory democracy in history, the Paris Commune, we must emphasize the sense in which the interplay of voices directly characterizes the technology of production and thereby strengthen the relation that Marx establishes between emancipation and control of the means of production. Because we are linguistic animals, voice characterizes not only our discursive practices but also our nondiscursive activities. Just as the syntax of language is ultimately describable in terms of whether a linguistic exchange is dialogical or hierarchical, so a piece of equipment is always part of the syntax of communication that characterize a workplace—for example, a democratic or, in contrast, a management-regulated workplace. Because of this communicative dimension of the technology of production, full democratization of the workplace is the prerequisite of any other type of emancipation, including Marx's notion of the development of human capacities.[33] The dialogue that characterizes the relation between the members of the community, therefore, is not only a means to other ends but the way we are a community on the level of our discursive and nondiscursive activities.[34]

Marx's narrative also leads him to concentrate on class voices as the means of gaining control over the apparatus of production in the name of society as a whole. Despite the importance of class, however, exclusive or primary emphasis upon it muffles other radical voices; for example, those of racial minorities, women, and groups marginalized because of their lifestyles, such as gays and lesbians. Fulfillment of the demands of these groups is also necessary for the free interplay of the voices of the community, and it is not clear that liberating the means of production would be sufficient to accomplish this. For these three reasons, then, we must give only a provisional status to Marx's role as our emancipatory oracle, one that is continually critiqued from within while it guides us toward a classless society.

The third implication of the affirmation of the creative tension of voices—and now, along with it, the provisional oracle of Marx's historical materialism—concerns the exclusion of certain members from the linguistic community. To affirm the creative play of voices may mean the simultaneous endorsement and dissolution of oracles and the ongoing contestation of voices, but it does not entail the affirmation of those who would deny the status of voice to other members of the community. Even if the oracle of the hegemonic class is inculcated into the other voices of the linguistic community, the members of that class still grant the status of voice to the other members of the community and leave open the possibility of hearing them and being influenced by them. In contrast, racism, sexism, and similar tendencies deny vocal standing to other members of the community. Affirmation of the creative tension of voices, therefore, logically excludes such doctrines as these, at least in their recalcitrant forms, from participatory representation in the dialogue of the community.[35]

All of these considerations suggest that democracy is neither a consensus nor a mere plurality of voices but the continual affirmation of what we already are, a creative tension of voices. Because this creative tension involves both a synchronic and a diachronic dimension, its affirmation is the continual reachievement of itself, the constant overturning of oracles to increase the audibility of the voices that have been marginalized or otherwise suppressed, to hear them in the sense that simultaneously gives life to our voices and yet places our identity at risk, and in this way to celebrate the play of voices of which we are a part. Two of these voices are embodied in the works of Marx and Nietzsche, and it is through their provocative relation to one another that we find a discourse on democracy, a discourse that resists congealing into either one of them taken separately or into any of the other oracles that arise as necessary accompaniments of the ongoing play of voices.[36]

NOTES

1. Both Marx and Nietzsche recognize the centrality of language for individual and social existence. Marx, for example, says that "language *is* practical consciousness" [1845], *The German Ideology,* in R. Tucker, *The Marx-Engels Reader,* 3d ed. (New York: W. W. Norton, 1978), p. 158, and that language is both a product of society and the very presence [*Dasein*] of the community, "a presence that goes without saying" [1939], *Grundrisse,* trans. M. Nicolaus (New York: Vintage, 1973), p. 490. In a similar vein, Nietzsche states that "consciousness has developed only under the pressure of the need for communication. . . . Consciousness is really only a net of communication between human beings" [1882], *The Gay Science,* trans. W. Kaufmann (New York: Vintage, 1974), p. 298. Although the role they assign to language does not amount to an endorsement of the notion of "voice" that I am developing here, it indicates that this notion, on the one hand, and Marx's notion of the "mode of production" and Nietzsche's notion of the "will-to-power" or the "active" and "reactive forces" that compose society, on the other, might be more compatible than one would expect. In the section of this paper on the responses of Marx and Nietzsche to liberal democracy, I will indicate how "voice" extends down into the nondiscursive relations of society, for example, into the apparatus of production, and how the interplay of voices, particularly the opposition between "oracles" and "voices," is similar to Nietzsche's notion of a "will-to-power" while still maintaining the spirit if not always the letter of Marxism.

2. A more complete account of this "creative tension of voices" than I can give here would also have to refer to the "dialogical" character of the linguistic community. Not only is each voice established by its difference from all the rest, but each voice is always a direct response to another voice and indirectly to each of the actual and possible voices that make up the linguistic community. We are therefore members of the linguistic community in our formal relation to the other voices of the community and in our participation in a community dialogue that carries us along as we articulate it. Moreover, the "lateral" mutual establishment of voices provides us directly with a sense of the *possible* voices and discursive practices to which we may respond, while our status as participants in the ongoing dialogue of the community provides us directly with a sense of which responses are *appropriate* at any moment of the dialogue. In this way, our membership in the linguistic community accounts for our communicative and, more generally, our cognitive competence, and there is no need for the computational activity that cognitive science

specifies as the foundation of our cognitive competence.

3. M. Bakhtin [1963], *Problems of Dostoyevski's Poetics,* trans. C. Emerson (Minneapolis: University of Minnesota Press, 1984).

4. M. Bakhtin [1975], "Discourse in the Novel," in *The Dialogic Imagination: Four Essays,* ed. Michael Holquist, trans. Caryl Emerson and M. Holquist, Slavic Series, no. 1 (Austin: University of Texas Press, 1981), p. 273. Quoted in K. Hirschkop, "A Response to the Forum on Mikhail Bakhtin," in *Bakhtin: Essays and Dialogues on His Work,* ed. Gary Saul Morson (Chicago: University of Chicago Press, 1981), p. 78.

5. On this point, see Hirschkop, "Response," p. 78.

6. R. Sennett, *The Fall of Public Man: On the Social Psychology of Capitalism* (New York: Vintage Books, 1974) p. 81.

7. D. M. Wolfe, ed., *Leveller Manifestoes of the Puritan Revolution* (New York: Thomas Nelson, 1944), p. 73. Quoted in A. Arblaster, *Democracy* (Minneapolis: University of Minnesota Press, 1987) p. 33.

8. See Arblaster, *Democracy,* p. 34.

9. Quoted in Arblaster, *Democracy,* p. 40.

10. R. B. Morris, ed., *Alexander Hamilton and the Founding of the Nation* (New York: Harper Torchbook, 1969), p. 131. Quoted in Arblaster, *Democracy,* p. 40.

11. A. Gouldner, *The Future of Intellectuals and the Rise of the New Class* (New York: The Seabury Press, 1979), p. 24.

12. K. Marx and F. Engels [1848], *The Communist Manifesto,* in R. Tucker, *Reader,* p. 491.

13. Marx says that the ideology of the bourgeoisie in liberal society—the doctrine of "abstract rights," property, and the legal code—allows men and women freedom for the possession of property but not from property (Marx [1843], *On the Jewish Question,* in Tucker, *Reader,* p. 56) and that John Stuart Mill's political economy separates production from distribution in order to guarantee the bourgeoisie's continued ownership and control of the means of production while still holding out the alluring possibility of a fairer distribution of society's products (Marx and Engels, *Manifesto,* pp. 348, 385). In relation to this last point, Marx argues that "[the economists'] object is rather to represent production in contradistinction to distribution—see Mill, for example—as subject to eternal laws independent of history, and then to substitute bourgeois relations, in an underhand way, as immutable natural laws of society *in abstracto*" (Marx, *Grundrisse,* p. 87).

14. In a recent article ("The Value of Narrativity in the Representation of Reality," in W. J. T. Mitchell, ed., *On Narrative* [Chicago: University of Chicago Press, 1981]) Hayden White argues that narration implies the imposition of "an order of meaning" upon events, and he specifies that this meaning must also appear (1) to "speak from the events themselves" (p. 3), (2) to provide "closure" to the sequence of events (p. 5), and, most important for White, (3) to be "intimately related to, if not a function of, the impulse to moralize reality, that is, to identify [reality] with the social system that is the source of any morality that we can imagine" (p. 14). With regard to this last implication, White says that the narrator experiences events as a *demand* for some form of closure; that is, the narrator experiences events as the focus of a conflict between contesting powers who are seeking narratives of moral legitimation for their actions or views with respect to those events. I will use the term *narrative* in a sense very close to White's characterization of it.

15. Thus Marx says, "This conception of history depends on our ability to expound the real process of production, starting out from the material production of life itself, and to comprehend the form of intercourse connected with this and created by this mode of production (i.e., civil society in its various stages), as the basis of all history; and to show it in its action as State, to explain all the different theoretical products and forms of consciousness, religion, philosophy, ethics, etc., etc., and trace their origins and growth from that basis; by which means, of course, the whole thing can be depicted in its totality

(and therefore, too, the reciprocal action of these various sides on one another)." *German Ideology,* p. 164; also cited in M. Jay, *Marxism and Totality* (Berkeley: University of California Press, 1984), p. 63.

16. In class-stratified societies, these social relations involve a "division of labor." This division of labor, in turn, is originally based on the separation of mental from physical labor in production (Marx, *German Ideology,* p. 159), ultimately the division between those who control the means of production and those who follow the directives of the controllers.

17. Marx, *German Ideology,* p. 191.

18. Not only will the proletarian revolution help achieve the full realization of human capacities—"a complete and no longer restricted self-activity, which consists in the appropriation of a totality of capacities" (Marx, *German Ideology,* p. 191)—but it will also rid the proletariate and society of the bourgeois consciousness and rationality, "of all the muck of ages" (p. 193) that have helped maintain the division of labor and exploitation.

19. In *German Ideology,* Marx states very clearly that the mode of cooperation is part of the forces of production as well as the structure of the social relations of production: "It follows from this that a certain mode of production, or industrial stage, is always combined with a certain mode of co-operation, or social stage, and this mode of co-operation is itself a 'productive force' " (p. 157). Thus one of the changes in the forces of production that can fire a social revolution is a change in the desires and outlook of the proletariate itself.

20. Thus Marx states that the proletariat "must first conquer for itself political power in order to represent its interest in turn as the general interest, which in the first moment it is forced to do" (*German Ideology,* p. 161).

21. In order to appropriate the productive forces, to rejoin what capitalism has split in twain, to replace the history of exploitation with human history, and to allow all members of society to develop their capacities and their unity, Marx declares that social action and revolution are necessary, not the mere disputation of ideas. One must overthrow the limiting ideologies of the bourgeoisie and the technocrats by hastening the change from the current mode of production into one characterized by a classless society and a unity rather than a division of labor. Against many of the left Hegelians (particularly Feuerbach), therefore, Marx argues forcefully that ideology cannot be changed on the level of consciousness itself, on the level of the "criticism of ideas," but requires social revolution: "[Historical materialism] comes to the conclusion that all forms and products of consciousness cannot be dissolved by mental criticism, by resolution into 'self-consciousness' or transformation into 'apparitions,' 'specters,' 'fancies,' etc., but only by the practical overthrow of the actual social relations which gave rise to this idealistic humbug; that not criticism but revolution is the driving force of history, also of religion, of philosophy and all other types of theory" (*German Ideology,* p. 164). In his *Theses on Feuerbach* [1845] (in Tucker, *Reader*), moreover, Marx states not only that "the human essence" is the ensemble of social relations involved in production, but that "the point" is to change, rather than merely interpret, these relations (p. 145). Combining this point with that of the last note, then, revolution requires both the appropriate material conditions and the consciousness of the proletariat, with the proviso that the latter is conditioned by the former.

22. Thus Nietzsche states that "this, then, is quite the contrary of what the noble man does, who conceives the basic concept 'good' in advance and spontaneously out of himself and only then creates for himself an idea of 'bad'! This 'bad' of noble origin and that 'evil' out of the caldron of unsatisfied hatred—the former an after-production, a side issue, a contrasting shade, the latter on the contrary the original thing, the beginning, the distinctive *deed* in the conception of a slave morality—how different these words 'bad' and 'evil' are" [1887], *On the Genealogy of Morals,* trans. W. Kaufmann (New York: Vintage, 1967), vol. 1, sec. 11. Even the concept of "happiness" is determined by whether it comes from self-affirmation or from *ressentiment:* "The 'well-born' *felt* themselves to be the 'happy'; they did not have to establish their happiness artificially by examining their

enemies, or to persuade themselves, *deceive* themselves, that they were happy (as all men of *ressentiment* are in the habit of doing); and they likewise knew, as rounded men replete with energy and therefore *necessarily* active, that happiness should not be sundered from action—being active was with them necessarily a part of happiness (whence *eu prattein* takes its origin)—all very much the opposite of 'happiness' at the level of the impotent, the oppressed, and those in whom poisonous and inimical feelings are festering, with whom it appears as essentially narcotic, drug, rest, peace, 'sabbath,' slackening of tension and relaxing of limbs, in short *passively*" (vol. 1, sec. 10). Finally, Nietzsche equates *ressentiment* with a negative "value-positing eye": "This inversion of the value-positing eye—this *need* to direct one's view outward instead of back to oneself—is of the essence of *ressentiment:* in order to exist, slave morality always first needs a hostile external world; it needs, physiologically speaking, external stimuli in order to act at all—its action is fundamentally reaction" (vol. 1, sec. 10).

23. For Nietzsche, the value code of these "ascetic priests" extends even to the scientific employment of the notion of "truth": "The truthful man, in the audacious and ultimate sense presupposed by the faith in science, *thereby affirms another world* than that of life, nature, and history, and insofar as he affirms this "other world," does this not mean that he has to deny its antithesis, this world, *our* world? . . . It is still a *metaphysical faith* that underlies our faith in science—and we men of knowledge of today, we godless men and anti-metaphysicians, we, too, still derive *our* flame from the fire ignited by a faith millennia old, the Christian faith, which was also Plato's, that God is truth, that truth is *divine (Genealogy,* vol. 3, sec. 24).

24. Prior to the "self-overcoming" of nihilism, Nietzsche states, the struggle between the "deification of life" and the "worship of a beyond" must continue at a "higher level": "The two *opposing* values 'good and bad,' 'good and evil' have been engaged in a fearful struggle on earth for thousands of years; and though the latter value has certainly been on top for a long time, there are still places where the struggle is as yet undecided. One might even say that it has risen ever higher and thus become more and more profound and spiritual: so that today there is perhaps no more decisive mark of a *'higher nature,'* a more spiritual nature, than that of being divided in this sense and a genuine battleground of these opposed values" (*Genealogy,* vol. 1, sec. 16).

25. Even if humanity chooses the route of the "last man," Nietzsche makes clear that even this amounts to one of the ways in which humanity maintains or declares its existence: "We can no longer conceal from ourselves *what* is expressed by all that willing which has taken its direction from the ascetic ideal: this hatred of the human, and even more of the animal, and more still of the material, this horror of the senses, of reason itself, this fear of happiness and beauty, this longing to get away from all appearance, change, becoming, death, wishing, from longing itself—all this means—let us dare to grasp it—a *will to nothingness,* an aversion to life, a rebellion against the most fundamental presuppositions of life; but it is and remains a *will!* . . . And, to repeat, in conclusion to what I said at the beginning: man would rather will *nothingness* than *not* will" (*Genealogy,* vol. 3, sec. 28).

26. In *The Will to Power* [1883–1888], trans. W. Kaufmann and R. Hollingdale (New York: Vintage, 1967), secs. 22, 23, 29, and *On the Genealogy of Morals* (vol. 3, secs. 17–19), Nietzsche distinguishes between active and passive strategies of preserving a nihilistic form of life. G. Deleuze [1962], *Nietzsche and Philosophy,* trans. H. Tomlinson (New York: Colombia University Press, 1983) argues that Nietzsche distinguishes between three forms of nihilism, negative, reactive, and passive.

27. Nietzsche, *Will to Power,* sec. 865.

28. "The herd man in Europe today gives himself the appearance of being the only permissible kind of man and glorifies his attributes, which make him tame, easy to get along with, and useful to the herd, as if they were the truly human virtues: namely, public spirit, benevolence, industriousness, moderation, indulgence, and pity." Nietzsche [1886],

Beyond Good and Evil, trans. W. Kaufmann, (New York: Vintage, 1966), p. 111. Nietzsche also speaks of anarchists, democrats, and socialists as being "at one . . . in their thorough and instinctive hostility to every other form of society except that of the autonomous herd." Ibid, p. 116. Both of these quotations are also presented in Love, *Marx, Nietzsche, and Modernity* (New York: Columbia University Press, 1986), and I have benefited greatly from her discussion of Nietzsche's treatment of democracy.

29. Nietzsche, *Beyond Good and Evil,* p. 139.

30. Nietzsche, [1883–1892], *Thus Spoke Zarathustra,* in *The Portable Nietzsche,* ed., trans. W. Kaufmann (New York: Viking Press, 1968). This creative tension between the "controverting gods" is also captured in Nietzsche's image of the ancient Greek *polis* as an "agon" or contest, in which any member who becomes *best* at something would immediately be ostracized to another community: "That is the core of the hellenic notion of the contest: it abominates the rule of one and fears its dangers; it desires, as a *protection* against the genius, another genius." "Homer's Contest," in *Portable Nietzsche,* p. 37.

31. A recurrent problem in Marxism concerns the status of the person prior to the achievement of a classless society. During such a preliminary period, do we have any status other than that of instruments to be used to achieve communism? Although it is clear that Marx did not view persons as instruments during any stage of the journey to a classless society, nothing in his historical materialism prevents one from interpreting persons in this light and using that interpretation to justify a Stalinist interpretation of the "dictatorship of the proletariat." By emphasizing the ontological and moral primacy of the creative tension of voices, one can provide an "ends in themselves" status of persons within an otherwise Marxist framework. Because persons gain this status through the mutual establishment of the voices they articulate, one does not need to resort to the liberal ploy of assigning persons abstract rights that seem to come from nowhere or from some Kantian transcendental sphere. Because the status of the individual on this view comes through the community, one does not lapse back into the liberal form of individualism either.

32. Marx, in Tucker, *Reader,* p. 146.

33. This democratization of the workplace would require worker and consumer councils, councils composed of workers or their elected representatives and charged with running the affairs of their production unit. See A. Smith, "Habermas and History: The Institutionalization of Discourse as Historical Project," in *At the Nexus of Philosophy and History,* ed. Bernard Dauenhauer (Athens: University of Georgia Press, 1987) and M. Albert and R. Hahnel, *Socialism Today and Tomorrow* (Boston: South End Press, 1981). It would also require technology designed to discourage demand hierarchies as part of their inherent structure; for example, solar as opposed to nuclear energy systems, personal computer as opposed to mainframe-based organizations, small farms as opposed to agribusinesses. See L. Winner, *The Whale and the Reactor: A Search for Limits in an Age of High Technology* (Chicago: Chicago University Press, 1986).

34. The tendency to dismiss the synchronic dimension of society, to think of the interplay of voices as a means and never as an end, is also evident in the technocratic form of rule advocated by Plato. Whereas Socrates' dialogues were open-ended, Plato built an end or "death" into his version of them. Instead of valuing dialogue for its own sake, Plato subordinated it to the goal of revealing the univocal and unchanging forms or ideals that he felt provided an autonomous basis for human knowledge and the governance of societies. The achievement of the theoretical goal of the dialogue logically entailed the termination of the interchange between the participants. On the basis of this view of dialogue, Plato constructed his famous republic, one that mandated a strict hierarchical division between social classes and a single source of ideology. Because Plato placed the management of this society in the hands of a special class of experts, the guardians, his society foreshadows the contemporary tendency toward technocracy.

35. Because the view of democracy put forward here rests on a philosophical view of

the self and community, it differs from the foundationless and "intersubjective reflective equilibrium" or "end of ideology" view put forward by such thinkers as Rawls ("Justness and Fairness: Political Not Metaphysical," *Philosophy and Public Affairs* 14[1985]) and Rorty ("The Priority of Democracy to Philosophy," unpublished paper, 1988). Whereas the creative tension of voices provides a rationale for excluding some voices from participation in the linguistic community, Rawls and Rorty appear to go much further than that, excluding all philosophical views of the self and of the meaning of life on the basis of a felt preference for the U.S. liberal tradition (cf. Rorty, p. 18, n. 20). Such an exclusionary view of democracy seems to be the antithesis of democracy as the interplay of voices and to reflect a strident political insularity despite its otherwise "tolerant" tone.

36. Marx and Nietzsche are the primary sources of two contemporary philosophical movements, respectively, Western Marxism and poststructuralism. Both of these movements provide the richest critiques of contemporary society and culture that we have today. Although they differ from one another as much as do Marx and Nietzsche, one would hope that the members of both movements could see their differences as resources for their common goal and for the continuation of their separate identities.

III

Feminism

9

A Feminist Aspect Theory
of the Self

ANN FERGUSON

T he contemporary women's movement has generated major new theories of the social construction of gender and male power. The feminist attack on the masculinist assumptions of cognitive psychology, psychoanalysis, and most of the other academic disciplines has raised questions about some basic assumptions of those fields. For example, feminist economists have questioned the public-private split of much of mainstream economics that ignores the social necessity of women's unpaid housework and child care.[1] Feminist psychologists have challenged cognitive and psychoanalytic categories of human moral and gender development, arguing that they are biased toward the development of male children rather than female children.[2] Feminist anthropologists have argued that sex-gender systems, based on the male exchange of women in marriage, have socially produced gender differences in sexuality and parenting skills that have perpetuated different historical and cultural forms of male dominance.[3] Feminist philosophers and theorists have suggested that we must reject the idea of a gender-free epistemological standpoint from which to understand the world.[4] Finally, radical feminists have argued that the liberal state permits a pornography industry that sexually objectifies women, thus legitimizing male violence against women.[5]

Though all of these feminist approaches to understanding the social perpetuation of male dominance are insightful, they are based on overly simplistic theories of the self and human agency. As a result, they tend to give us misleading ideas of what is required for social change. For one thing, they don't allow us to understand how women who are socialized into subordinate gender roles nonetheless can develop the sense of self-respect and the personal power necessary to be strong feminists able to change institutional sexism. In order to grasp what is necessary to develop a strong and powerful sense of self, we must have the correct theory of what the self is. I shall defend an aspect theory of the self.

Developing a Sense of Self

Most feminists would take it as a truism that women's sense of self-worth, and consequently personal power, has been weakened by a male-dominant society that has made us internalize many demeaning images of women. Thus, part of every feminist program must involve a process of feminist education that allows women to develop—some would say reclaim—a self-integrity and self-worth that will provide each of us with the psychological resources we need to develop full self-realization. Since individuals who lack a sense of self-worth are timid and afraid to take risks, women face the problem of contributing to our own subordination because of not even trying to achieve goals we really want, thus falling victim to the adage "Nothing ventured, nothing gained." But how do we conceive of the process of constructing self-respect? In what follows, I am going to present three theories of the self feminist theories have presupposed. I shall give the answers they give to the question of how women can develop a strong sense of self, critique the first two, and defend my view.

The Rational-Maximizer Theory of the Self

There is a view of self prevalent in American society today that derives from the views of such classical liberal philosophers as John Locke and Thomas Jefferson. This view, characteristic of many contemporary Americans, both liberal and conservative, holds that the self is a unified rational thinking subject possessed of free will and the ability to choose life goals and means to achieve them, as long as fate or external social coercion does not interfere. Examples of such social coercion include government legal restrictions against certain actions or strong social groups (e.g., large corporations or community groups) whose actions or policies restrict one from certain courses of action.

On this view of self, which I call the *rational-maximizer* view, humans are unified selves, rational maximizers, who operate to maximize their self-interest as defined by their goals within the external constraints laid down by force of circumstance, government, or society. Social oppression of a group—for example, women or black people—is then explained by external constraints placed in the way of individuals achieving their goals. These constraints can range from the personal prejudices of employers and potential friends and lovers to the institutional sexism involved in lesser pay for work defined socially as "women's work" or the fact that housework, defined as women's work, is unpaid labor, which makes the exchanges between men and women in the household economy unequal.

On the rational-maximizer view of self, women do not differ from men in personal identity and the human ability to choose reasonable goals and means to them. Thus, if men and women make different choices how to develop what economists call their human capital, that is, their skills and abilities, including their degree of formal education and job training, this is due not to innate gender preferences and skills (e.g., that men are more competitive and aggressive and women more nurturant and submissive). Rather, it is a result of the realistic options that society and the individual circumstances of women provide. Thus, more men than women choose to pursue graduate studies or careers in management and other high-paying careers in business, politics, and medicine because women choosing as men do would have to face much sexism and would have to work twice as hard and be twice as lucky to succeed. In a male-dominant society, it is not rationally maximizing for women to make the same choices as men, especially since most women want to be wives and mothers—whether this is socialized or innate—and these goals are more difficult to combine with the typical high-paying masculine career.

The explanation of women's lesser sense of self-worth on this view is that women lack the skills that are highly valued in our society as well as access to the wages that are necessary to achieve status and economic independence in our society. Furthermore, men, because of their comparative social and economic advantage, treat women as inferiors.

On the view that both men and women are rational maximizers, there are two social conditions necessary to develop a better sense of self for women. First is a feminist social policy that makes it less worth men's while to continue their sexist treatment of women, and second are feminist education programs that compensate women for the lack of skills society has denied them by encouraging the development of those skills necessary to compete in a man's world.

Affirmative-action programs are a good example of feminist social policy that provides opportunities for qualified women to learn the skills hitherto reserved for men in higher education and in on-the-job training. Such opportunities help those women involved to change their self-concept. Men will be persuaded to overcome their sexist attitudes when they see that women can do men's jobs as well as men and will stop treating women as inferiors.

Another kind of training need is psychological retraining. Women need consciousness-raising types of education like assertiveness training and counseling programs that advocate the goal of economic indepen- dence for women. Such programs can provide the survival skills to replace those self-denigrating traditional skills that are characteristic of most women under patriarchy, those that involve habits of deference to men and the myriad skills of indirect manipulation we have been taught to create the greater likelihood of "catching a man" and in gaining indirect power through men's favors in a patriarchal world.

Since most women want to be wives and mothers, feminists must support state legislation providing affordable, quality child-care centers. At the same time, feminist education must combat the traditional prejudice against combining a career with motherhood. The most important feminist goal, in this view, should be to create social structures that help women learn to become more like men—in motivations, personalities, and job skills—so that we can get ahead in the system and thus achieve economic parity with men.

Difference Theory

The second theory of the self is that of those I call the *difference* theorists. Unlike rational-maximizer theory, which argues that men and women are basically the same underneath, though we develop different skills and goals as means to achieving social success, this theory argues that there really are extreme personality and skills differences between the genders. These differences, whether innate or socialized in early infancy, are so much a part of the identities of men and women that they cannot be changed. People's identities are not analogous to little atoms of consciousness that can, chameleonlike, take on or shed their personal properties as it is expedient. Rather, since human personal identity is essentially relational, a personal identification with one's gender is an essential characteristic of personal identity. Men and women essentially define themselves in relation to different social standards learned in childhood. Since a man's or woman's sense of self-worth is essentially connected to success or failure in meeting gender-related standards, women's sense of self-worth cannot be ultimately achieved by imitating men or by adopting masculine goals and skills. Rather, women must find collective ways to revalorize feminine-identified values and skills in order that individual women can reclaim a sense of self-worth denied by patriarchy.

There are two schools of thought among difference theorists on the question of the inevitability of gender differences. One school, the biological determinist—those such as Mary Daly,[6] Mary O'Brien,[7] and others[8]—maintain that it is inevitable that masculine traits and sense of self be different from feminine ones. Testosterone makes men more aggressive then women, while women's reproductive biology not only creates womb envy in men but makes women more nurturant and altruistic in relation to others.[9] Thus, universally, men have a motivation to dominate women and the personality skills capable of doing so, while women have a motivation to relate more to children than to men (thus setting up a universal conflict in male and female motivations) as well as to each other (as like understands and empathizes better with like). Thus, given these biologically based gender conflicts, systems of compulsory heterosexuality are set up for the benefit of men to keep women from bonding with each other and children to the exclusion of men.

The social schools of difference include feminist psychoanalytic theory as well as some radical feminist theory.[10] These theorists argue that the personality differences between men and women, though they are central to personal identity and difficult to change, are not biological. Rather, they are socially produced through the sexual division of labor, particularly in parenting. This sexual division creates in women a more altruistic and relational sense of self than in men, who are produced with a more oppositional and autonomous, hence more competitive and self-interested, sense of self.

The biological determinist school of feminism tends toward a separatist solution for women. Men, after all, are incorrigible! Indeed, in her latest book, Mary Daly goes so far as to suggest that they are tantamount to a separate species from women, and consequently women owe them no personal or political obligations.[11] Women should learn to value our authentic selves by relating to each other as friends and lovers, thus dropping out of and thereby challenging the dominant patriarchal culture by providing an example to other women of freer life, one more in tune with women-centered values.

Not all difference theorists believe that such an extreme separatism is the political solution for feminists. Jan Raymond, in her latest book, *A Passion for Friends*,[12] maintains that women have an authentic Self (her *S*) different from men's. Thus if women are to be true to themselves, they must prioritize being for other women. This means that we should prioritize friendships with women rather than accept the socially constructed patterns of what she calls heteroreality, all of which socialize women to define ourselves and our meaning in life in relationships with men.

Though Raymond wants a certain kind of cultural separatism for women, she does not advocate a drop-out separatism. Rather than dropping out of the world, women must strive to change the political and economic priorities of a patriarchal society by working in careers that have hitherto involved only males and male-defined values.

It is never made clear in Raymond's book whether she thinks women's authentic Self is more like other women's than like men's for biological or for social reasons. Other difference theorists who clearly reject the biological gender difference argument are Nancy Chodorow,[13] Dorothy Dinnerstein,[14] Carol Gilligan,[15] and Sara Ruddick.[16] These thinkers argue that the psychology of women differs from that of men because women mother. By *mothering* they do not mean childbearing, the biological function that women cannot share with men, but mothering in the social sense of the nurturing and direct physical care for infants in early childrearing. The fact that women and not men mother in this sense creates a different sense of self in little girls than in little boys. Girls have an immediate role model for what it is to be female: one who is engaged in the concrete chores involved in housework and regular nurturant interaction with children. Consequently the girl defines a sense of self that is relational or incorporative (i.e., I am like Mom in these ways). Girls also must identify with, rather than absolutely oppose, that aspect of mother which is resented and feared: the fact that she can never meet all of the infant's myriad needs. This tends to make females turn anger originally directed at mother inward on themselves in ways that weaken self-esteem.

Gender identity for the boy comes out differently. Society teaches him that to be male is not to be female, and due to the relative or complete absence of his father, he lacks a male role model as immediate for him as is the mother for the little girl. Thus he learns to define himself oppositionally instead of relationally (I am not-mother, I am not-female). He can thus project infantile anger not only on mother but on women in general. Thus, the cross-cultural constant, the asymmetrical parenting of women, explains the cross-cultural male deprecation of women.

Carol Gilligan argues that women tend to have a different style of moral reasoning than men—what she calls a different moral voice. When presented with hypothetical moral dilemmas, females tend to find a contextual solution, while males formulate abstract principles and prioritize justifying one solution rather than the other.

The idea that women have a different moral voice is pursued by Sara Ruddick, who argues that the socialization for, and actual experience of, mothering creates a maternal thinking in women that prioritizes the life preservation, growth, and social acceptability of the child under her care.

When women generalize from the values embedded in this concrete mothering experience, they develop a more care-oriented ethic, concerned with peacemaking and concrete life preserving, than men. Men, with their gender identity and masculine training in the abstract skills necessary to do well in competitive male groups and careers, are more likely to fall prey to the militaristic thinking of the sort that justifies war, the arms race, and other life- and species-endangering activities.

Social-difference theory has two conflicting tendencies within it in regard to the question of how individual women can reclaim a personal power denied by the standards of femininity built into heterosexual desires. Feminist psychoanalytic theory suggests that women should have recourse to feminist therapy to undo the damages of being denied the proper nurturance for self-autonomy in early childhood. The collective strategies of radical feminism, however, tend to reject this individual solution in favor of a collective process in which women bond with other women to revalue feminine work and values, thus allowing women's self, based as it is on the worth of the feminine itself, to gain power. Thus the importance of comparable worth campaigns and women-only peace protests that reclaim the value of maternal thinking as opposed to militaristic thinking.

The general strategy of this line of difference thought is opposed to the strategies of those liberal feminists who assume a rational-maximizer theory of self. Rather than striving to make women more like men so we have a better chance of succeeding in a male-dominant world, the feminist empowerment process involves affirming the socially insufficiently recognized value of the feminine. Indeed, ideally, men should become more like women by committing themselves to learn so-called feminine skills. Only by so identifying with the feminine can they cease their deprecation of women. Further, only by an individual commitment of this sort—for example, the commitment to learn mothering skills by coparenting—can a man create the kind of love relationship with a woman that will allow her the maximum opportunity of obtaining a sense of self-worth.

But it is at this point that difference theory can provide us with no clear answers on how and why men are going to be motivated to make such a dramatic change in the conception of masculinity. And even if they are, how can they be expected to succeed in learning feminine skills if these demand a permeable, or incorporative, personality as opposed to an oppositional one? And, given these problems, why and how can women who are concerned to increase their sense of self-worth work with individual men to encourage change?

Problems with the First Two Theories of the Self

Although both the rational-maximizer and difference theories of the self have important insights, they are inadequate in other ways. Though the first explains why women remain oppressed because of the external constraints that society places on them, it cannot explain why those few women in economically and socially privileged positions in society still defer to men. Why, if a woman is independently wealthy, would she be content to be a wife and mother rather then embarking on a professional or political career that would give her an even greater social effect on the world? Why do some such women allow themselves to be battered wives? Such behavior does not seem to be rationally maximizing! Why, then, do these women, who are economically independent, continue to pursue less rewarding lives that require deferring to men? And why do many women who can afford higher education choose less well-paying careers in literature, nursing, and elementary-school teaching rather than business, physics, medicine, or engineering? In short, the rational-maximizer theory underestimates the way people are not rational maximizers when it comes to their ultimate goals in life, which for most are gender-defined and socially engineered.

Though the difference school can answer this question—women are constructed with essentially different senses of self, skills, and desire from men—this group is overly deterministic about the static nature of this social molding. Consequently they cannot answer the historical question of how and why a women's movement should have arisen just now in American history. If women are so different from men, why should women now be demanding the opportunity to enter male spheres? Why should the idea of developing independence and autonomy, long considered the special purview of masculine identity, suddenly be a goal for feminists as well?

My view is at odds with both the rational-maximizer and difference theories. Both are *static* and *essentialist*. That is, they conceive of the self as a given unity with certain fixed qualities, though they disagree about what those fixed qualities are. Thus, they have *atomistic* views of the self. Whether the self is a rational calculator or a phenomenal center that defines itself in relation to others, the self is seen as having an essence fixed by human nature or by early childhood.

Many difference theorists maintain that there is a split between the authentic and inauthentic parts of the self. This model does suggest that radical change is possible by spurning the inauthentic self. But their claim that there is such an authentic aspect of self and speculations as to the nature of its preferences and interests are wildly metaphysical and unprovable. Indeed, they have seemed elitist and culture-bound to some.

For example, since most women continue to prefer men to women as lovemates, how can it be proved that it is more authentic for those women to prefer women, as some difference theories maintain? How do we decide whether the authentic female self is a lesbian, heterosexual, pansexual, or asexual?

The Aspect Theory of Self

My alternative theory, which I call the *aspect* theory of self, rejects the idea that the self is an unchanging, unified consciousness that has a two-tiered set of properties: those that are necessary and essential, and those that are accidental. Rather, conscious selfhood is an ongoing process in which both unique individual priorities and social constraints vie in limiting and defining one's self-identity.[17]

Humans may be rational maximizers if placed in the sort of social practices that encourage such a type of thinking strategy. But that is only one aspect of a self that is more like a bundle of parts or aspects than it is like a unidimensional means-ends calculator. Gender differences in personality, life choices, and moral reasoning are characteristic of only one aspect of a complicated human psyche that is often at odds with itself, and therefore cannot be thought, comfortably, to have only one essence.

If we think of the self as having many parts or aspects, some of which are in conflict, we can make better sense of Gilligan's claim that there is a dichotomy of masculine and feminine moral voices. Most male and female psyches, created in standard gender-dichotomous childrearing practices, have at least one characteristic difference that is reflected by a difference in moral voices. But many adult women who engage in similar social practices with adult men (e.g., as business or professional colleagues) may also share with them the so-called masculine voice of moral reasoning. And men influenced enough by feminist women to attempt coparenting may develop a feminine voice of moral reasoning. These men and women will have both so-called masculine and feminine aspects of self as developed by their ongoing social practices, and while they will be likely to find these opposing perspectives incongruous and indeed inharmonious, there is no reason to say that they are thus "denying their essence" in the social practice in which they are doing the gender-anomalous job.

If the self is seen as having many aspects, it cannot be determined universally which are prior, more fundamental, or more or less authentic. Rather, aspects of our selves are developed by participating in social practices that insist on certain skills and values. Furthermore, the *contents* of masculinity and femininity vary with the social practices they are connected to. A woman defending her child against attack (for example, in the movie *Cujo* or *Aliens*) is supposed to be showing her feminine protective maternal instinct. But a similar aggressive, perhaps violent act against a man who has made deprecating sexist remarks is not considered feminine.

Where different social practices encourage skills and values that are in conflict, those participating in them will develop conflicting aspects of self. And where certain social practices are taken to be paradigmatic of one's personal identity (as in self-effacing mothering activities for women in our society and self-aggrandizing aggressive or competitive activities for men), those who develop gender-anomalous aspects of self can be disempowered by attributing the inharmonious combination of the two aspects to a personal neurosis. Though the feminist strategy of conceiving of certain aspects of self as inauthentic (for example, manipulative skills or heterosexual charm) is a more empowering approach than this, it does not follow that the view of self as having an authentic core and inauthentic outer layers is correct. Rather, one's sense of self and one's core values may change at different times and in different contexts. How, then, do we understand what it is to increase a sense of self-worth and personal power when the self is conceived of, as the aspect theory suggests, as an *existential process* in which incongruities and lack of power are due to participation in conflicting social practices? Let us take a concrete example to discuss.

Professional women in the helping professions are a good example of those whose concrete social practices are in conflict. Those in higher education, nursing, and social work must develop an ability to empathize with concrete others—students, patients, or clients—to do the job well. But since most work in large bureaucratic settings where impersonal rules of the game apply to hiring, promotions, and allocations, they must develop a competitive, impersonal meritocratic set of values and principles in self-defense. Thus one aspect of the jobs encourages the caring ethic connected to a contextual concern for concrete others that Gilligan claims is typical of the feminine role, and another aspect requires adopting the masculine ethic characterized by a universalistic rights-justice approach. Thus we have two moral voices, both in unhappy and unharmonious juxtaposition in our consciousness. What is alienating is not that our authentic self is thus denied but the psychological incongruity of having to operate with conflicting values.

This contradiction in ways of thinking and valuing is a feature not only of women's work in the helping professions but of the work of those in male-dominated fields like business, politics, and law who face the second-shift problem as working mothers.

Ironically, the juggling of incorporative aspects of self in nurturant work at home with oppositional and individualistic ways of being in such careers is also a problem for men who in sharing housework and child care with feminist partners find their modus operandi different from their more conservative male colleagues at the office. Black and other minority women, whether employed or not, could be expected to develop a rights-justice orientation in self-defense against the social opposition of racist whites toward whom they cannot afford to take a simple caring orientation.

The way to understand personal empowerment of an oppressed group faced with social practices that involve conflicting values is to combine the insights of the rational-maximizer and difference theories of self with a historical perspective. The traditional division of labor by gender in public and private spheres is breaking down for many women and some men. Where it is no longer clear what is men's and women's work, gender identities defined in terms of the different standards of self-worth attached to men's and women's work are put in crisis. It is this developing conflict in gender roles, in conjunction with the American democratic ideology of the right of equality for all based on merit, that has spawned both the women's movement and the possibility for greater empowerment for women. Though the initial phase of capitalist development in America perpetuated male dominance by relegating women to the private, less socially valued, dependent, and relatively powerless sphere of the home, advanced capitalism and consumerist standards of living have been pulling women into part- and full-time labor. Though this has created the second-shift problem for working mothers and the incongruity of women placed in impersonal and uncaring bureaucracies and anonymous institutions, it has also allowed many women to gain economic independence from men.

An existential process of resolving this incongruity of personal identity can take many forms. The New Right women may decide that homemaking in economic social dependency on a man is a better way to resolve the incongruity in her life than to strive for career and economic independence. As Phyllis Schlafly notes, most women would really rather cuddle a baby than a typewriter!

If the aspect theory of the self is correct, the feminist cannot challenge the New Right woman's choice by claiming it is inauthentic, for there is no way to prove what the authentic female self would choose. Nonetheless, due to the social crisis in gender roles, all women in the United States today are likely to have developed rational-maximizer as well as incorporative (traditionally feminine) aspects of self. This is so because when traditional lifestyles are no longer rigidly followed, individuals are forced to a more self-conscious means-ends calculation of what in the long run will serve their interests.

Feminists can appeal to the rational-maximizer aspect of women to argue that women who take the New Right solution to the gender crisis face a high risk of failing to achieve their goals of security and well-being. This is so because of the rise in divorce rates, low welfare payments, low-paying wage-labor work for most women, and the small amount of child support most women receive from former husbands. Thus a woman who places all her eggs in the homemaker basket is increasingly likely to end up a single mother who is one of the statistics in the feminization of poverty.

With respect to women's traditional feminine identification as nurturers, feminists can argue that the only way to have these values today is not to retreat to private motherhood but to influence public policy by gaining individual and collective power in careers and politics that will allow for a public challenge to a militarism spawned by an excessive masculine thinking. Only by gaining public power as women can we have the collective power, through unionizing women and feminist political networks, to demand that those feminine values of caring and contextual moral decision making be incorporated into the rules of our economic and government institutions. In the long run, only a more decentralized worker's (and client, patient, and student) type of decision making can incorporate the caring and contextual considerations needed into the more abstract meritocratic but often inhumane rules by which our public institutions operate.

Such a feminist program will require radical structural changes in the present relation between public and private. We will need to educate the American public to the idea that the raising of children is not a private luxury but a public responsibility. Employers should thus be required to reorganize wage work to allow flex-time jobs, with no career penalty for mothers and fathers of young children, as well as maternity and paternity leave and affordable child care.

Our ultimate goal must be the degenderizing of every aspect of social life. Only this can empower women to develop our potentials as unique individuals not constrained by a social definition that sees our essential nature to be to serve men. However, we cannot achieve this goal without a collective, public process that first empowers women by creating a higher public value for feminine skills and interests. Though assertiveness training and economic independence are key for women, they must be supplemented by comparable worth, social security for homemakers, and other such campaigns that set a higher value on women's traditional work.

While feminist collective networking and public feminist political campaigns can start the empowerment process that allows a woman to redefine a core sense of self that can perceive itself as valuable and able to control her life independently of men, there are many other private issues that remain to be negotiated if she is to develop full personal empowerment.

For example, should a woman cut herself off from, or just try to ignore, her parents if they are sexist? Should she pursue motherhood, given the social costs and dangers of motherhood, indeed the likelihood of being a single mother in a sexist world? Should she give up a heterosexual lifestyle and choose a woman lover to create a more equal context for love? Should she choose an alternative living arrangement with a man that does not involve marriage to avoid the sexist social and psychological expectations that may be involved? Or should she eschew sexual love relationships altogether and prioritize platonic friendships with women (and perhaps men)?[18]

There is no general answer to which of these paths a woman should take to personal empowerment. Only trial and error and the experience of juggling the various aspects of her self by trying different private commitments can lead to what is most personally empowering to different women. The aspect theory of the self, based as it is on the view that the self is an existential process whose integration may be different for different women, must assume an ethical pluralism on such matters of personal choice.

The position of ethical pluralism is a consequence of the rejection of the essentialist idea that all women have the same inner and authentic self, which can only be empowered by the same choices. But nonetheless, we can still draw a few important generalizations about what this empowerment process must minimally entail for women in the contemporary United States: first, collective networking with other women around feminist campaigns; second, prioritizing friendships with other women that value personal autonomy and the elimination of self-definitions that define self-worth exclusively in terms of relationships with men, whether they be fathers, employers, sons, workmates, friends, husbands, or lovers. Given the fragmented aspects of self and the general deprecation of the feminine that pervades all our social life, these steps are necessary to empower both the rational maximizing aspect of self, which gains when women find ways to gain material equality with men, and the incorporative aspect of self, which finds empowerment when it finds a secure yet self-affirming way to ally one's self-interests in nurturing and supportive connections to others.

NOTES

1. For a survey of this literature, see Natalie Sokoloff, *Between Money and Love: The Dialectics of Women's Home and Market Work* (New York: Praeger, 1980). See also Heidi Hartmann, "The Unhappy Marriage of Marxism and Feminism," in Lydia Sargent, ed., *Women and Revolution* (Boston: South End Press, 1981), the responses to Hartmann in the same volume; Christine Delphy, *Close to Home: A Materialist Analysis of Women's Oppression* (Amherst: University of Massachusetts Press, 1984), and the articles by Jean Gardiner, "Women's Domestic Labor," Batya Weinbaum and Amy Bridges, "The Other Side of the Paycheck: Monopoly Capital and the Structure of Consumption," Heidi Hartmann, "Capitalism, Patriarchy and Job Segregation by Sex," and Margery Davies, "Women's Place Is at the Typewriter: The Feminization of the Clerical Labor Force," in Zillah R. Eisenstein, ed., *Capitalist Patriarchy and the Case for Socialist-Feminism* (New York: Monthly Review Press, 1979).

2. See Nancy Chodorow, *The Reproduction of Mothering* (Berkeley: University of California Press, 1978); Carol Gilligan, *In a Different Voice* (Cambridge: Harvard University Press, 1982); Jean Baker Miller, *Toward a New Psychology of Women* (Boston: Beacon Press, 1976); Jean Baker Miller, ed., *Psychoanalysis and Women* (Baltimore: Penguin, 1973).

3. Perhaps the most original and influential article of the new feminist anthropology is that by Gayle Rubin, "The Traffic in Women," in Rayna Reiter, ed., *Toward a New Anthropology of Women* (New York: Monthly Review Press, 1975). Other important contributions are the rest of the articles in Reiter as well as those in Michelle Zimbalist Rosaldo and Louise Lamphere, eds., *Woman, Culture and Society* (Stanford: Stanford University Press, 1974). See also Peggy Reeves Sanday, *Female Power and Male Dominance: On the Origins of Sexual Inequality* (New York: Cambridge University Press, 1981).

4. See Nancy Hartsock, *Money, Sex and Power* (New York: Longman, 1983); Mary O'Brien, *The Politics of Reproduction* (Boston: Routledge & Kegan Paul, 1981); Sandra Harding and Merrill Hintikka, eds., *Discovering Reality: Feminist Perspectives on Epistemology, Metaphysics, Methodology and Philosophy of Science* (Boston: Reidel, 1983); Sandra Harding, *The Science Question in Feminism* (Ithaca, N.Y.: Cornell University Press, 1987).

5. See Andrea Dworkin, *Womanhating* (New York: Dutton, 1974); Andrea Dworkin, *Pornography: Men Possessing Women* (New York: Perigee, 1981); Kathleen Barry, *Female Sexual Slavery* (Englewood Cliffs, N.J.: Prentice-Hall, 1979); Susan Griffin, *Pornography and Silence* (New York: Harper, 1981); Laura Lederer, ed., *Take Back the Night: Women on Pornography* (New York: Morrow, 1980); Andrea Dworkin, "Against the Male Flood: Censorship, Pornography and Equality" and Catharine A. MacKinnon, "Pornography, Civil Rights and Speech," in Dworkin and MacKinnon, *The Reasons Why* (Cambridge: Harvard Law School, 1985).

6. Mary Daly, *Gyn/Ecology: The Meta-ethics of Radical Feminism* (Boston: Beacon Press, 1978).

7. Mary O'Brien, *The Politics of Reproduction* (Boston: Routledge & Kegan Paul, 1981).

8. Simone de Beauvoir, *The Second Sex* (New York: Bantam, 1952); Laurel Holliday, *The Violent Sex: Male Psychobiology and the Evolution of Consciousness* (Guerneville, Calif.: Bluestocking Press, 1978).

9. Alice Rossi, "A Biosocial Perspective on Parenting," *Daedulus* 106(2)(Spring 1977), pp. 1–32; Melvin Konner, "She & He," *Science* (September 1982), pp. 54–61; Adrienne Rich, *Of Woman Born* (New York: Norton, 1976).

10. Nancy Chodorow; Juliet Mitchell, *Psychoanalysis and Feminism* (New York: Pantheon, 1974); Janice Raymond, *The Transsexual Empire: The Making of the She-Male*

(Boston: Beacon, 1979); Carol Gilligan, *In a Different Voice* (Cambridge: Harvard University Press, 1982).

11. Mary Daly, *Pure Lust: Elemental Feminist Philosophy* (Boston: Beacon Press, 1984).

12. Janice Raymond, *A Passion for Friends: Toward a Philosophy of Female Affection* (Boston: Beacon Press, 1986).

13. Nancy Chodorow, *The Reproduction of Mothering* (Berkeley: University of California Press, 1978).

14. Dorothy Dinnerstein, *The Mermaid and the Minotaur: Sexual Arrangements and Human Malaise* (New York: Harper, 1976).

15. Carol Gilligan, *In a Different Voice* (Cambridge: Harvard University Press, 1982).

16. Sara Ruddick, "Maternal Thinking," *Feminist Studies* 6(2)(Summer 1980) pp. 342–67; reprinted in Joyce Trebilcot, ed., *Mothering: Essays in Feminist Theory* (Totowa, N.J.: Rowman and Allenheld, 1984).

17. See my books, *Blood at the Root: Motherhood, Sexuality and Male Dominance* (London: Pandora/Harper Collins, 1989); and *Sexual Democracy: Women, Oppression and Revolution* (Boulder: Westview, 1991); as well as Ferguson, "Motherhood and Sexuality: Some Feminist Questions," *Hypatia: Journal of Feminist Philosophy* 1(2)(Fall 1986), p. 322.

18. For a discussion of some of these feminist ethical questions, see Ferguson, *Blood at the Root,* and the articles in Ann Ferguson, ed., "Motherhood and Sexuality," *Hypatia: Journal of Feminist Philosophy* 1(2)(Fall 1986).

10

Feminist Thought and Action

KATHRYN PYNE ADDELSON

T he final test of political and social theory lies in action, and the justification of theory building lies in the usefulness of the theory. It is political action that sets the problems that political theory helps resolve. Since feminist political action takes place on many fronts and through many means, there are many feminist political theories counseling different avenues of action. So too, a feminist theory may be useful for some feminist political communities but not others.

In some of the classic scholarly sources, feminist political theories have been classified as liberal, Marxist, socialist, and radical—although we have to add varieties of lesbian feminism, anarcha-feminism, eco-feminism, and others. Liberal, Marxist, and socialist feminisms, according to the scholarly analysis, correspond to the general political theories that go by those names, though the feminist versions require radical revision of the originals to rid them of male bias and support of male dominance. Radical feminism is an original theory taking patriarchy as the fundamental structural characteristic of human societies and male dominance as the basic dominance to be overthrown. Anarcha-feminism and eco-feminism grow out of the anarchist tradition.

Contemporary feminist theory in the United States has its roots in the political action of the women's movement of the 1960s and 1970s. For this reason, though the theories differ, they share certain central themes and concerns: a focus on analyzing and overcoming male dominance; a general objection to dominance structures on the societal level; and a discomfort with hierarchy and authority on the organization-al or group level. These criticisms of political and social order grow out of the commitment to respect women's experience and to empower women.

During the 1970s, the main strategies of social change and empowerment involved building nonhierarchically organized workgroups and collectives. This is an anarchist strategy. But the commitment was widespread in all varieties of feminism. Even today, although the liberal group the National Organization for Women cannot embody the principles of decentralism and internal democracy, it carries on the feminist commitment in being structured to prevent domination by a small elite and by working to maximize participation by rank-and-file members. In general, the organizations of the women's movement have not suffered bureaucratization.[1]

Respecting women's experience relates directly to empowering women and to the objections to hierarchy, authority, and dominance. One of the key ways a group dominates others is by controlling definitions of experience and action, by defining the world and all its peoples from the dominant group's perspective. Once the world is defined, a dominant group can get its way by persuasion, keeping force and violent coercion more or less veiled, as a backup.

Some of the best-known feminist scholarly work has criticized Western culture and science (and the classic authorities on these things) for defining women and the world through dominant male eyes.[2] This dominance involves the exercise of a cognitive authority, an authority to define knowledge and the world.[3] Dominance in this sense makes women's experience invisible—and the experiences of many other subordinate groups. But the commitment to respect women's experience is surrounded with tensions and dilemmas.

On the political-action side, nonhierarchical collectives committed to serving women classically run up against the distinction between the servers and the served, the staff and the client. The problem is exacerbated when the feminist collective has to accept federal or state funding or funding from agencies like the United Way. The ways the collective must show its accountability (thus worthiness to receive funds) are defined by social-service professionals. They are based on hierarchical forms in which the client's experience is defined in professional terms and the client runs a danger of being "rehabilitated" rather than empowered. The client's problems and the solutions are defined in the official professional vocabulary—which may incorporate the definitions of groups who are gender, race, and class dominant. The feminists in the collective must continually balance on the razor's edge. This widespread problem in feminist political action offers a problem for feminist theory as well.[4] Feminist theory must somehow take account of it in a way that offers aid to activists.

Feminist theorists have their own razor's edges. Those theorists who hold positions in the academy exercise cognitive authority by virtue of their positions in establishment institutions. The tension here is between the dominant traditions and definitions in which they have been trained and the commitment to doing work that empowers women.

There is a certain model of choice and action that operates in the social-service professionals' definitions and the definitions of many feminist theorists. It is a voluntarist model in the sense that a person comes to a problematic situation with moral or pragmatic principles in mind, then uses the principles as guides to action. In the professional-client relationship, the aim may be to educate the client so that she grasps principles and is able to act on them—according to her own choice. For example, the solution of the teen-pregnancy problem in sex education takes this route. In the theoreticians' use, the model deeply underlies both theory and method. It may take the form of understanding political theory as an abstract linguistic structure that activists should read, grasp, and act upon. In theories relating to personal choice and personal morality, it makes a division between thought and action, mind and body, person and group. Despite the fact that it is the model used in political and legal systems in the United States and by most Anglo-American philosophers, feminist or not, it is a model that is philosophically and scientifically mistaken. I'll call it the *philosophers' model.*

The individualist, voluntarist philosophers' model of choice is politically pernicious because it does not allow feminist activists to see how the structures of dominance define women's experience. Because of this, it acts as an obstacle to empowering women. It also allows us the illusion that all women suffer under the same oppressive male dominance and that all women share their essential experience as subordinate. This is very far from the truth; empirical study as well as direct testimony shows us that the experiences and the very selves of women of different classes, races, and ages are constructed differently. I will demonstrate some of these things in this chapter.

I will use case studies of pregnant teens to make my point in the context of service agencies. My view is that moral choice, and moral explanation (and the categories of explanation), are constructed in social interactions. When we examine those interactions, we find that systemic social and political relations are created and maintained in the process of the construction. I will use Carol Gilligan's ethics of responsibility and care as my sample of a feminist theory that mistakenly uses the philosophers' model. Carol Gilligan's work took off from anomalies she discerned in Lawrence Kohlberg's widely used theory of moral development. Kohlberg incorporated a technical philosophical ethics (of the rights-and-obligations sort) into a basically Piagetian model of moral development.

Gilligan was concerned that the style of moral explanation Kohlberg favored and the scoring method he used did not do justice (so to speak) to the moral thinking of women students and women subjects. In her now well known abortion study, she dropped the hypothetical-dilemma approach and interviewed women about their abortion experiences, recorded their explanations, then developed both moral categories and a scoring manual out of the interview material. She claims that her subjects think in terms of care and responsibility rather than justice and obligation, and a "psychologic logic of relationships" rather than the abstract logic suited to deriving decisions from principles or to solving hypothetical dilemmas.[5] Both women and men use the care-responsibility orientation, but women tend to use it more. Both men and women use the justice-obligation orientation, but men tend to use it more. She speaks of a gestalt switch—the same relationships seen from two orientations.

Gilligan's analysis does seem to give an empirical grounding to feminist ethics. It does, that is, if we suppose that accommodating moral explanations reported by individual women can alter accounts of the moral institution of life so that gender bias is overcome and women are taken seriously. But to suppose that is to give the game away. The reason isn't that women might be forgetful or self-deceptive in their reports, or that there is a white middle-class bias and other women might explain things differently (though both of those factors are present). The reason is that the women's very explanations have been constructed as a part of a process of interaction that itself brings into existence gender, age, class, and race relations. The explanations Gilligan uncovers cannot give us a fair and nonsexist account of the moral institution of life because those explanations themselves are products of processes by which gender, age, class, race, and other systemic, social-political relations are created and maintained. It is that process that must be examined if we are even to begin to understand the moral institution of life. As C. Wright Mills once said, the explanations people offer are themselves in need of explanation.[6]

I shall argue these claims on the basis of sociological field studies. But serious objections can also be made to shortcomings of the general models that are presupposed. Two main objections relate to the accounts of individual decision, choice, or action and to the accounts of how individual moral explanation is social.

As for individual decision, both the classic analysis and many of the revisionist ones are voluntaristic, in the sense that the person comes to the situation with a grasp of moral explanations and uses them as guides to action. In the paradigm case of explicit moral reasoning, one weighs principles, then makes the moral decision. Or one ponders responsibilities and relationships, then chooses. In nonparadigm cases the thinking need not be explicit, and in other voluntarist accounts, one merely reads the situation and acts out of virtue or habit. There might not be a major objection to such voluntarism if we had some explanation of how it works materially in the moral institution of life. As I'll say in the conclusion to this chapter, we have none.[7]

Nearly all of the accounts, from "classical" to feminist, also presuppose that moral explanation by individuals is social, in this sense: There are categories, principles, narratives, paradigm cases, language games, or other devices that are (or ought to be) shared in some group of people (or all humanity); individual members explain their moral activities in those group terms. In this light, Gilligan corrected Kohlberg's overgeneralization of the rights-obligations ethics by showing that there are two kinds of moral explanations used by members of humanity. But this is a sociologically mistaken view of the relationship of individual to "group culture." It is a mistaken view of the relationship of individual to the moral institution of life. Let me begin by offering a more appropriate sociological account.

The sociological tradition I shall rely upon is called *symbolic interactionism*. The tradition began its development early in the century at the University of Chicago; its practitioners are now widely dispersed. My work has been with Howard Becker, and theoretically I rely particularly on writings by his teachers, Herbert Blumer and Everett Hughes.[8] The tradition is marked by using methods of participant observation to do small group studies.

One basic premise, which Blumer articulates well, is that any human social world consists of the actions and experiences of its people. Furthermore, the nature of both the social and the natural environment, and the objects composing them, is set by the meanings they have for those people.[9] This sort of claim has become common enough in recent years, but it would be a mistake to leap to saying that the meanings are given in terms of the group rules or language games (as Winch and other Wittgensteinians do) or that they are given in terms of institutionalized norms that are interiorized through socialization (as even social constructionalists like Berger and Luckmann do).[10] The interactionist approach is to study actual processes of interaction by which the meanings are constructed: It is the social process in group life that creates and upholds the rules, not the rules that create and uphold group life.[11] These social processes are studied by participant observation of small groups. They include processes that will aid in understanding the moral institution of life.

To investigate the processes involved in moral explanation, we need a perspicuous working notion. I shall use the notion of a moral passage.

As I use it, it is derivative on the notion of a career, which is widely used in interactionist studies.[12]

A career covers both an individual's movement through an activity (in biographical terms) and the general pattern followed by any person going through "that sort of thing." The pattern is displayed in the movements from one *step* to another, so that a career is a pattern of steps. Howard Becker explains the steps in terms of career contingencies—continuing in the career is contingent on moving to the next in the series of steps.[13] The steps are uncovered by field investigation, and they need not match the steps subjects take to be definitive. Nor do they explain psychological or moral differences among the people who finish the career and those who do not. The steps are contingencies in the sense that what people who make the passage have in common is that they pass through those steps.

Prudence Rains did several field studies in the late 1960s, which she reported and discussed in her book *Becoming an Unwed Mother.* They included studies of mainly white and middle-class young women at a home for unwed mothers and of black, mainly poor teenagers at a day school for unwed mothers. Rains opens the book with this statement.

> Becoming an unwed mother is the outcome of a particular sequence of events that begins with forays into intimacy and sexuality, results in pregnancy, and terminates in the birth of an illegitimate child. Many girls do not have sexual relations before marriage. Many who do, do not get pregnant. And most girls who get pregnant while unmarried do not end up as unwed mothers. Girls who become unwed mothers, in this sense, share a common career that consists of the steps by which they came to be unwed mothers rather than brides, the clients of abortionists, contraceptively prepared lovers, or virtuous young ladies.[14]

Rains studied one line of passage in this network of passages in the seas of young womanhood: becoming an unwed mother. Fieldworkers must limit themselves. But her understanding of the place of unwed motherhood in a larger network of passages gives us a way to make a schema of social options.

Figure 10.1 represents Rains's remarks. Rains names the common starting point "the situation of moral jeopardy." The starting point is important and problematic. The schema in figure 10.1 represents patterns of moral passages in the late 1960s when Rains did her studies. There are branching paths to abortion because restrictive abortion laws made abortion illicit in all but a few circumstances (or places). The figure operates as a guide to further empirical study. It is not a decision-making tree, nor does it define social options. But it does offer a way to take women's circumstances seriously.[15] Figure 10.1 provides a guide to empirical study.

The figure allows me to make a methodological distinction that is important. The terms *pregnant, abortion, unwed motherhood,* and others appear on the chart. Now, Rains's subjects were involved in pregnancy, and some thought about abortion and other possible passages. The young women (and those around them) used the words *pregnancy* and *abortion* as *folk terms.* Folk terms are used by people in organizing their social interactions, and they carry with them assumptions about what activities are involved, what cast of characters is important, what courses might be followed. They offer guides about what to expect.

The notion of a moral passage is a construct to be used by the scholarly investigator, not the "folk" who are being studied. The scholarly investigators use what Herbert Blumer calls *sensitizing concepts.* Blumer contrasts sensitizing concepts with definitive concepts—the sort philosophers usually concern themselves with. Definitive concepts refer to a class of objects, and they carry with them criteria or "benchmarks" by which one can tell whether something belongs to the class. Sensitizing concepts are not designed to offer such criteria but to offer guidance in approaching empirical instances.

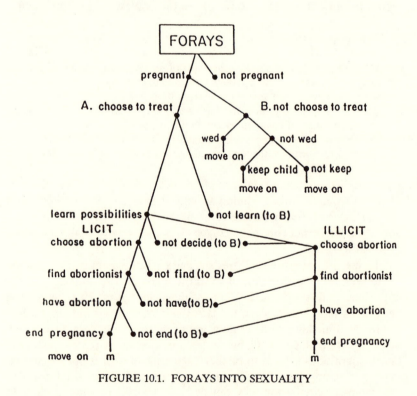

FIGURE 10.1. FORAYS INTO SEXUALITY

Blumer goes on to say that even if definitive concepts were possible to construct in sociology, they would not be proper for sociologists to use in describing the human social world. Definitive concepts give what is common to the instances. With sensitizing concepts, "we seem forced to reach what is common by accepting and using what is distinctive to the given empirical instance."[16] This, he says, is due not to the immaturity of the discipline of sociology but to the nature of the empirical world that is its object of study.

In a certain way, Blumer takes meaning to be use—not use by the subject population but use by the sensitized researcher. He says that by taking concepts as sensitizing, his line of approach

> seeks to improve concepts by naturalistic research, that is, by direct study of our natural social world wherein empirical instances are accepted in their concrete and distinctive form. It depends on faithful reportorial depiction of the instances and on analytical probing into their character. As such its procedure is markedly different from that employed in the effort to develop definitive concepts. Its success depends on patient, careful and imaginative life study, not on quick shortcuts or technical instruments. While its progress may be slow and tedious, it has the virtue of remaining in close and continuing relations with the natural social world.[17]

This is a statement of sociological theory as well as sociological field method.

In my theoretical reconstruction of Rains's work, I would say that as a field researcher, she uses *unwed mother* and *pregnant* as sensitizing concepts—though she does not speak in these terms, nor does she distinguish her use from her subjects' use of those terms. However, her studies show how the meanings of *pregnant* and *unwed mother* come to be constructed as folk terms among her subjects, and so it is theoretically necessary to take her to be using sensitizing concepts. In this light, I should remind readers that *who* gets pregnant is more a social than a biological question.[18]

To write *Becoming an Unwed Mother,* Prudence Rains did three field studies. Two were the extended studies that form the core of the book. These are the study at Hawthorne House, the home run by social workers for mostly white middle-class young women and the study at the Project, a day school for pregnant black young women. In addition to these two, Rains briefly studied a traditional maternity home, which she called Kelman Place. The restrictions on her data gathering there were severe because of secrecy requirements at the home, and she ultimately used the study only to contrast traditional homes with the situations at

Hawthorne House and the Project.[19]

Rains's view is that illicit pregnancy is "the incidental product of the way sexual activity is *normally* organized among unmarried girls in this society."[20] She names the common situation out of which unwed mothers begin their careers "The Situation of Moral Jeopardy." (Fig. 10.1) Somehow, in passing from childhood to womanhood, a girl must learn how to become the kind of women she would be.[21] The learning takes place on many fronts, but girls (and boys) must come to change their early childish ways to ways suitable to the adult world—and given our society, that means finding a place in a heterosexual world, though not necessarily as a heterosexual. In the process, the girl begins (with others) to construct her place as a woman in the adult world—a construction that includes her understanding of both self and world as well as other people's understanding of her. These things are not simple opinions or beliefs, for they exist in interactions, in the activities and doings that make up her life. Rains says that a central moral experience for the young women she studied is the ambivalence they feel when they find themselves acting in ways they only recently, as children, disapproved.

Rains says, "The central feature of these girls' moral careers as unwed mothers is the experience of coming to realign themselves with the conventional, respectable world; the central theme of this book has to do with the ways in which the maternity homes sponsor and organize this experience of moral realignment."[22]

Becoming pregnant was a blatant way of going public about things customarily hidden in the journey from childhood to adulthood (and hidden in adulthood). For the young men involved, it was usually relatively easy to restrict the range of the publicity. For a young woman, it required major institutionalized methods to deal with the publicity. And it had to be dealt with because of what would be jeopardized by going public in an unrestricted way. The passages of Rains's unwed mothers show how managing the publicity was essential not only to the girls' future but to the social organization of morality.

Kelman Place

Rains quotes a remark by a spokesperson for a Florence Crittenden home that indicates the policy of traditional homes like Kelman Place: "These are your loving, trusting girls in here. Your other girl who is probably doing the same thing doesn't get caught because she is too smart. . . . What is needed is more understanding on the part of the parents and the general public. I don't mean condoning. I mean understanding . . . that this kind of thing can happen and these girls do need help."[23] This "philosophy" was shared by staff at Kelman Place. One staff member put it this way: "I talk a lot with the girls. In general, with the whole group, I would say they know what they have done is not condoned by society and never will be—never. I do not condemn a girl for making one mistake. I just hope they learn a lesson."[24] These remarks capture the major features of a classic sort of moral explanation. We do not condemn a person of good character who has made a mistake, will learn from the mistake, and is determined not to make the mistake again.

In the context, the explanation carries an old-fashioned image of a nice girl led astray, whose mistake is punishment enough in itself. This sort of explanation presupposes that reputation, self-respect, and respectability are risked by getting pregnant out of wedlock. It is not the simple getting pregnant that is the problem. It is the woman herself—her character or the motive one derives from traits of her character. Illicit pregnancy is a visible mark of character that somehow must be dealt with.

At both Kelman Place and Hawthorne House, the young women's explanations of their own pregnancies came to be in harmony with this venerable story. Rains quotes her field notes from Hawthorne House. "Louise asked during group meeting, 'Can you remember what you thought of unwed mothers in places like this before? I mean, think of what we thought, before we came here, about unwed mothers and maternity homes.' " Peg said, "That's right. Whenever I thought of places like this, I always thought, 'Well, I'm not that type of girl.' Everyone looked agreeing to this."[25] Rains says, "Girls enter maternity homes expecting to confront the concrete proof of what they have become and encounter instead a reminder of what they 'really' are, what they presumably have been all along."[26]

There is, however, a certain ominous tone in the staff member's remark, "I do not condemn a girl for making one mistake. I just hope they learn a lesson." The remark raises the awful specter that the event may happen again if the girl doesn't learn from it. This specter was raised at each of the three locations Rains studied, but it was dealt with differently at each of them. But interestingly enough, the young women at each of the locations begin with the same explanation: there were two kinds of girls—respectable and "that kind." (Fig. 10.2) They then modified the explanation so that the "nice girl" category might contain a loop covering the passage through unwed motherhood, after which the girl returns to respectability if she learns her lesson. It was a loop they believed could only be taken once, otherwise the chart would have been the passage of "that type of girl." (Fig. 10.3)

At Kelman Place, the young women's self-respect and reputation

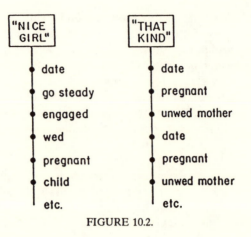

FIGURE 10.2.

were rescued by this explanation. I do not mean that the verbal explanation rescued them by magically changing people's opinions. Kelman Place had the material wherewithal to let the young women "move on" back to their normal lives with their reputations saved by concealing their mistakes—and in fact, Kelman Place was part of the *institutionalized* means in the society for that kind of moral rescue.

An important part of the Kelman Place rescue turned on the ways a young woman's public interaction was altered. During her stay at a traditional home, secrecy was preserved as much as possible so that the young woman might reenter respectable society without her mistake "ruining" her. Her passage was hidden by her physically leaving her usual public locations of home, school, and so on. It was also hidden by

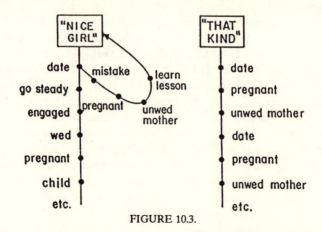

FIGURE 10.3.

cover stories.[27]

Which authorities had to be dealt with varied with the young woman's previous life. For women in school, they included principals and counselors, truant officers, and police; for women in college, they included deans, teachers, and registrars. For all of the young women, they included physicians, lawyers, adoption-agency and birth-registry officials, as well as the maternity-home staff, whose stance was one of stern but benign rescue. Because of the way the rescue was institutionalized, the outside authorities involved were either kept in ignorance or were parties to the conspiracy. This was part of the standard operating procedure of maternity homes. The Kelman Place staff's judgment on character was accepted, and the category of "nice girl who made a mistake" was socially real, not a matter of opinion. The young women could accept authorities at face value because they could simply and unconsciously count on their protection in this hidden salvage operation. The institutional salvage included dealing with the public reminder of the "mistake"—the child—for nearly all of the girls gave their babies up for adoption. The entire operation confirmed the fact that the girl's past was really that of a nice girl who had made a mistake by creating the possibility for her to be a respectable young woman in the future.

Hawthorne House

In entering Hawthorne House, the young women changed their public interactions in the same way the Kelman Place women did, for both homes had the same institutional status and connections. Hawthorne House staff generally dealt with authorities such as judges, lawyers, hospital personnel, and adoption-agency staff by the same institutional means used at the traditional homes. However, Hawthorne House was operated by professional social workers whose disciplinary training was aimed at bringing people to face emotional and psychological realities and the truth about their motives.

The social workers regarded becoming an unwed mother as having its cause in a prior unhealthy psychological state. Their task was to help the young women uncover and correct that state so that it would not continue to operate in the future, with the risk of repeated illicit pregnancies. When one father expressed reservations about "the girls" returning to dating, a staff member said, "We expect girls will resume their heterosexual relationships in the manner of dating, but we feel that if they have learned something during their stay here, they can communicate better with their parents and they don't need to act out in inappropriate ways."[28]

Rains says that the social workers were concerned that the young women accept responsibility for their behavior and acknowledge the seriousness of the consequences. For the girls to accept the traditional explanation that they were trusting young women who had made a mistake counted as denial. Understanding the emotional roots of their actions was necessary to avoid another illicit pregnancy. This amounts to a straightforward criticism of the traditional maternity homes. The criticism shows that the responsibility the social workers wanted was not responsibility for being a respectable woman in the traditional sense—and this marks a deep difference from the Kelman Place approach.

In criticizing traditional maternity-home practices of extreme secrecy and protection, one staff member said,

> "After all, girls come here because they acted irresponsibly to start with, particularly now that ways to prevent getting pregnant are so common. And I don't think we should encourage that kind of thing. A lot of what we try to do is based on this philosophy that girls should be encouraged to accept responsibility for themselves, and to take responsibility."[29]

This is not the traditional moral view that premarital sex in itself is either irresponsible or promiscuous. In fact, it appears to be a liberated view that takes young women seriously as moral agents who autonomously choose their moral principles and make their own lives.

From Rains's report, all the Hawthorne House women seem to accept the benign, helpful posture of the social workers, and they accepted the intrusion of these authorities into areas that are customarily hidden and private. This does not mean that they all accepted the psychotherapeutic explanation. One young woman said,

> "My social worker is always trying to convince me. . . . I keep telling here that it doesn't seem to me to be true, and she'll agree, but there's always the implied idea that there was an emotional reason. It's insinuated all the time, in every question. I just keep wondering where the explanation came from to begin with. I mean I wonder what girl they knew well enough to arrive at this idea, this explanation."[30]

But another girl responded, "I know I felt that way when I came, but I feel now that if you don't know why you're here, you'll end up here again."[31]

The first girl questions the social worker's redefinition of the past, and the second accepts it. On the social-worker picture, the first girl will return to the fog of denial. (Fig. 10.4)

The adequacy of psychotherapeutic explanation does not turn on there *always* being a hidden explanation for illicit pregnancy, for there may be many classes of exceptions. However, what *is* essential to the viewpoint is the contrast between the inner truth and everyday ways of explaining things. The professional social worker's job is to unveil the truth that is hidden under the illusions of "nice girl" and "that kind of girl." The body of knowledge that the professional learns through her training penetrates to the underlying realities. Everyone *can* come to know those kinds of truths, but with the expert's help. This is different from the Kelman Place staff's reliance on "what everyone knows," but like the Kelman Place explanation, it overlooks the effect of the arrangements for maintaining secrecy about the young woman's future.

The Project

The black teenagers of the Project dealt with the public reality in ways quite different from those used by the mainly white middle-class women of the maternity homes—in part because of differences in their options and their relationships with authorities. The Project teenagers' passages were public in two ways from those of the maternity-home women. They were public in the sense that the teenagers continued to live at home, so the pregnancy was widely known, and questions of respectability and responsibility had to be handled in school, on the street, and in the kitchen. They were also public in the sense that public

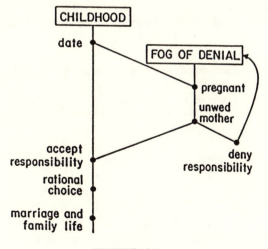

FIGURE 10.4.

officials and public records defined an *official* reputation for the young women.

At the time Rains did her study, the Project was funded as a pilot school for pregnant teens located in a black ghetto of a large midwestern city—handling a maximum of about thirty-five teenagers (roughly fourteen-year-olds) at a time.[32] The Project staff included two teachers (one black, one white), a white psychiatric nurse, and a black social worker.

The social worker had standard professional views on how group discussions should be handled, what sorts of problems should be discussed, and what the discussion should accomplish—views much like those of the social workers at Hawthorne House. She tried to encourage the girls to express themselves, and she hoped to help the girls develop abstract skills to help them take responsibility for their lives. Accordingly, her style in running the meetings was one of "moral neutrality," encouraging the girls to speak of their feelings. Rains says that the style "was simultaneously unbelievable, unbelieved, misunderstood, and unacceptable to the Project girls."[33] Rains quotes one of the young women: "Dorene said, 'I mean why do social workers want to ask you all kinds of personal questions, but you can never ask them back?' "[34] They saw asking questions as implying a right to know—and they believed the social worker had no right to know some of the things she asked. This seemed to be because she was an adult and because she was in a position of official authority.

The Project clients' experience with authorities was quite different from that of the young women at the maternity homes. They had developed a warranted disbelief in moral neutrality and questions asked "for their own good." Here is part of a transcript of one of Rains's interviews:

> "The truant officer asked me all sorts of questions—had I been picked up for curfew, had I ever been in jail, the boy's name, where I lived, did I work after school. He say he didn't know if they would let me stay in school or throw me out." (How did you feel?) "He just be screaming at you like you was some slut dog."[35]

One of the young women said about official questioners, "They keep records."

The records the truant and probation officers kept were accessible records. They made up a public reputation that allowed authorities to meddle in the girl's future life. Was she an incorrigible and fit for reform school? Was she a fit mother? Were her claims that she was raped or assaulted to be given credence? Was an employer to be wary of offering her a job? Even social workers kept records, and the privacy that the middle-class people believed in was much less plausible in an agency that for all of its humanitarian concerns, was part of a public effort to deal with the social problems of being poor and black, young, and pregnant. In the mid-1960s, neither being middle-class and white nor being an illicitly pregnant refined girl constituted a social problem.

In the Project girls' circumstances, there was no chance of rescue by redefining the past psychotherapeutically. The teenagers *did* consider themselves girls who had made a mistake, however.

Salvaging one's reputation did not have the same meaning for the black teenagers of the Project because reputation in the black community did not offer the same protection that it did for the middle-class women. Since the pregnancies of black women were not kept secret, the "mistake" view didn't function to preserve future options by salvaging their past reputations, but it did serve to say that they were not condemned to carry out the common fate they saw around them—women on welfare struggling to support their children, with or without a husband. Rains said, "An illegitimate pregnancy jeopardized more than moral respectability for these girls; it lessened their chances for continuing in school and possibly attaining a better way of life. Marriage was seen by many Project girls and their parents as more of an obstacle than a solution to this other sort of respectability. As one girl put it:

> "Some of these girls just don't think ahead. They think they'll get married and leave school and they don't think that maybe their husband won't stay around and then where will they be when they can't do anything. Some of them don't even graduate from grammar school. What kind of mother could you be not even out of grammar school? If your kid has work from school, you can't even help him, maybe can't even read. At least that's one thing I've learned. When I got pregnant, my mother talked to me. She told me that everybody's ship is going to come in sometime, but that you had to be there when it came 'cause you can only get it once. She said I was only part way up the gangplank. I think it is foolish to get married with so much ahead of you."[36]

Going to the Project school was not simply an illusion of this other sort of respectability. It was *in fact* continuing on the path to respectable adult life by continuing in *school.* At fourteen, school was a major step toward a respectable life.

Nearly all of the black young women kept their babies. The social workers regarded it as their responsibility to point out the possibility of adoption or foster-home placement. But often girls and their mothers regarded the suggestion as a moral affront. Here are May's remarks.

"She talked to my mother first—asked her did she want me to give the baby up for adoption. My mother say, 'No, May be a nice mother. Yes, she love that child and she feel about it like it was hers. She was mad about it at first.'" These feelings show in differences in the ways children were raised.

For most of the middle-class young women, "moving on" was publicly moving back to the original position of "respectable young woman." The passage was a loop. For the young black women of the Project, moving on was moving from "pregnant girl" to "girl with a baby." It was this transformation that in the end stifled public comment. From Rains's quotes, it appears that the Project girls gained strength from their *own* love and pride in the baby. ("'I love my baby enough that I don't care what they say.'")[37] But also they gained from other people's love of babies—their interest focused on baby rather than girl. ("They just like babies.") Rains describes the situation:

> The Project girls shared a way of life in which motherly responsibilities were usually diffused among a number of persons. The Project girls themselves had been involved in caring for their younger brothers and sisters and were themselves cared for by a variety of aunts, stepfathers and stepmothers, mothers—persons who for reasons of blood relationship or sense of kinship took interest in them. The Project girls' babies thus did not so much enter the world to an exclusive relation to a single mother, as to a web of persons with a variety of interests and concerns in their welfare.[38]

There is much to be learned from Rains's cases. I'll begin with some further explanation why relying on women's own accounts, as Gilligan does, is not sufficient for understanding the moral institution of life or for correcting bias in analysis. I'll go on to insist that academics ask serious questions about their authority and responsibility and conclude with a mention of some positive contributions from my own approach.

We should note that the young women of Kelman Place and Hawthorne House certainly regarded getting pregnant as a moral matter that required explanation. But their explanations changed over time, through the process of the young woman's interactions with others—her intimates, neighbors, the other pregnant young women she met—and particularly through her interaction with authorities. The young women reported the explanations and changes as belonging to themselves and to their own perceptions. (See remarks quoted above in the sections on Kelman Place and Hawthorne House.) Yet these explanations were socially constructed, with the help of upstanding members of the general community at Kelman Place and the guidance of social workers at

Hawthorne House. They were constructed differently in different social locations—differently in the maternity homes than at the Project and with different effect. Let me discuss the social workers because their model is in many ways the philosopher's model in ethics.

The authority the social workers exercised was a professional authority that had been politically won during the 1920s in the course of the struggle to have the occupation designated a profession. Theirs was a chapter in the great movement of professionalization that began in the United States after the Civil War, a movement that transformed our democracy. Professionalization produced new and powerful authorities who worked at defining health and disease, law and justice, nature and the good life—authorities that came to include not only doctors and lawyers but physicists, botanists, psychologists, and philosophers.[39] The professional authorities eventually replaced the clergymen and the "educated laymen of good character" as advisors to the nation. The social workers' debunking of the "nice girl" explanation has a place in the secularization of "the moral institution of life" that was concurrent with the professionalization process in the United States.[40] Nonetheless, they retained the basic religious model of explaining human activity: explanation in terms of preconditions of the activity, preconditions that exist somehow within the individual. They differed in the classifications of preconditions, using technical categories of their profession: preconditions may be irrational, as when a person is acting out, but with the social workers' help, the emotional preconditions may be dealt with, and then the young woman may make free and reasonable choices. That is where the philosophers come in.

I am not disputing the truth of psychotherapeutic explanations. Rather I am saying that truth does not come in a bottle with a label on it that says TRUTH. What we call truth is based on the authority of someone or other. Some truths are based on "what everyone knows" ("everyone" here referring to some selection of people). Some truths may be based on firsthand experience. But in professionalized fields the confirmation or falsification of truths is handled by professionals. What is relevant here is the authority the social workers had in constructing the explanations of the young women's pasts—explanations accepted by the young women at Hawthorne House and rejected by the young women at the Project (though despite this rejection, the social worker's explanation carried the day in the official records).

The rational action the social workers postulated as the fruit of overcoming denial is in fact the model of moral activity that many philosophers presuppose as the way that moral reasoning or moral explanation relates to moral activity. In this model, preconditions exist in the explicit reasoning process that the agent goes through, although people are also said to act out of preconditions of habit, unexpressed motive, good character, and so on. Even unarticulated preconditions can supposedly be retroactively captured in explanations. This is quite a realist view, for it presupposes that the preconditions of the act are objectively there to be uncovered later, by the person herself or an outside judge. It requires, for the paradigm cases at least, that one's moral reasoning actually be applied in a situation to bring about one's action.

Unfortunately, there is no adequate explanation of how moral reasoning is applied by a rational agent in an actual situation. Philosophers don't usually raise the question. Psychologists have not even hypothesized such a model, much less discovered the actual mechanisms. But even if there *were* such a model, we would have to ask on whose authority do we use this model in explaining our activities? By what social means is that authority exercised? And what consequences does its use have? All of these questions have answers in Rains's studies, and we see that consequences differ by class and race. These questions have answers, even when Rains's subjects come to report the explanations as their own.

Gilligan doesn't obviously use the philosophers' "precondition" model. Her interest lies more in tracing the women's changing explanations and their relationship to changing conceptions of self. Her approach may be analogous to that of multitudes of social scientists who investigate folk explanations while remaining agnostic whether they pick out existing objects or acts—phlogiston and witches are time-worn examples. It is a peculiar sort of bracketing (to use the phenomenologist's term). Gilligan herself developed the responsibilities-care orientation by seeing that the Kohlberg scheme imposed gender dominance. She saw that moral reasoning was being socially constructed in the Kohlberg "laboratory" and classroom. But in developing her new "orientation," she did not relinquish the supposition that group members individually apply the concepts she defines in understanding their own moral activities (or in understanding what other group members do). In assuming this, she removes the moral institution of life from the social and political institutions of life. She ignores the processes by which explanations come to be socially constructed. It is within those processes that systemic relations of gender, age, class, and race come into existence and come to be preserved.

If theorists use these models, they contribute to the processes and the preservation of systemic gender, age, class, and race divisions. Their authority to publish and teach their opinions is a professional authority, politically won and it is politically maintained.[41] They cannot simply assume that "academic freedom" allows them to teach and publish whatever definitions of the moral institution their graduate schools supported. Academic freedom is a political instrument, and it should not be used unless academics make explicit their moral, social, and political responsibilities. At a minimum, that requires knowing the implications of our work, and it requires asking by what authority we define the moral institution of life.

But I want to end this chapter on a joyous note about what we begin to see if we pay heed to what is hidden and the means by which it is hidden. My discussion of Rains's cases makes it evident that life cannot be understood by looking at moral explanations and ignoring silences and secrets.[42] The moral superiority of the respectable higher classes owes less to money than to the wealth of secrecy they control and use to cover their moral mistakes. The secrecy required is an official as well as a private family one. The advantage of this wealth is evident when we see the consequences of lacking it—for example, in the publicity the young Project women faced both in their neighborhoods and in the official records. Their experiences went on record not in their own terms but in the terms of the professionals.

Rains's study points out differences in the public selves of the young white women and the young black women. It shows how the professional vocabularies recycled the white women's experience and their understandings of themselves, their lives, their world. It shows how different the case was for the young black women, who had separate "public selves"—one in the home neighborhood, the other official. This knowledge might offer the beginnings of help to activist feminists in their efforts to undermine the recycling of women's experience into official categories. Studies done today would be able to show us how things have changed for young white and black women, and they might show us a little about what empowerment might mean and how it might be accomplished.

I began this chapter by saying that the final test of political and social theory lies in action and that the justification of theory building itself lies in the usefulness of the theory. It is political action that sets the problems that political theory helps resolve. This means that the philosophers' model of decision and action also has to be rejected as a model of how theory relates to action. But to speak of "theory in relation to action" is to run a serious danger of falling into the philosophers' model. What I really mean is how theorists relate to activists. The relationship has to be a direct one of human beings in interaction, constructing action and theory, one in which theorists are involved in action and activists are there to help make the theory—and to criticize it. This is true not only for feminist political theory but for any political theory. When the theorists hold positions in the academy, it is very difficult to make a direct relationship. The structure of academic work operates against it. But if the feminists in the collectives can struggle with their problems, theoreticians in the academy can struggle with theirs. In the end, we will do better theory and be better people for it.

NOTES

The major part of this chapter was originally published as "Moral Passages," in *Women and Moral Theory,* edited by Eva Feder Kittay and Diana T. Meyers (Rowman and Littlefield, 1987). For this volume, the introductory section is new, and the concluding section has been revised.

    1. Joyce Gelb and Marian Tief Palley, *Women and Public Policies* (Princeton, N.J.: Princeton University Press, 1987).

    2. For a classic criticism of Enlightenment views of women, science, and nature, see Susan Griffin, *Woman and Nature* (New York: Harper and Row, 1978); for interdisciplinary accounts, see Ellen Messer-Davidow and Joan Hartman, eds., *Engendering Knowledge* (Knoxville: University of Tennessee Press, 1991), and Julia Sherman and Evelyn Beck, eds., *The Prism of Sex* (Madison: University of Wisconsin Press, 1979). See also the essays in S. Harding and M. Hintikka, eds., *Discovering Reality* (Norwell, Mass.: D. Reidel, 1983).

    3. Kathryn Pyne Addelson, "The Man of Professional Wisdom," in Harding and Hintikka.

    4. Dorothy Smith, *The Everyday World as Problematic* (Boston: Northeastern University Press, 1987).

    5. Carol Gilligan, "In a Different Voice: Women's Conceptions of Self and of Morality," *Harvard Educational Review* 47(4), pp. 481–517. Later work by Gilligan and others shows that the care orientation also exists in presentation of dilemmas. See Gilligan, "Remapping Development: The Power of Divergent Data," in L. Cirillo and S. Wapner, eds., *Value Presuppositions in Theories of Human Development* (Hillside, N.J.: Erlbaum, 1984).

    6. C. Wright Mills, *Power Politics and People: The Collected Essays of C. Wright Mills,* ed. Irving Louis Horowitz (New York: Ballantine, 1963).

    7. For a psychologist's case that we have none, see Augusto Blasi, "Bridging Moral Cognition and Moral Action: A Critical Review of the Literature," *Psychological Bulletin* 88(1)(July 1980). See also papers in *Ethics* 92, no. 3 (April 1982). I give a sociologist's case here, and more fully in my book in progress. Mills and Aubert (*The Hidden Society* [Bedminster Press, 1965]) are provocative, but Blumer (*Symbolic Interactionism: Perspective and Method* [Englewood Cliffs, N.J.: Prentice-Hall, 1969]) offers my theoretical basis. Hauerwas's analysis in terms of narratives is an attempt to overcome what I would call a free-will analysis of the moral institution. I am not saying we do not have free will (nor is Hauerwas). I'm saying there is no psychological or sociological model for either free or unfree will, i.e., that the notion should be jettisoned and our decisions and choices must be otherwise analyzed. That would require jettisoning most of philosophical ethics.

    8. I also owe more than I can say to Arlene Kaplan Daniels.

    9. Blumer, pp. 11, 35.

    10. Peter Winch, *The Idea of a Social Science* (London: Routledge and Kegan Paul, 1958); Peter Berger and Thomas Luckmann, *The Social Construction of Reality* (London: Penguin, 1967).

    11. Blumer, p. 19.

12. The concept of a career came initially from the sociology of occupations, particularly as it was developed by Everett Hughes and his students. It very quickly came to have a broader use, referring to patterns of changes over time, which were common to members of a variety of social categories, not merely occupational ones. For example, Howard Becker described the career of a marijuana user; Prudence Rains described the career of an unwed mother; Erving Goffman described the career of a mental patient.

Goffman takes a different emphasis than Becker, though the notion of a career is in many ways similar. In his paper "The Moral Career of the Mental Patient," Erving Goffman puts forth reasons why the notion is valuable. "One value of the concept of career is its two-sidedness. One side is linked to internal matters held dearly and closely, such as the image of self and felt identity; the other side concerns official position, jural relations, and style of life, and is part of a publicly accessible institutional complex. The concept of career, then, allows one to move back and forth between the personal and the public, between the self and its significant society, without having to rely overly for data upon what the person says he thinks he imagines himself to be." "The Moral Career of the Mental Patient," in *Asylums* (Garden City, N.Y.: Doubleday, 1961), p. 127. Goffman calls his paper "an exercise in the institutional approach to the self."

13. Howard Becker, *Sociological Work: Method and Substance* (Chicago: Aldine, 1970), p. 24.

14. Prudence Mors Rains, *Becoming an Unwed Mother* (Chicago: Aldine, 1971), p. 1.

15. See Beverly Wildung Harrison, *Our Right to Choose: Toward a New Ethic of Abortion* (Boston: Beacon Press, 1984); Caroline Whitbeck, "The Moral Implications of Regarding Women as People," in *The Concept of Person and Its Implications for the Use of the Fetus in Biomedicine* (Norwell, Mass.: D. Reidel, 1982).

16. Blumer, p. 152.

17. Ibid.

18. See Kristin Luker, *Taking Chances: Abortion and the Decision Not to Contracept* (Berkeley: University of California Press, 1975); Harrison, *Our Right.*

19. A fourth source of information was a small pilot study of contraceptive use among sexually experienced college women, which Rains used to supplement the published literature in giving the setting, or the origin point, from which unwed mothers begin their careers.

20. Rains, p. 4.

21. This "situation must be placed within systematic social themes." Rains does not do so. In the larger work from which this chapter is drawn, I use the sensitizing concept of procreative responsibility to place it.

22. Ibid., p. 34.

23. Ibid., p. 48.

24. Ibid., p. 49.

25. Rains, pp. 43–44.

26. Ibid., p. 54.

27. Cover stories were used to explain a young woman's absence from home ground and to explain her pregnancy in the new public life—for example, wearing a wedding ring and calling herself Mrs. saved embarrassment at temporary jobs, or while out shopping. Within the maternity home, secrecy was maintained by not using last names, by using letter drops, and by various other means.

28. Ibid., p. 98.

29. Ibid., p. 63.

30. Rains, p. 92.

31. Ibid.

32. It was jointly sponsored by the city's boards of mental health and education. The services offered under the Project included a day school for the girls, prenatal care (at

public clinics), and counseling. Initially, the school was limited to black girls in elementary school. The girls were from low-income backgrounds, and many had records of truancy. When Rains did the major part of her study, most of them were about fourteen — many of them old for their grade because they had been "held back."

33. Rains, p. 132.

34. Ibid., p. 133.

35. Ibid., p. 134.

36. Ibid., pp. 39–40.

37. Rains, p. 169.

38. Ibid., p. 171.

39. Addelson, "The Man" and "Moral Revolution," in Marilyn Pearsall, *Women and Value* (San Diego: Wadsworth, 1986).

40. Paul F. Boller, *American Thought in Transition* (Washington: University Press of America); Thomas L. Haskell, *The Emergence of Professional Social Science* (Urbana: University of Illinois Press, 1977).

41. Ibid.

42. Adrienne Rich, *On Lies, Secrets, and Silence: Selected Prose, 1966–1978* (New York: Norton, 1979).

11

Impartiality and the Civic Public: Some Implications of Feminist Critiques of Moral and Political Theory

IRIS MARION YOUNG

Many writers seeking emancipatory frameworks for challenging both liberal individualist political theory and the continuing encroachment of bureaucracy on everyday life, claim to find a starting point in unrealized ideals of modern political theory. John Keane, for example, suggests that recent political movements of women, oppressed sexual and ethnic minorities, environmentalists, and so on return to the contract tradition of legitimacy against the legalistic authority of contemporary state and private bureaucracies. Like many others, Keane looks specifically to Rousseau's unrealized ideals of freedom and cooperative politics.

> According to Rousseau, individualism could no longer be seen as consisting in emancipation through mere competitive opposition to others; its authentic and legitimate form could be constituted only through the communicative intersubjective enrichment of each bodily individual's qualities and achievements to the point of uniqueness and incomparability. Only through political life could the individual become this specific, irreplaceable individual "called" or destined to realize its own incomparable capacities.[1]

There are plausible reasons for claiming that emancipatory politics

139

should define itself as realizing the potential of modern political ideals that have been suppressed by capitalism and bureaucratic institutions. No contemporary emancipatory politics wishes to reject the rule of law as opposed to whim or custom or fails to embrace a commitment to preserving and deepening civil liberties. A commitment to a democratic society, moreover, can plausibly look upon modern political theory and practice as beginning the democratization of political institutions that we can deepen and extend to economic and other nonlegislative and nongovernmental institutions.

Nevertheless, in this chapter I urge proponents of contemporary emancipatory politics to break with modernism rather than recover suppressed possibilities of modern political ideals. Whether we consider ourselves continuous or discontinuous with modern political theory and practice can only be a choice, more or less reasonable given certain presumptions and interests. Since political theory and practice from the eighteenth to the twentieth centuries is hardly a unity, making even the phrase *modern political theory* problematic, contemporary political theory and practice both continues and breaks with aspects of the political past of the West. From the point of view of a feminist interest, nevertheless, emancipatory politics entails a rejection of modern traditions of moral and political life.

Feminist did not always think this. Since Mary Wollstonecraft, generations of women and some men wove painstaking arguments to demonstrate that excluding women from modern public and political life contradicts the liberal democratic promise of universal emancipation and equality. They identified the liberation of women with expanding civil and political rights to include women on the same terms as men and with the entrance of women on an equal basis into the public life dominated by men.

After two centuries in which the ideal of equality and fraternity included women has still not brought emancipation for women, contemporary feminists have begun to question the faith itself.[2] Recent feminist analyses of modern political theory and practice increasingly argue that ideals of liberalism and contract theory such as formal equality and universal rationality are deeply marred by masculine biases about what it means to be human and the nature of society.[3] If modern culture in the West has been thoroughly male-dominated, these analyses suggest, then there is little hope of laundering some of its ideals to make it possible to include women.

Women are by no means the only group that has been excluded from the promise of modern liberalism and republicanism. Many nonwhite people of the world wonder at the hubris of a handful of Western nations to claim liberation for humanity at the same time that they enslaved or subjugated most of the rest of the world. Just as feminists see in male domination no mere aberration in modern politics, so many others have come to regard racism as endemic to modernity.[4]

In this chapter I draw out the consequences of two strands of recent feminist responses to modern moral and political theory and weave them together. Part I is inspired by Gilligan's critique of the assumption that a Kantian-like "ethic of rights" describes the highest stage of moral development, for women as well as men.[5] Gilligan's work suggests that the deontological tradition of moral theory excludes and devalues women's more particularist and affective experience of moral life. In her classification, however, Gilligan retains an opposition between universal and particular, justice and care, reason and affectivity, that I think her insights clearly challenge.

Thus in part I, I argue that an emancipatory ethics must develop a conception of normative reason that does not oppose reason to desire and affectivity. I pose this issue by questioning the deontological tradition's assumption of normative reason as impartial and universal. I argue that the ideal of impartiality expresses what Theodor Adorno calls a logic of identity that denies and represses difference. The will to unity expressed by this ideal of impartial and universal reason generates an oppressive opposition between reason and desire or affectivity.

In part II, I seek to connect this critique of the way modern normative reason generates opposition with feminist critiques of modern political theory, particularly as exhibited in Rousseau and Hegel. Their theories make the public realm of the state express the impartial and universal point of view of normative reason. Their expressions of this ideal of the civic public of citizenship rely on an opposition between public and private dimensions of human life, which corresponds to an opposition between reason, on the one hand, and the body, affectivity, and desire on the other.

Feminists have shown that the theoretical and practical exclusion of women from the universalist public is no mere accident or aberration. The ideal of the civic public exhibits a will to unity and necessitates the exclusion of aspects of human existence that threaten to disperse the brotherly unity of straight and upright forms, especially the exclusion of women. Since man as citizen expresses the universal and impartial point of view of reason, moreover, someone has to care for his desires and feelings. The analysis in part II suggests that an emancipatory conception of public life can best ensure the inclusion of all persons and groups not by claiming a unified universality but by explicitly promoting heterogeneity in public.

In part III, I suggest that Habermas's theory of communicative action offers the best direction for developing a conception of normative reason that does not seek the unity of a transcendent impartiality and thereby does not oppose reason to desire and affectivity. I argue, however, that despite the potential of his communicative ethics, Habermas remains too committed to the ideals of impartiality and universality. In his conception of communication, moreover, he reproduces the opposition between reason and affectivity that characterizes modern deontological reason.

Finally, in part IV, I sketch some directions for an alternative conception of public life. The feminist slogan "The personal is political" suggests that no persons, actions, or attributes of persons should be excluded from public discussion and decision making, although the self-determination of privacy must nevertheless remain. From new ideals of contemporary radical political movements in the United States, I derive the image of a heterogeneous public with aesthetic and affective as well as discursive dimensions.

I. The Opposition between Reason and Affectivity

Modern ethics defines impartiality as the hallmark of moral reason. As a characteristic of reason, impartiality means something different from the pragmatic attitude of being fair, considering other people's needs and desires as well as one's own. Impartiality names a point of view of reason that stands apart from any interests and desires. Not to be partial means being able to see the whole, how all the particular perspectives and interests in a given moral situation relate to one another in a way that because of its partiality, each perspective cannot see itself. The impartial moral reasoner thus stands outside and above the situation about which he or she reasons with no stake in it or is supposed to adopt an attitude toward a situation as though he or she were outside and above it. For contemporary philosophy, calling into question the ideal of impartiality amounts to questioning the possibility of moral theory itself. I will argue, however, that the ideal of normative reason as standing at a point transcending all perspectives is both illusory and oppressive.

Both the utilitarian and deontological traditions of modern ethical theory stress the definition of moral reason as impartial.[6] Here I restrict my discussion to deontological reason for two reasons. Utilitarianism, unlike deontology, does not assume that there is a specifically normative reason. Utilitarianism defines reason in ethics in the same way as in any other activity: determining the most efficient means for achieving an end—in the case of ethics, the happiness of the greatest number. I am interested here in modern efforts to define a specifically normative reason. Second, I am interested in examining the way a commitment to impartiality results in an opposition between reason and desire, and this opposition is most apparent in deontological reason.

The ideal of an impartial normative reason continues to be asserted by philosophers as "the moral point of view." From the ideal observer to the original position to a spaceship on another planet,[7] moral and political philosophers begin reasoning from a point of view they claim as impartial. This point of view is usually a counterfactual construct, a situation of reasoning that removes people from their actual contexts of living moral decisions, to a situation in which they could not exist. As Michael Sandel argues, the ideal of impartiality requires constructing the ideal of a self abstracted from the context of any real persons: The deontological self is not committed to any particular ends, has no particular history, is a member of no communities, has no body.[8]

Why should normative rationality require the construction of a fictional self in a fictional situation of reasoning? Because this reason, like the scientific reason from which deontology claims to distinguish itself, is impelled by what Theodor Adorno calls the logic of identity.[9] In this logic of identity reason does not merely mean having reasons or an account, or intelligently reflecting on and considering a situation. For the logic of identity, reason is *ratio*, the principled reduction of the objects of thought to a common measure, to universal laws.

The logic of identity consists in an unrelenting urge to think things together, in a unity, to formulate a representation of the whole, a totality. This desire itself is at least as old as Parmenides, and the logic of identity begins with the ancient philosophical notion of universals. Through the notion of an essence, thought brings concrete particulars into unity. As long as qualitative difference defines essence, however, the pure program of identifying thought remains incomplete. Concrete particulars are brought into unity under the universal form, but the forms themselves cannot be reduced to unity.

The Cartesian ego founding modern philosophy realizes the totalizing project. This *cogito* itself expresses the idea of pure identity as the reflective self-presence of consciousness to itself. Launched from this point of transcendental subjectivity, thought now more boldly than ever seeks to comprehend all entities in unity with itself and in a unified system with each other.

But any conceptualization brings the impressions and flux of experience into an order that unifies and compares. It is not the unifying force of concepts per se that Adorno finds dangerous. The logic of identity goes beyond such an attempt to order and describe the particulars of experience. It constructs total systems that seek to engulf the alterity of things in the unity of thought. The problem with the logic of identity is that through it thought seeks to have everything under control, to eliminate all uncertainty and unpredictability, to idealize the bodily fact of sensuous immersion in a world that outruns the subject, to eliminate otherness. Deontological reason expresses this logic of identity by eliminating otherness in at least two ways: the irreducible specificity of situations and the differences among moral subjects.

Normative reason's requirement of impartiality entails a requirement of universality. The impartial reasoner treats all situations according to the same rules, and the more rules can be reduced to the unity of one rule or principle, the more this impartiality and universality will be guaranteed. For Kantian normality, to test the rightness of a judgment, the impartial reasoner need not look outside thought but only seek the consistency and universalizability of a maxim. If reason knows the moral rules that apply universally to action and choice, then there will be no reason for one's feelings, interests, or inclinations to enter in making moral judgments. This deontological reason cannot eliminate the specificity and variability of concrete situations to which the rules must be applied; by insisting on the impartiality and universality of moral reason, however, it renders itself unable rationally to understand and evaluate moral contexts in their particularity.[10]

The ideal of an impartial moral reason also seeks to eliminate otherness in the form of a differentiated moral subject. Impartial reason must judge from a point of view outside the particular perspectives of persons involved in interaction, able to totalize these perspectives into a whole, or general will. This is the point of view of a solitary transcendent God.[11] The impartial subject need acknowledge no other subjects whose perspective should be taken into account and with whom discussion might occur.[12] Thus the claim to be impartial often results in authoritarianism. By asserting oneself as impartial, one claims authority to decide an issue in place of those whose interests and desires are manifest. From this impartial point of view, one need not consult with any other because the impartial point of view already takes into account all possible perspectives.[13]

In modern moral discourse, being impartial means especially being dispassionate, being entirely unaffected by feelings in one's judgment. The idea of impartiality thus seeks to eliminate alterity in a different sense, in the sense of the sensuous, desiring, and emotional experiences that tie me to the concreteness of things, which I apprehend in their particular relation to me. Why does the idea of impartiality require the separation of moral reason from desire, affectivity, and a bodily sensuous relation with things, people, and situations? Because only by expelling desire, affectivity, and the body from reason can impartiality achieve its unity.

The logic of identity typically generates dichotomy instead of unity. The move to bring particulars under a universal category creates a distinction between inside and outside. Since each particular entity or situation has both similarities with and differences from other particular entities or situations and they are neither completely identical or absolutely other, the urge to bring them into unity under a category or principle necessarily entails expelling some of the properties of the entities or situations. Because the totalizing movement always leaves a remainder, the project of reducing particulars to a unity must fail. Not satisfied to admit defeat in the face of difference, the logic of identity shoves difference into dichotomous normative oppositions: essence-accident, good-bad, normal-deviant. The dichotomies are not symmetrical, however, but stand in a hierarchy. The first term designates the positive unity on the inside; the second, less-valued term designates the leftover outside.[14]

For deontological reasons, the movement of expulsion that generates dichotomy happens this way. As I have already discussed, the construct of an impartial point of view is arrived at by abstracting from the concrete particularity of the person in a situation. This requires abstracting from the particularity of bodily being, its needs and inclinations, and from the feelings that attach to the experienced particularity of things and events. Normative reason is defined as impartial, and reason defines the unity of the moral subject, both in the sense of knowing the universal principles of morality and in the sense of what all moral subjects have in common in the same way. This reason thus stands opposed to desire and affectivity as what differentiates and particularizes persons. In the next section I will discuss a similar movement of the expulsion of persons from the civic public to maintain its unity.

Several problems follow from the expulsion of desire and feeling from moral reason. Because all feeling, inclinations, needs, desires, become thereby equally irrational, they are all equally inferior.[15] By contrast, premodern moral philosophy sought standards for distinguishing good and bad interests, noble and base sentiments. The point of ethics in Aristotle, for example, was to distinguish good desires from bad and to cultivate good desires. Contemporary moral intuitions, moreover, still distinguish good and bad feelings, rational and irrational desires. As Lawrence Blum argues, deontological reason's opposition of moral duty to feeling fails to recognize the role of sentiments of sympathy, compassion, and concern in providing reasons for and motivating moral action.[16] Our experience of moral life teaches us, moreover, that without the impulse of deprivation or anger, for example, many moral choices would not be made.

Thus as a consequence of the opposition between reason and desire, moral decisions grounded in considerations of sympathy, caring, and an assessment of differentiated need are defined as not rational, not "objective," merely sentimental. To the degree that women exemplify or are identified with such styles of moral decision making, then, women are excluded from moral rationality.[17] The moral rationality of any other groups whose experience or stereotypes associate them with desire, need, and affectivity is also suspect.

By simply expelling desire, affectivity, and need, deontological reason finally represses them and sets morality in opposition to happiness. The function of duty is to master inner nature, not to form it in the best directions. Since all desiring is equally suspect, we have no way of distinguishing which desires are good and which bad, which will expand the person's capacities and relations with others and which stunt the person and foster violence. In being excluded from understanding, all desiring, feeling, and needs become unconscious but certainly do not thereby cease to motivate action and behavior. Reason's task thereby is to control and censure desire.

II. The Unity of the Civic Public

The dichotomy between reason and desire appears in modern political theory in the distinction between the universal, public realm of sovereignty and the state, on the one hand, and the particular, private realm of needs and desires on the other. Modern normative political theory and political practice aim to embody impartiality in the public realm of the state. Like the impartiality of moral reason, this public realm of the state attains its generality by the exclusion of particularity, desire, feeling, and those aspects of life associated with the body. In modern political theory and practice this public achieves a unity in particular by the exclusion of women and others associated with nature and the body.

As Richard Sennett and others have written, the developing urban centers of the eighteenth century engendered a unique public life.[18] As commerce increased and more people came into the city, the space of the city itself was changed to make for more openness, vast boulevards where people from different classes mingled in the same spaces.[19] As Habermas has argued, one of the functions of this public life of the mid–nineteenth century was to provide a critical space where people discussed and criticized the affairs of the state in a multiplicity of newspapers, coffeehouses, and other forums.[20] While dominated by bourgeois men, public discussion in the coffeehouses admitted men of any class on equal terms.[21] Through the institution of the salons, moreover, as well as by attending the theater and being members of reading societies, aristocratic and bourgeois women participated and sometimes took the lead in such public discussion.[22]

Public life in this period appears to have been wild, playful, and sexy. The theater was a social center, a forum where wit and satire criticized the state and predominant mores. This wild public to some degree mixed sexes and classes, mixed serious discourse with play, and mixed the aesthetic with the political. It did not survive republican philosophy. The idea of the universalist state that expresses an impartial point of view transcending any particular interests is in part a reaction to this differentiated public. The republicans grounded this universalist state in the idea of the civic public that political theory and practice institutionalized by the end of the eighteenth century in Europe and the United States to suppress the popular and linguistic heterogeneity of the urban public. This institutionalization reordered social life on a strict division of public and private.

Rousseau's political philosophy is the paradigm of this ideal of the civic public. He develops his conception of politics in reaction to his experience of the urban public of the eighteenth century,[23] as well as in reaction to the premises and conclusions of the atomistic and individualist theory of the state expressed by Hobbes. The civic public expresses the universal and impartial point of view of reason, opposed to and expelling desire, sentiment, and the particularity of needs and interests. From the premises of individual desire and want we cannot arrive at a strong enough normative conception of social relations. The difference between atomistic egoism and civil society does not consist simply in the fact that the infinity of individual appetite has been curbed by laws enforced by threat of punishment. Rather, reason brings people together to recognize common interests and a general will.

The sovereign people embodies the universal point of view of the collective interest and equal citizenship. In the pursuit of their individual interests people have a particularist orientation. Normative reason reveals an impartial point of view, however, that all rational persons can adopt, that expresses a general will not reducible to an aggregate of particular interests. Participation in the general will as a citizen is an expression of human nobility and genuine freedom. Such rational commitment to collectivity is not compatible with personal satisfaction, however, and for Rousseau this is the tragedy of the human condition.[24]

Rousseau conceived that this public realm ought to be unified and homogeneous, and indeed suggested methods of fostering among citizens commitment to such unity through civic celebrations. While the purity, unity, and generality of this public realm require transcending and repressing the partiality and differentiation of need, desire, and affectivity, Rousseau hardly believed that human life can or should be without emotion and the satisfaction of need and desire. Man's particular nature as a feeling, needful being is enacted in the private realm of domestic life over which women are the proper moral guardians.

Hegel's political philosophy developed this conception of the public realm of the state as expressing impartiality and universality as against the partiality and substance of desire. For Hegel, the liberal account of social relations as based on the liberty of self-defining individuals to pursue their own ends properly describes only one aspect of social life, the sphere of civil society. As a member of civil society, the person pursues private ends for himself and his family. These ends may conflict with those of others, but exchange transactions produce much harmony and satisfaction. Conceived as a member of the state, on the other hand, the person is not a locus of particular desire but the bearer of universally articulated rights and responsibilities. The point of view of the state and law transcends all particular interests to express the universal and rational spirit of humanity. State laws and action express the general will, the interests of the whole society. Since maintaining this universal point of view while engaged in the pursuit of one's particular interests is difficult if not impossible, a class of persons is necessary whose sole job is to maintain the public good and the universal point of view of the state. For Hegel, these government officials are the universal class.[25]

Marx was the first to deny the state's claim to impartiality and universality. The split between the public realm of citizenship and the private realm of individual desire and greed leaves the competition and inequality of that private realm untouched. In capitalist society application of a principle of impartiality reproduces the position of the ruling class because the interests of the substantially more powerful are considered in the same manner as those without power.[26] Despite this critique, as powerful as it ever was, Marx stops short of questioning the ideal of a public that expresses an impartial and universal normative perspective; he merely asserts that such a public is not realizable in a capitalist society.

I think that recent feminist analyses of the dichotomy of public and private in modern political theory imply that the ideal of the civic public as impartial and universal is itself suspect. Modern political theorists and politicians proclaimed the impartiality and generality of the public and at the same time quite consciously found it fitting that some persons—namely women, nonwhites, and sometimes those without property—be excluded from participation in that public. If this was not just a mistake, it suggests that the ideal of the civic public as expressing the general interest, the impartial point of view of reason, results in exclusion. By assuming the reason stands opposed to desire, affectivity, and the body, the civic public must exclude bodily and affective aspects of human existence. In practice, this assumption forces a homogeneity of citizens upon the civic public. It excludes from the public those individuals and groups that do not fit the model of the rational citizen who can transcend body and sentiment. This exclusion is based on two tendencies that feminists stress: the opposition between reason and desire and the association of these traits with kinds of persons.

In the social scheme expressed by Rousseau and Hegel, women must be excluded from the public realm of citizenship because they are the caretakers of affectivity, desire, and the body. Allowing appeals to desires and bodily needs to move public debates would undermine public deliberation by fragmenting its unity. Even within the domestic realm, moreover, women must be dominated. Their dangerous heterogeneous sexuality must be kept chaste and confined to marriage. Enforcing chastity on women will keep each family a separated unity, preventing the chaos and blood mingling that would be produced by illegitimate children. These chaste, enclosed women can then be the proper caretakers of men's desire by tempering its potentially disruptive impulses through moral education. Men's desire for women threatens to shatter and disperse the universal rational realm of the public and to disrupt the neat distinction between the public and private. As guardians of the private realm of need, desire, and affectivity, women must ensure that men's impulses do not remove them from the universality of reason. The moral neatness of the female-tended hearth, moreover, will temper the possessively individualistic impulses of the particularistic realm of business and commerce, which like sexuality constantly threatens to explode the unity of society under the umbrella of universal reason.[27]

The bourgeois world instituted a moral division of labor between reason and sentiment, identifying masculinity with reason and femininity with sentiment and desire.[28] As Linda Nicholson has argued, the modern sphere of family and personal life is as much a modern creation as the modern realm of state and law, and part of the same process.[29] The impartiality and rationality of the state depend on containing need and desire in the private realm of the family.[30] While the realm of personal life and sentiment has been thoroughly devalued because it has been excluded from rationality, it has nevertheless been the focus of increasingly expanded commitment. Modernity developed a concept of "inner nature" that needs nurturance and within which is to be found the authenticity and individuality of the self rather than in the conformity, regularity, and universality of the public. The civil public excludes sentiment and desire, then, partly to protect their "natural" character.

Not only in Europe but in the early decades of the United States the white male bourgeoisie conceived republican virtue as rational, re-strained, and chaste, not yielding to passion, desire for luxury. The designers of the American Constitution specifically restricted the access of the laboring class to this rational public because they feared disruption of commitment to the general interests. Some, like Jefferson, even feared developing an urban proletariat. These early American republicans were also quite explicit about the need for the homogeneity of citizens, which from the earliest days of the republic involved the relationship of the white republicans to the black and Native American people. These republican fathers, such as Jefferson, identified the red and black people in their territories with wild nature and passion just as they feared that women outside the domestic realm were wanton and avaricious. They defined moral, civilized republican life in opposition to this backward-looking uncultivated desire they identified with women and nonwhites.[31]

To summarize, the ideal of normative reason, moral sense, stands opposed to desire and affectivity. Impartial civilized reason characterizes the virtue of the republican man who rises above passion and desire. Instead of cutting bourgeois man entirely off from the body and affectivity, however, this culture of the rational public confines them to the domestic sphere that also confines women's passions and provides emotional solace to men and children. Indeed, within this domestic realm sentiments can flower, and each individual can recognize and affirm his particularity. Because virtues of impartiality and universality define the public realm, it ought not to attend to our particularity. Modern normative reason and its political expression in the idea of the civic public, then, has unity and coherence by its expulsion and confinement of everything that would threaten to invade the polity with differentiation: the specificity of women's bodies and desire, the difference of race and culture, the variability of heterogeneity of the needs, the goals and desires of each individual, the ambiguity and changeability of feeling.

III. Habermas as Opposing Reason and Affectivity

I have argued that the modern conception of normative reason derived from the deontological tradition of moral and political theory aims for a unity that expels particularity and desire and sets feeling in opposition to reason. To express that impartiality and universality, a point of view of reasoning must be constructed that transcends all situation, context, and perspective. The identification of such a point of view with reason, however, devalues and represses the concrete needs, feelings, and interests persons have in their practical moral life and thus imposes an impossible burden on reason itself. Deontological reason generates an opposition between normative reason, on the one hand, and desire and affectivity on the other. These latter cannot be entirely suppressed and reduced to the unity of impartial and universal reason, however. They sprout out again, menacing because they have been expelled from reason.

Because the ideal of impartiality is illusory and because claims to assert normative reason as impartial and universal issue practically in the political exclusion of persons associated with affectivity and the body, we need a conception of normative reason that does not hold this ideal and does not oppose reason to affectivity and desire. I think that Habermas's idea of communicative ethics provides the most promising starting point for such an alternative conception of normative reason. Much about the way he formulates his theory of communicative action, however, retains several problems that characterize deontological reason.

In his theory of communicative action Habermas seeks to develop a conception of rationality with a pragmatic starting point in the experience of discussion that aims to reach an understanding. Reason in such a model does not mean universal principles dominating particulars but more concretely means giving reasons, the practical stance of being reasonable, willing to talk and listen. Truth and rightness are not something known by intuition or through tests of consistency but achieved only from a process of discussion. This communicative ethics eliminates the authoritarian monologism of deontological reason. The dialogic model of reason supplants the transcendental ego sitting at a height from which it can comprehend everything by reducing it to synthetic unity.

In the theory of communicative action Habermas also seeks directly to confront the tendency in modern philosophy to reduce reason to instrumental reason, a tendency that follows from its assumption of a solitary reasoning consciousness. He insists that normative, aesthetic, and expressive utterances can be just as rational as factual or strategic ones but differ from the latter in the manner of evaluating their rationality. For all these reasons Habermas's theory of communicative action has much more to offer a feminist ethic than modern ethical and political theory. Habermas's communicative ethics remain inadequate, however, from the point of view of the critique of deontological reason I have made, for he retains a commitment to impartiality and reproduces in his theory of communication an opposition between reason and desire.

A dialogic conception of normative reason promises a critique and abandonment of the assumption that normative reason is impartial and universal. Because there is no impartial point of view in which a subject stands detached and dispassionate to assess all perspectives, to arrive at an objective and complete understanding of an issue or experience, all perspectives and participants must contribute to its discussion. Thus dialogic reason ought to imply reason as contextualized, where answers are the outcome of a plurality of perspectives that cannot be reduced to unity. In discussion speakers need not abandon their particular perspectives or bracket their motives and feelings. As long as the dialogue allows all perspectives to speak freely and be heard and taken into account, the expression of need, motive, and feelings will not have merely private significance and will not bias or distort the conclusions because they will interact with other needs, motives, and feelings.

Habermas reneges on this promise to define normative reason contextually and perspectivally, however, because he retains a commitment to the ideal of normative reason as expressing an impartial point of view. Rather than arbitrarily presuppose a transcendental ego as the impartial reasoner, as does the deontological tradition, he claims that an impartial point of view is actually presupposed by a normative discussion that seeks to reach agreement. A faith in the possibility of consensus is a condition of beginning dialogue, and the possibility of such consensus presupposes that people engage in discussion "under conditions that neutralize all motives except that of cooperatively seeking truth."[32] Habermas claims here to reconstruct a presumption of impartiality implicitly carried by any discussion of norms that aims to reach consensus. I take this to be a transcendental argument since he poses this abstraction from motives and desires as a condition of the possibility of consensus. Through this argument Habermas reproduces the opposition between universal and particular, reason and desire, characteristic of deontological reason. A more thoroughly pragmatic interpretation of dialogic reason would not have to suppose that participants must abstract from all motives in aiming to reach agreement.[33]

Communicative ethics also promises to break down the opposition between normative reason and desire that deontological reason generates. Individual needs, desires, and feelings can be rationally articulated and understood no less than facts about the world or norms.[34] A possible interpretation of communicative ethics, then, can be that normative claims are the outcome of the expression of needs, feelings, and desires that individuals claim to have met and recognized by others under conditions where all have an equal voice in the expression of their needs and desires. Habermas stops short of interpreting normative reason as the dialogue about meeting needs and recognizing feelings, however. As Seyla Benhabib argues, because Habermas retains a universalistic understanding of normative reason, he finds that norms must express shared interests.[35] In his scheme, discussion about individual need and feeling is separate from discussion about norms.

I suggest that Habermas implicitly reproduces an opposition between reason and desire and feeling in his conception of communication itself because he devalues and ignores the expressive and bodily aspects of communication. The model of linguistic activity Habermas takes for his conception of communicative action is discourse, or argumentation. In argumentation we find the implicit rules underlying all linguistic action, whether teleological, normative, or dramaturgical. In discourse people make their shared activity the subject of discussion to come to agreement about it. People make assertions for which they claim validity, give reasons for their assertions, and require reasons of others. In the ideal model of discourse, no force compels agreement against that of the better argument. This model of the communication situation, which any attempts to reach understanding presupposes, defines the meaning of utterances: The meaning of an utterance consists in the reasons that can be offered for it. To understand the meaning of an utterance is to know the conditions of its validity.[36]

In Habermas's model of communication, understanding consists of participants understanding the same meaning by an utterance, which means that they agree that the utterance refers to something in the objective, social, or subjective world. The actors

> seek consensus and measure it against truth, rightness and sincerity, that is, against the "fit" or "misfit" between the speech act, on the one hand, and the three worlds to which the actor takes up relations with his utterances, on the other.[37]
>
> The term "reaching understanding" means, at the minimum, that at least two speaking and acting subjects understand a linguistic expression in the same way. . . . In communicative action a speaker selects a comprehensible linguistic expression only in order to come to an understanding *with* a hearer *about* something and thereby to make *himself* understandable.[38]

Behind this apparently innocent way of talking about discourse lies the presumption of several unities: the unity of the speaking subject that knows himself or herself and seeks faithfully to represent his or her feelings, the unity of subjects with one another that makes it possible for them to have the same meaning, and the unity, in the sense of fit or correspondence, between an utterance and the aspects of one or more of the "worlds" to which it refers. By this manner of theorizing language Habermas exhibits the logic of identity I discussed in part I, or what Derrida calls the metaphysics of presence.[39] This model of communication presumes implicitly that speakers can be present both to themselves and one another and that signification consists in the re-presentation by a sign of objects. To be sure, Habermas denies a realist interpretation of the function of utterances; it is not as though there were worlds of things apart from situated human and social linguistic life. Nevertheless he presumes that utterances can have a single meaning, understood in the same way by speakers, because they affirm that it expresses the same relation to a world. As writers such as Michael Ryan and Dominick LaCapra have argued, such a conception of meaning ignores the way meaning arises from the unique relationship of utterances to one another and thereby ignores the multiple meaning that any movement of signification expresses.[40]

I suggest, moveover, that this model of communication reproduces the opposition between reason and desire because like modern normative reason, it expels and devalues difference: the concreteness of the body, the affective aspects of speech, the musical and figurative aspects of all utterances, which all contribute to the formation and understanding of their meaning. John Keane argues that Habermas's model of discourse abstracts from the specifically bodily aspects of speech—gesture, facial expression, tone of voice, rhythm. One can add to this that it also abstracts from the material aspects of written language, such as punctuation, sentence construction, and so on. This model of communication also abstracts from the rhetorical dimensions of communication, that is, the evocative terms, metaphors, dramatic elements of the speaking, by which a speaker addresses himself or herself to this particular audience.[41] When people converse in concrete speaking situations, when they give and receive reasons from one another with the aim of reaching understanding, gesture, facial expression, tone of voice (or in writing, punctuation, sentence structure, etc.), as well as evocative metaphors and dramatic emphasis, are crucial aspects of their communication.

In the model of ideal discourse that Habermas holds, moreover, there appears to be no role for metaphor, jokes, irony, and other forms of communication that use surprise and duplicity. The model of communication Habermas operates with holds an implicit distinction between "literal" and "figurative" meaning and between a meaning and its manner of expression. Implicitly this model of communication supposes a purity of the meaning of utterances by separating them from their expressive and metaphorical aspects.

He considers irony, paradox, allusion, metaphor, and so on as derivative, even deceptive modes of linguistic practice, thus assuming the rational literal meaning in opposition to these more playful, multiple, and affective modes of speaking.[42] In the practical context of communication, however, such ambiguous and playful forms of expression usually weave in and out of assertive modes, together providing the communicative act.

Julia Kristeva's conception of speech provides a more embodied alternative to that proposed by Habermas that might better open a conception of communicative ethics. Any utterance has a dual moments in her conception—the "symbolic" and "semiotic" moments. The symbolic names the referential function of the utterance, the way it situates the speaker in relation to a reality outside him or her. The semiotic names the unconscious, bodily aspects of the utterance, such as rhythm, tone of voice, metaphor, word play, and gesture.[43] Different kinds of utterances have differing relations of the symbolic and the semiotic. Scientific language, for example, seeks to suppress the semiotic elements, while poetic language emphasizes them. No utterance is without the duality of a relation of the symbolic and semiotic, however, and it is through their relationship that meaning is generated.

This understanding of language bursts open the unity of the subject that Habermas presupposes as the sender and receiver and negotiator of meaning. The subject is in process, positioned by the slipping and moving levels of signification, which is always in excess of what is grasped or understood discursively. The heterogeneous semiotic aspects of utterances influence both speakers and hearers in unconscious, bodily, and affective ways that support and move the expressing and understanding of referential meaning. Kristeva is quite clear in rejecting an irrationalist conception that would hold that all utterances are equally sensible and simply reduce speech to play. The point is not to reverse the privileging of reason over emotion and body that it excludes but to expose the process of the generation of referential meaning from the supporting valences of semiotic relations.

> Though absolutely necessary, the thetic [i.e., proposition or judgment] is not exclusive: the semiotic, which also precedes it, constantly tears it open, and this transgression brings about all the various transformations of the signifying practice that are called "creation." Whether in the realm of metalanguage (mathematics, for example) or literature, what remodels the symbolic order is always the influx of the semiotic.[44]

What difference does such a theory of language make for a conception of normative reason grounded in a theory of communicative action? As I understand the implications of Kristeva's approach to language, it means that communication is motivated not only by the aim to reach consensus, a shared understanding of the world, but also and even more basically by a desire to love and be loved. Modulations of eros operate in the semiotic elements of communication that put the subject's identity in question in relation to itself, its past and imagination, and to others in the heterogeneity of their identity. People do not merely hear, take in, and argue about the validity of utterances. Rather we are affected, in an immediate and felt fashion, by the other's expression and its manner of addressing us.

Habermas has a place in his model of communication for making feelings the subject of discourse. Such feeling discourse, however, is carefully marked off in his theory from factual or normative discourse. There is no place in his conception of linguistic interaction for the feeling that accompanies and motivates all utterances. In actual discussions, tone of voice, facial expression, gesture, the use of irony, understatement, or hyperbole all serve to carry with the propositional message of the utterance another level of expression relating the participants in terms of attraction or withdrawal, confrontation or affirmation. Speakers not only say what they mean but say it excitedly, angrily, in a hurt or offended fashion, and so on, and such emotional qualities of communication contexts should not be thought of as non- or prelinguistic. Recognizing such an aspect of utterances, however, involves acknowledging the irreducible multiplicity and ambiguity of meaning. I am suggesting that only a conception of normative reason that includes these affective and bodily dimensions of meaning can be adequate for a feminist ethics.

IV. Toward a Heterogeneous Public Life

I have argued that the distinction between public and private as it appears in modern political theory expresses a will for homogeneity that necessitates the exclusion of many persons and groups, particularly women and racialized groups culturally identified with the body, wildness, and irrationality. In conformity with the modern idea of normative reason, the idea of the public in modern political theory and practice designates a sphere of human existence in which citizens express their rationality and universality, abstracted from their particular situations and needs and opposed to feeling. This feminist critique of the exclusionary public does not imply, as Jean Elshtain suggests, a collapse of the distinction between public and private.[45] Indeed, I agree with those writers, including Elshtain, Habermas, Wolin, and many others, who claim that contemporary social life itself has collapsed the public and that emancipatory politics requires generating a renewed sense of public life. Examination of the exclusionary and homogeneous ideal of the public in modern political theory, however, shows that we cannot envision such renewal of public life as a recovery of Enlightenment ideals. Instead, we need to create a distinction between public and private that does not correlate with an opposition between reason and affectivity and desire, or universal and particular.

The primary meaning of *public* is what is open and accessible. For democratic politics this means two things: There must be public spaces and public expression. A public space is any indoor or outdoor space to which any persons have access. Expression is public when third parties may witness it within institutions that give these others an opportunity to respond to the expression and enter a discussion and through media that allow anyone to enter the discussion. Expression and discussion are political when they raise and address issues of the moral value or human desirability of an institution or practice whose decisions affect a large number of people. This concept of a public, which indeed is derived from aspects of modern urban experience, expresses a conception of social relations in principle not exclusionary.

The traditional notion of the private realm, as Hannah Arendt points out, is etymologically related to *deprivation*. The private, in her conception, is what should be hidden from view or what cannot be brought to view. The private, in this traditional notion, is connected with shame and incompleteness, and as Arendt points out, implies excluding bodily and personally affective aspects of human life from the public.[46]

Instead of defining privacy as what the public excludes, privacy should be defined, as an aspect of liberal theory does, as that aspect of his or her life and activity that any individual has a right to exclude others from. I mean here to emphasize the direction of agency, the individual withdrawing rather than being kept out. With the growth of both state and nonstate bureaucracies, defense of privacy in this sense has become not merely a matter of keeping the state out of certain affairs but asking for positive state action to ensure that the activities of nonstate organizations, such as corporations, respect the claims of individuals to privacy.

The feminist slogan "The personal is political" does not deny a distinction between public and private, but it does deny a social division between public and private spheres, with different kinds of institutions, activities, and human attributes. Two principles follow from this slogan: (1) no social institutions or practices should be excluded a priori as proper subjects for public discussion and expression; (2) no persons, actions, or aspects of a person's life should be forced into privacy.

1.   The contemporary women's movement has made public issues out of many practices claimed too trivial or private for public discussion: the meaning of pronouns, domestic violence against women, men opening doors for women, the sexual assault on women and children, the

division of housework by gender, and so on. Radical politics in contemporary life consists of taking many actions and activities deemed properly private and making public issues out of them.

2. The second principle says that no person or aspects of persons should be forced into privacy. The modern conception of the public, I have argued, creates a conception of citizenship that excludes from public attention most particular aspects of a person. Public life is supposed to be "blind" to sex, race, age, and so on, and all are supposed to enter the public and its discussion on identical terms. Such a conception of a public has resulted in the exclusion of persons and aspects of persons from public life.

Ours is still a society that forces persons or aspects of persons into privacy. Repression of homosexuality is perhaps the most striking example. In the United States today most people seem to hold the liberal view that people have a right to be gay as long as they remain private about their activities. Calling attention in public to the fact that one is gay, making public displays of gay affection, or even publicly asserting needs and rights for gay people provoke ridicule and fear in many people. Making a public issue of heterosexuality, moreover, by suggesting that the dominance of heterosexual assumptions is one-dimensional and oppressive can rarely get a public hearing even among feminists and radicals. In general, contemporary politics grants entrance into the public to all on condition that they do not claim special rights or needs or call attention to their particular history or culture and that they keep their passions private.

The new social movements of the 1960s, 1970s, and 1980s in the United States have begun to create an image of a more differentiated public that directly confronts the allegedly impartial and universalist state. Movements of racially oppressed groups, including black, Chicano, and American Indian liberation, tend to reject the assimilationist ideal and assert the right to nurture and celebrate in public their distinctive cultures and forms of life, and to assert special claims of justice deriving from suppression or devaluation of their cultures or compensating for the disadvantage in which the dominant society puts them. The women's movement too has claimed to develop and foster a distinctively women's culture; both women's bodily needs and situation in a male-dominated society require attending in public to special needs and unique contributions of women. Movements of the disabled, the aged, and the gay and lesbian have all produced an image of public life in which persons stand forth in their difference and make public claims to have specific needs met.

The street demonstrations that in recent years have included most of these groups, as well as traditional labor groups and advocates of environmentalism and nuclear disarmament, sometimes create heterogeneous publics of passion, play, and aesthetic interest. Such demonstrations always focus on issues they seek to promote for public discussion, and these issues are discussed, claims made and supported. The style of politics of such events, however, has many less discursive elements: gaily decorated banners with ironic or funny slogans, guerrilla theater or costumes serving to make political points, giant puppets standing for people or ideas towering over the crowd, chants, music, song, dancing. Liberating public expression means not only lifting formerly privatized issues into the open of public and rational discussion that considers the good of ends as well as means but also affirming in the practice of such discussion the proper place of passion and play in public.

As the 1970s progressed and the particular interests and experience expressed by these differing social movements matured in their confidence, coherence, and understanding of the world from the point of view of these interests, a new kind of public has become possible that might persist beyond a single demonstration. This public is expressed in the idea of a "rainbow coalition." Realized to some degree only for sporadic months during the 1983 Mel King campaign in Boston and the 1984 Jesse Jackson campaign in certain cities, this is an idea of a political public that goes beyond the ideal of civic friendship in which persons unite for a common purpose on terms of equality and mutual respect.[47] While it includes commitment to equality and mutual respect among participants, the idea of the rainbow coalition specifically preserves and institutionalizes in its form of organizational discussion its heterogeneous groups. In this way it is quite unlike the Enlightenment ideal of the civil public (which might have its practical analogue here in the idea of the "united front"). As a general principle, this heterogeneous public asserts that the only way to ensure that public life will not exclude persons and groups it has excluded in the past is to give specific recognition to the disadvantage of those groups and bring their specific histories into the public.[48]

I have been suggesting that the Enlightenment ideal of the civil public where citizens meet in terms of equality and mutual respect is too rounded and tame an ideal. This idea of equal citizenship attains unity because it excludes bodily and affective particularity as well as the concrete histories that make groups unable to understand one another. Emancipatory politics should foster a conception of public that in principle excludes no persons, aspects of persons' lives, or topic of discussion and encourages aesthetic as well as discursive expression. In such a public, consensus and sharing may not always be the goal but the recognition and appreciation of differences in the context of confrontation with power.[49]

NOTES

1. John Keane, "Liberalism under Siege: Power, Legitimation, and the Fate of Modern Contract Theory," in his *Public Life in Late Capitalism* (Cambridge: Cambridge University Press, 1984), p. 253. Andrew Levine is another writer who finds in Rousseau an emancipatory alternative to liberalism. See "Beyond Justice: Rousseau Against Rawls," *Journal of Chinese Philosophy* 4(1977), pp. 123–42.

2. I develop the contrast between commitment to a feminist humanism and reaction against belief in women's liberation as the attainment of equality with men in formerly male-dominated institutions in "Humanism, Gynocentrism and Feminist Politics," *Hypatia: A Journal of Feminist Philosophy*, 3, special issue of *Women's Studies International Forum*, 8(5)(1985).

3. The literature on these issues has become vast. My understanding of them is derived from reading, among others, Susan Okin, *Women in Western Political Thought* (Princeton, N.J.: Princeton University Press, 1978); Zillah Eisenstein, *The Radical Future of Liberal Feminism* (New York: Longman, 1979); Lynda Lange and Lorrenne Clark, *The Sexism of Social and Political Theory* (Toronto: University of Toronto Press, 1979); Jean Elshtain, *Public Man, Private Woman* (Princeton: Princeton University Press, 1981); Alison Jaggar, *Human Nature and Feminist Politics* (Totowa, N.J.: Rowman and Allenheld, 1983); Carole Pateman, "Feminist Critiques of the Public/Private Dichotomy," in S. I. Benn and G. F. Gaus, eds., *Public and Private in Social Life* (New York: St. Martin's Press, 1983), pp. 281–303; Hannah Pitkin, *Fortune Is a Woman* (Berkeley: University of California Press, 1984); Nancy Hartsock, *Money, Sex and Power* (New York: Longman, 1983); Linda Nicholson, *Gender and History* (New York: Columbia University Press, 1986).

4. See Cornel West, *Prophesy Deliverance* (Philadelphia: Westminster Press, 1983) and "The Genealogy of Racism: On the Underside of Discourse," *The Journal* (Society for the Study of Black Philosophy) 1(1)(Winter–Spring 1984), pp. 42–60.

5. Carol Gilligan, *In a Different Voice* (Cambridge, Mass.: Harvard University Press, 1982).

6. Bentham's utilitarianism, for example, assumes something like an "ideal observer" that sees and calculates each individual happiness and weighs them all in relation to one another, calculating the overall utility. This stance of an impartial calculator is like that of the warden in the panopticon that Foucault takes as expressive of modern normative reason. The moral observer towers over and is able to see all the individual persons in relation to each other, while remaining itself outside of their observation. See Foucault, *Discipline and Punish* (New York: Vintage, 1977).

7. Bruce Ackerman, *Social Justice in the Liberal State* (New Haven: Yale University Press, 1980).

8. Michael J. Sandel, *Liberalism and the Limits of Justice* (Cambridge: Cambridge University Press, 1982); see also Theodor Adorno, *Negative Dialectics* (New York: Continuum, 1973), pp. 238–39.

9. Theodor Adorno, "Introduction," in Adorno, *Negative Dialectics.*

10. Roberto Unger identifies this problem of applying universals to particulars in modern normative theory. See *Knowledge and Politics* (New York: Free Press, 1974), pp. 133–44.

11. Thomas A. Spragens, Jr., *The Irony of Liberal Reason* (Chicago: University of Chicago Press, 1981), p. 109.

12. Rawls's original position is intended to overcome his monologism of Kantian deontology. Since by definition in the original position everyone reasons from the same perspective, however, abstracted from all particularities of history, place and situation, the original position is monological in the same sense as Kantian reason. I have argued this in "Toward a Critical Theory of Justice," *Social Theory and Practice* 7(3)(Fall 1981), pp.

279–301; see also Sandel, *Liberalism,* pp. 59–64, and Benhabib, "The Generalized and the Concrete Other."

13. Adorno, *Negative Dialectics,* pp. 242, 295.

14. I am relying on a reading of Jacques Derrida's *Of Grammatology* (Baltimore: Johns Hopkins University Press, 1976) in addition to Adorno's *Negative Dialectics* for this account. Several writers have noted similarities between Adorno and Derrida in this regard. See Fred Dallmayr, *Twilight of Subjectivity: Contributions to a Post-Structuralist Theory of Politics* (Amherst: University of Massachusetts Press, 1981), pp. 107–14, 127–36, and Michael Ryan, *Marxism and Domination* (Baltimore: Johns Hopkins University Press, 1982), pp. 73–81.

15. T. A. Spragens, *Irony of Liberal Reason,* 250–56.

16. Lawrence A. Blum, *Friendship, Altruism and Morality* (London: Routledge and Kegan Paul, 1980).

17. This is one of Gilligan's points in claiming there is a "different voice" that has been suppressed; see Benhabib, "The Generalized and the Concrete Other"; see also Lawrence Blum, "Kant's and Hegel's Moral Rationalism: A Feminist Perspective," *Canadian Journal of Philosophy* 12(June 1982), pp. 287–302.

18. Richard Sennett, *The Fall of Public Man* (New York: Random House, 1974).

19. See Marshall Berman, *All That Is Solid Melts Into Air* (New York: Simon and Schuster, 1982).

20. Jürgen Habermas, "The Public Sphere: An Encyclopedia Article," *New German Critique* 1(3)(Fall 1974), pp. 49–55.

21. Sennett, *Fall of Public Man,* chap. 4.

22. See Joan Landes, "Women and the Public Sphere: The Challenge of Feminist Discourse," paper presented as part of Bunting Institute Colloquium, April 1983.

23. Charles Ellison, "Rousseau's Critique of Codes of Speech and Dress in Urban Public Life: Implications for His Political Theory," unpublished manuscript, University of Cincinnati.

24. Judith Shklar, *Men and Citizens* (Cambridge: Cambridge University Press, 1969).

25. See Z. A. Pelczynski, "The Hegelian Conception of the State," in Pelczynski, ed., *Hegel's Political Philosophy: Problems and Perspectives* (Cambridge: Cambridge University Press, 1971), pp. 1–29, and Anthony S. Walton, "Public and Private Interests: Hegel on Civil Society and the State," in Benn and Gaus, eds., *Public and Private in Social Life,* pp. 249–66.

26. There are many texts in which Marx makes these sorts of claims, including "On the Jewish Question" and "Critique of the Gotha Program." For some discussion of these points, see Shlomo Avineri, *The Social and Political Thought of Karl Marx* (Cambridge: Cambridge University Press, 1968), pp. 41–48.

27. For feminist analyses of Hegel, see works by Okin, Elshtain, Einstein, Lange, and Clark cited in note 3. See also Joel Schwartz, *The Sexual Politics of Jean-Jacques Rousseau* (Chicago: University of Chicago Press, 1984).

28. See Genevieve Lloyd, *The Man of Reason: "Male" and "Female" in Western Philosophy* (Minneapolis: University of Minnesota Press, 1984); Lynda Glennon, *Women and Dualism* (New York: Longman, 1979).

29. Nicholson, *Gender and History.*

30. Eisenstein claims that the modern state depends on the patriarchal family; see *The Radical Future.*

31. Ronald Takaki, *Iron Cages: Race and Culture in Nineteenth Century America* (New York: Knopf, 1979).

32. Jürgen Habermas, *The Theory of Communicative Action,* vol. 1, *Reason and the Rationalization of Society* (Boston: Beacon Press, 1983), p. 19. In the footnote to this passage Habermas explicitly connects this presumption to the tradition of moral theory

seeking to articulate the impartial "moral point of view."

33. Richard Bernstein suggests that Habermas vacillates between a transcendental and empirical interpretation of his project in many respects. See *Beyond Objectivism and Relativism* (Philadelphia: University of Pennsylvania Press, 1983), pp. 182–96.

34. Habermas, *Theory of Communicative Action*, vol. 1, pp. 91–93.

35. Seyla Benhabib, "Communicative Ethics and Moral Autonomy," presented at American Philosophical Association, December 1982.

36. Habermas, *Theory of Communicative Action*, vol. 1, pp. 115, 285–300.

37. Ibid., p. 100.

38. Ibid., p. 307.

39. I am thinking here particularly of Derrida's discussion of Rousseau in *Of Grammatology*. I have dealt with these issues in much more detail in "The Ideal of Community and the Politics of Difference," unpublished.

40. For critiques of Habermas's assumptions about language from a Derridian point of view, which argue that he does not attend to the difference and spacing in signification that generates undecidability and ambiguity, see Michael Ryan, *Marxism and Deconstruction* (Baltimore: Johns Hopkins University Press, 1982); Dominick LaCapra, "Habermas and the Grounding of Critical Theory," *History and Theory* (1977), pp. 237–64.

41. John Keane, "Elements of a Socialist Theory of Public Life," in Keane, *Public Life*, pp. 169–72.

42. Habermas, *Theory of Communicative Action*, vol. 1, p. 331.

43. Julia Kristeva, *Revolution in Poetic Language* (New York: Columbia University Press, 1984), pp. 124–47.

44. Kristeva, *Revolution*, p. 291.

45. Elshtain, *Public Man*, part 2.

46. Hannah Arendt, *The Human Condition* (Chicago: University of Chicago Press, 1958).

47. See Drucilla Cornell, "Toward a Modern/Postmodern Reconstruction of Ethics," *University of Pennsylvania Law Review* 133(2)(1985), pp. 291–380.

48. Thomas Bender promotes a conception of a heterogeneous public as important for an urban political history that would not be dominated by the perspective of the then and now privileged; "The History of Culture and the Culture of Cities," paper presented at meeting of the International Association of Philosophy and Literature, New York City, May 1985.

49. I am grateful to David Alexander for all the time and thought he gave to this essay.

IV

Postmodernism

12

Postmodernism and Politics

ROBERT HOLLINGER

Any adequate discussion of postmodernism and politics must deal with at least the following questions: What is postmodernism? What is the political? What is the connection between postmodernist thought and practice? What sorts of political practices does postmodernist thought suggest?

All of these questions have been discussed in the recent literature. Unfortunately, the literature on postmodernism is vast, multivocal, and for the most part inconclusive. And while many discussions about postmodernist politics have been interesting, very little direct attention has been focused on the radical changes in the notion of the political that postmodernist writings often embody. So while there are almost as many answers to the question, What is postmodernism? as there are writers discussing it, there is very little effort to answer the question, How do we understand the political within postmodernist thought?

In addition, there are other complex subquestions that make it even more difficult to summarize, let alone assess, the responses to these and related questions. In this brief overview I shall therefore limit myself to providing an impressionistic gloss on some of the main problems and issues that must be addressed as part of any effort to deal with the basic issues mentioned above.

What Is Postmodernism?

One of the difficulties in answering this question involves the connections between it and three other questions: (1) What is modernism? (2) What is modernity? (3) What is the interrelationship between modernity and modernism? Many of the varied and indeterminate results of the attempts to define *postmodernism* and to evaluate it stem from the fact that characterizations and assessments of modernism and modernity are almost as varied as responses to the question about postmodernism.

Modernism and *modernity* have been characterized in both functional and temporal terms ("periodization"), and literary writers and philosophers tend to differ about its nature and origins. Modernism in philosophy is often associated with Descartes and the rise of modern philosophy and science. Within this framework, modernism is defined in terms of notions such as transcendental subjectivity or self, scientific humanism, the growing dominance of scientific method on culture, the Enlightenment project of universalism, scientific culture and political liberalism, combined with the privatization and even the aestheticization of personal lifestyle.

Literary authors usually characterize modernism's beginnings in the writings of Baudelaire, Mallarmé, and other literary figures active in late nineteenth-century Paris. Literary or aesthetic modernism can be seen as an outgrowth of philosophical modernism, just as romanticism was. The emphasis on subjective experience, the critique of mass society, bourgeois liberalism, rebellion and/or withdrawal, the "new," and so on that characterize aesthetic modernism is already prefigured by writers such as Kierkegaard. This stance is arguably just the other side (perhaps the dark side) of the modernism started by Descartes, its negation, but a negation that accepts the framework of modernism and thus remains caught up in it. In Heidegger's jargon, the literary or aesthetic modernism of a Baudelaire and the "subjectivism" of a Kierkegaard are merely inversions of the rationalism of a Descartes. In Hegelian language, these expressions of "subjectivity" are the antithesis of the thesis of modern philosophy. Modernism is thus inherently ambivalent and gives rise to variations that oscillate between the extreme subjectivism and rebelliousness of aesthetic modernism to the standard liberal views of a Mill that seek to combine loyalty to the "objective" sciences and a liberal society with the aesthetics of the private.

The most interesting and troublesome variations on the paradigm of modernity, exemplified in the writings of Lionel Trilling, Richard Rorty, and others, is the combination of a commitment to the Enlightenment project of bourgeois liberalism, science, and instrumental reason with a romantic notion of the private sphere, values, and lifestyle. Sometimes this combination of scientific humanism and aestheticism is used to justify an adversary culture; at other times it is used to privatize criticism of society, emphasizing the idea that we need to preserve the framework of liberal society and confine our criticisms of it to the private realm of the imaginary.

This ambivalence concerning the legitimacy of adversary culture is rooted in the ambivalent, perhaps internally incoherent framework of modernity. This difficulty stems from the problem of what Foucault called the "transcendental double": the ambivalent role of consciousness as both subject and object, both transcendental and empirical, both subjective and objective. In Heidegger's view, all variations on modernism, from Descartes to Kierkegaard to Mill to Sartre, are all variations on "subjectivism," so that the variations on such themes as the relation between the private and the public, the aesthetic and the political (seen in utilitarian terms) between the endorsement of the social order and its rejection, take place within a shared framework or paradigm. This is one reason why even conservatives such as Daniel Bell can be compared to modernists or even postmodernists.

This may or may not illustrate Derrida's claim that we cannot escape the language of Western metaphysics. But it does account partly for the difficulties of sharply separating modernism from postmodernism. In fact, things are more complex, since *antimodernism* can be a label for a nostalgic loyalty either to the "premodern" (Heidegger, Bell) or the antimodernism of writers often dubbed postmodernists (Foucault).

This makes it possible for Habermas to lump, say, Bell and Foucault together (as "neoconservative" and "young conservative"). If positivism and existentialism, the nostalgic conservativism of a Bell, and the political romanticism of a Benjamin are at bottom variations on a single modern paradigm, it is not surprising that there are similarities between ostensibly contradictory views. Further, the ambivalence in Nietzsche's distinction between complete and incomplete nihilism adds another dimension of ambivalence: Are the "radical" expressions of subjectivity and the new, characteristic of literary and aesthetic modernism, nothing more than the reinscription of modern ideas and values? That is, is aesthetic modernism not sufficiently radical? Is it a coincidence that right- and left-wing criticisms of liberal modern society and ideals have been almost identical since the beginning of the nineteenth century, that their ideals of community as *Gemeinschaft* have embodied similar (romantic?) ideals? I do not think so.

One illustration of these ambiguities, which allow both conservative and rebellious positions as well as an oscillation between technological rationality and aesthetic rebellion (more often, as in Weber, Trilling, and Rorty, an unstable synthesis of the two), can be seen by comparing modern architecture with "late-high" literary modernism, including, perhaps, the avant-garde. Architectural modernism does not criticize bourgeois society or its highest values, capitalism, technology, and utilitarianism, but embodies them. The artistic movements of dadaism, surrealism, and Italian futurism often rebel against these very ideals, although Italian futurism is a version of fascism. So we see how modern ideas can be combined with quite reactionary as well as quite revolutionary embodiments.

What Is Modernity?

Modernity is a sociological category that denotes modern societies, defined originally as Western societies. The transformations in "traditional" or "premodern" society in the West brought about by the scientific revolution, the French Revolution, the industrial revolution, the rise of capitalism, bourgeois liberalism, mass democracy, the division of labor, utilitarianism, and technical rationality are the hallmarks of modernity. *Modernization* names the process of transformation.

A great deal of sociological literature, cultural writings, and art, beginning with the German romantics, was concerned with understanding and evaluating this transformation and with modernity or modern society. Putting it very crudely, some—the romantics, both reactionary and not—thought that modernity was terrible and that traditional societies, real or imagined (e.g., classical Athens), were better and had been lost. Nostalgia for some real or imagined glorious *Gemeinschaft,* or for one that had not yet been realized (Benjamin) underlies the antimodernity of this group, which wanted modernity to go away or be transformed from a *Gesellschaft* into a *Gemeinschaft.* Others, mainly positivists and their successors (Comte, Spencer), were glad to be rid of the premodern and desired a scientific technological utopia and eventually a universal civilization where the last vestiges of the traditional were eliminated (the Enlightenment project). A third group (e.g., Durkheim, Weber, and sometimes Freud) were more ambivalent about modernity and tradition. Weber's "iron cage" metaphor embodies this ambivalence and seeks to reconcile the modern and traditional by privatizing traditional values in the personality of the individual. Durkheim believed that the modern would give rise, for evolutionary reasons, to a new type of *Gemeinschaft* that would, as it were, be functionally equivalent to the community values of traditional society but based upon the values of the modern: individualism and the division of labor. (Marx combines the romantic longing for community with historical materialism.) The similarities between *ideology* and *utopia* (in Mannheim's sense of the terms) illustrates the fact that *modernity* also gives rise to a kind of ambivalence that parallels and mirrors the ambivalence about "the modern" discussed earlier, that is part and parcel of the same broad framework adumbrated above.

Hence, critics of modernity are often reactionary and nostalgic, sometimes utopian but with a nostalgic twist (Benjamin's belief in the unrealized revolutionary messianism embodied in Western utopia is perhaps the clearest example of this stance). So being against modernity can amount to favoring the premodern or favoring something that has not yet been—the postmodern? Yet the term *postmodernity,* from a sociological perspective, has been given a more technical meaning, namely, *postindustrial society,* by both the conservative Daniel Bell and the much more radical Alain Touraine. Are those who speak of postmodernity in this sense conservatives or revolutionaries? Are they antimodern, premodern, postmodern in some totally new way?

At any event, it seems clear that writers like Habermas and Jameson who equate Daniel Bell's conservativism and postmodernism with the writings of, say, Lyotard or Baudrillard are assuming that the latter must be endorsing the postmodern in Bell's sense just because they are trying to describe it and explore its ramifications. This is similar to the attempt to label Nietzsche a nihilist because he spends so much time fleshing out the nihilistic nature of modern culture. However, Baudrillard and Lyotard do agree with Bell's description of postindustrial-postmodern society, with its emphasis on "modes of information," technological "end of ideology" politics, and so on. So their own assessment of the nature of the political and cultural, of the possible forms of political and cultural critique, take for granted the descriptive validity of Bell's analysis (not to mention present reality). And so the postmodernist concept of the political is not utopian or totalizing and moves beyond "humanist" political ideas precisely because these notions may be unable to gain a purchase in the world of postmodernity. A new conception of the political, or at least very new tactics and strategies and aspirations, may be needed today if adversary culture is to gain a foothold. If so, it may turn out that Habermas is more nostalgic and less "rational" than the postmodernists he criticizes. (Jameson is more sensitive to the difficulties here, which is why he remains unsettled about post-modernism.)

The postmodern appears to reject the notions that constitute the modern in philosophy, the arts, and modern society: the humanistic idea of the self, together with its dichotomies (transcendental-empirical, subject(ive)-object(ive), the dualism between science and art, the political and the aesthetic. It also thereby distances itself from the key terms and debates characteristic of modernism and modernity vis à vis culture, society, and politics. All forms of utopianism and nostalgia, all attempts at totality and *Gemeinschaft,* all foundationalisms, universalisms, and metanarratives are set aside. Unlike the modernists and closer to the avant-garde, it rejects the idea that modern society is divided into spheres—the cultural, scientific, moral—and that art (art for art's sake) is not political (or vice versa). It thus disagrees with Habermas's version of modernism, which accepts these divisions and seeks to find (Kantian) ways of relating them systematically so that each preserves its legitimate boundaries.

Does postmodernism thereby become nostalgic and conservative, a kind of latter-day romanticism? Does it thereby radically depart from modernism or bring it (especially its dark underbelly) to its culmination? Are these questions even well formed and legitimate? Are there neat, much less decidable or determinate, answers to them? Or are they best set aside?

Before focusing on one issue that might clarify these matters—the Enlightenment project—it should be made clearer just what are and are not uniquely postmodernist themes. One common theme (here I do not include Bell as a postmodernist since his views about economics, politics, and culture are attempts to combine modernism, premodernism, and postmodernism as he understands them) is a kind of pluralism that focuses the political on the goal of preserving the otherness of the other at all costs. The perspectivism of Nietzsche and Heidegger, combined with a rejection of what Heidegger called "the Europeanization of the Earth" and what Levinas dubs the violence of Western metaphysics against the otherness of the other (combined with ideas from Lacan, Deleuze, and Guattari, and Foucault on "normality" and a unified self reconciled to the reality principle) lead away from utopian politics (universalism, totality, identity, unity) to a notion of politics where community must preserve and be based upon the otherness of the other. This takes various forms (Bakhtin, Raymond Williams, Foucault, Levinas, Lyotard), but its core idea is to seek a conception of human interaction where difference is preserved and commonality is in some sense always a temporary stopping place that grows out of the interactions among the irreducibly other voices in the conversation.

There is no utopianism, no consolation, no telos to history, society, human life. Here the lessons from Nietzsche, Weber, and Freud come into play. The movement is beyond optimism and pessimism, ideology and utopia.

So the abandonment of the key ideas and ideals of modernism and modernity—and thus of its distinctions, attitudes, political options—is only to be expected. Hence, the debates about whether postmodernism is irrationalist, nihilistic, conservative, aesthetic decisionism as opposed to the standard antithesis to each of these modernist dualisms both begs the issue and misses the point. However, it may be that as Habermas and others (including, I think, Derrida) suggest, this in itself shows that

postmodernist thought cannot entirely transcend the modernist framework. But it can perhaps deconstruct it (forever?) or continue to beat it
at its own game and thus diffuse it. But this raises the questions about
the nature and point, not to say value, of postmodernist political
practice, tactics, and strategy.

What Is the Enlightenment?

Much of the recent debate about postmodernism and its politics
focus on the question "What is Enlightenment?" Both Foucault and
Habermas discuss the question explicitly (and explicitly against each
other), but much of the work of Derrida, Lyotard, Baudrillard, Deleuze,
and Guattari has rehearsed themes related to this question. I suggest—following, I think, some work by Foucault and Derrida—that we
need to distinguish between the spirit and the doctrines of the Enlightenment. While postmodernists such as Foucault and Derrida reject some
of the doctrines of the Enlightenment, they do so in the name of the
spirit of the Enlightenment. Their disagreements with Habermas, who
wants to defend the doctrines (by now the dogmas) of the Enlightenment—universalism, utopianism—are thus not rooted in "irrationalism."
In fact, one could argue that their rejection of many dogmas of the
Enlightenment project stem from the influence of Nietzsche, Weber, and
Freud, whose ethics of honesty led them to look at the will to truth in
a cold, clinical, harsh light and unmasked some of the more dogmatic,
perhaps even less rational, aspects of eighteenth-century thought, which
may not constitute the most important elements of the Enlightenment
project (or may indeed be incompatible with it).

Thus, Foucault's emphasis on the "despotism of reason," like
Nietzsche's analysis of "the will to truth," is undertaken in the name of
Enlightenment, in the name of the elimination of prejudices and dogma.
Hence Foucault talks about the enlightened limits of Enlightenment. At
the same time, Foucault rejects the question "for or against the
Enlightenment?" Habermas is more concerned to show that Adorno and
Horkheimer are less pessimistic and more rational than Nietzsche,
Foucault, and perhaps Weber since the former do not totally abandon
the Enlightenment project. Perhaps. But then what is this project? Who
are its true heirs? Who are its enemies? (Even Gadamer claims to be
defending the spirit of the Enlightenment when attacking its unhistorical
dogmas and defending prejudice and tradition.) Or is Foucault not right:
The question What is Enlightenment? admits of no clear, determinate
answer but is rather an "essentially contested concept." The entire
subject needs rethinking. It certainly cannot be settled by claiming that

Habermas defends the Enlightenment and that Foucault, Nietzsche, and others attack it in favor of some irrationalist version of premodern myth, nostalgia, and so on. This may be true of Hitler, perhaps even Heidegger. But Heidegger is a premodernist, not a postmodernist.

What Is the Political?

The critics of postmodernism tend to identify the politics of writers such as Foucault and Derrida within the confine of choices such as "young conservative" or "apolitical" or even nihilistic, irrational, and so on. Some similarities with, say, Popperian meliorism—except that the French version is more transgressive, sexier, and more negative—are hinted at. But these critics fail to realize that the question, What is the political? can no longer be taken for granted. The political must be rethought and not merely because of the political climate of the day. The failure of Marxism and liberalism, the changes in postindustrial society, the growing recognition that while not everything is political, many things usually not recognized as such (e. g, teaching, textual interpretation, the acquisition and transmission of knowledge) are.

To what extent do more familiar conceptions of the political fit or fail to fit postmodernist writings, practice, and contemporary society? Briefly, we can identify several notions of the political: (1) the classical notion, defended of late by Hannah Arendt and others (mainly hermeneutic writers who follow Gadamer or MacIntyre), that politics is dialogue, the realm of great speech, that revitalizes shared traditions; (2) epistemological behaviorism or pragmatism, (Rorty, Feyerabend, Walzer, Barber) in which politics is not grounded in epistemology but in changing practices and participants in a community need share nothing more than agreement in behavior to achieve consensus, solidarity; (3) politics as epistemology—politics must apply epistemological criteria in the realm of praxis (Platonism? positivism?); (4) politics as technique, a utilitarian view defended by many writers that culminates in the end-of-ideology thesis (recently defended by Rorty) and usually associated with some form of meliorism or "piecemeal social engineering"; (5) revolutionary utopianism (Marxism?); (6) conservativism; (7) libertarianism.

Does postmodernist politics fit in here? I'd like to suggest that "the politics of transgression," so characteristic of much postmodernism, involves the radicalization of the role of what Gramsci called the traditional intellectual. The most radical form of politics may not involve the "treason of the clerks" (i.e., advocacy stands by ideologically involved intellectuals, organic or traditional, conservative or radical). Rather, by combining the spirit of ruthless honesty in the work of Nietzsche, Weber, and Freud with the rigorous, almost clinical work of the traditional intellectual, guided only by the will to truth, postmodernists such as Derrida have managed to undermine traditional thought, and thus politics, by beating it at its own game, by undermining it from within, so to speak. The quite radical cultural and political implications of beating the will to truth at its own game—perhaps by showing how it undermines itself when pushed to its limit—may make the "political" dimensions of Derrida's work profoundly revolutionary. It is still too soon to tell.

But what about the negative, perhaps defeatist, certainly the dominant "transgressive" nature of politics for the postmodernist? Will it get us anywhere? Is it just zany kibitzing—a French version of the yippies of the sixties? But didn't *that* get us somewhere? But where should we be going? To a utopian vision? To local never-ending tactics of transgression and mucking things up? Toward never-ending indeterminacy? Nobody can say.

In any case, I agree with Foucault, who said that everything is dangerous. That is not the issue. The issue is whether Adorno's negative dialectics, Marcuse's great refusal, and the more recent postmodernist emphasis on transgression of boundaries and so on is a political practice that is reasonable. Is what Foucault called a politics of "hyper and pessimistic activism" worth anything? Can it allow the marginalized others of the world a voice? Can it enhance pluralism and otherness while also making some form of social solidarity viable? Can it move us past the tendency for politics to oscillate between utopian and apocalyptic visions? Might it lead us beyond optimism and pessimism, beyond nihilism, beyond the dualisms that Western culture, especially since modernism, have locked us (including the postmodernists) into? Can it finally allow us, in Freud's idiom, to grow up? One can only conclude that these possibilities cannot be dismissed, certainly not by calling postmodernists names or by criticizing them for rejecting outworn utopias.

13

Lyotard as Political Thinker

DAVID INGRAM

I t is difficult to assess the significance of a thinker whose philosophy is as singular and fluid as Lyotard's. Like any philosophy it is a product of its age. What sets it apart from others, however, is its obsessive concern with this fact. The modern age, Lyotard tells us, continually surpasses itself. It is an age whose course has been determined by the grand narratives of the Enlightenment. In one way or another, these narratives articulate the sobering disenchantment, critical reflexivity, and worldliness associated with reason. Reason questions parochial traditions from the universal standpoint of consensus; what all reasonable persons cannot assent to cannot be legitimate, or justifiable. Yet reason also questions its own demand for absolute foundations, thereby effacing the boundaries that ostensibly distinguish it from other, contingent discourses. The relative and irrational is thus made rational and universal.[1]

What Lyotard calls the postmodern condition is just this tendency of the modern age to undermine itself and affirm its other. He acknowledges that the contradictions and paradoxes that abound in his thought are symptomatic of this condition. Here we have a thinker who can find equal merit in, say, the idealism of Kant, the biologism of Nietzsche and Freud, and the pragmatic contextualism of Aristotle and the Sophists. Such, at any rate, is the postmodern syncretism of Lyotard's thought, which is at once rationalist and antirationalist, universalistic and particularistic.

Having noted the futility of approaching Lyotard's thought as a coherent theory, let me now turn to its figuration of the political. For Lyotard, the Kantian problematic of determining the rightful grounds and limits of reason is a political matter, a matter of justice. At issue is the totalitarian tendency of a rationalism that seeks to legislate a single political goal to be striven for regardless of circumstances. Lyotard shares Marx's hostility toward ideologies that legitimize patterns of oppression in the name of universal reason. Not surprisingly, liberalism is the paradigmatic ideology at which Lyotard aims his critique. However, Marxism also comes in for some rough treatment. Both of these traditions claim to advance the Enlightenment ideals of universal freedom, equality, and democracy. Yet both legitimize forms of oppression.

Liberalism degenerates into capitalism, which subsumes the diverse natural languages of moral identity under the universal lingua franca of performativity, namely, productive efficiency and exchange oriented toward "saving time." Democracy here serves as a mechanism for suppressing dissent. Conflict is managed, if not dissolved altogether, owing to the centripetal cohesiveness of mass party politics and public opinion formation. Even the political process is structured in accordance with the strategic laws of exchange and economic competition.

Marxism, on the other hand, withdraws into bureaucratic entropy. It manifests a tendency toward terror of the sort described by Hegel and Sartre in their analyses of the dialectic of revolutionary freedom. Loyalty to the revolution requires the discipline of a general will in which the absolute freedom of the individual coincides perfectly with the absolute freedom of the state. Practically speaking, the realization of such freedom terminates in the identification of the state with the solitary will of a dictator.

Finally, in opposition to the emancipatory ideologies of liberalism and Marxism, there is the totalitarian ideology of fascism. For Lyotard, fascism represents a perverted ideology, a rejection of reason that masquerades as science. Reacting to the bloodless and rootless abstraction of universal humanity celebrated by the Enlightenment, it seeks a return to traditional authority based upon identification with nation, family, and race. At the same time, however, it shows its allegiance to the principle of modernity in its *idealization* of exclusivity as a *universal* goal.[2]

The diagnosis of modernity to which Lyotard subscribes was first announced by Adorno and Horkheimer under the title "dialectic of enlightenment."[3] According to this diagnosis, the suppression of the other in all its manifestations—economic, cultural, political, and organic—is a symptom of totalitarian reason. Adorno later extended this critique to include conceptual thought.[4] His antitheoretical animus, which led him to appreciate the particularity of organic nature, finds parallel expression in Lyotard's early political philosophy. Indeed,

Lyotard continues to cite the micrological fragments of his predecessor in laying out the inherent diremption of rational discourse.[5]

The priority of practice over theory is a staple of Lyotard's thought dating back to the fifties when he was a member of the ultraleft group *Socialisme ou Barbarie.* The critique of Leninist forms of democratic centralism and the promotion of worker self-management that the members of this group undertook anticipated Lyotard's later involvement in the May Revolt of 1968. Lyotard's faith in spontaneous action during this period was reflected in his critique of structuralism. In *Discours, Figure,* published in 1971, Lyotard appealed to the phenomenology of Merleau-Ponty to argue against an intellectualist reduction of sense to linguistic structure.[6] He refused, in other words, to reduce the perceptible and sensible to a virtual system of signifiers. Conversely, he refused to reduce language to the constitutive acts, gestures, and spoken utterances of an embodied subject. The dualism of discourse and figure also led him to reject Lacan's reduction of the unconscious to the laws of the signifier. Although desire can be ideologically represented in the form of an illusory wish fulfillment, its chaotic, polymorphous nature, he insisted, resists the integrating power of discourse. Like Marcuse, then, Lyotard circumvented the aporia of a totalitarian discursive rationality by investing the figural images of preconscious artistic fantasy with subversive political power.[7]

Lyotard's anti-intellectualism reached its zenith in *Economie Libidinale.*[8] Published three years after *Discours, Figure,* this book propounded a metaphysics of the libido that owed much to the Nietzsche-inspired critique of Freud inaugurated by Georges Bataille and later developed by Gilles Deleuze and Felix Guattari.[9] It was more radical than their critique, however, since it abandoned not only the earlier dualism of discourse and figure but also the distinction between good and bad, revolutionary and fascist, desires.[10] If this dualism did not establish a basis for any positive political program, its uncompromising denial of reconciliation at least opened up a critical space for a disruptive politics. Here the Great Refusal announced by Blanchot and Marcuse could at least find political expression in the anarchist interventions of avant-garde artists.

In *Economie Libidinale,* by contrast, the "great ephemeral theatre" of consciousness, discourse, social structure—indeed capitalism itself—is viewed as a dissimulation of libidinal intensities. Lyotard likens this theater to a Möbius strip in which interior and exterior, obverse and reverse, compose a single surface of fluid energies. Conceptual thought is figuratively represented as a cooling of energy caused by the deceleration of a bar whose three-dimensional rotation traces a libidinal band. By totalizing the libidinal economy in this way, Lyotard smoothed out the Freudian dualism of life and death instincts so central to Marcuse's erotic politics. The negative teleological notion of desire as a lack striving for completion is here assimilated to the positive nonteleological notion of desire as energetic drive issuing in discharge. Rational critique is thus replaced by Nietzschean affirmation. Even consumer society has redeeming value on Lyotard's reading. Despite its reifying tendencies, it too embodies polymorphous intensities.

It did not take Lyotard long to realize that what *Economie Libidinale* amounted to was, in his own words, a metaphysics of force.[11] His recent turn toward recouping a postmodern conception of justice can thus be understood as an attempt to combine rational critique and prerational affirmation of the immediate in a politically more satisfactory way. Most important, it marks a reversal of priorities. Instead of developing a libidinal economy Lyotard now undertakes a conceptually rigorous critique of reason in the name of reason.

As this characterization suggests, Lyotard's new political philosophy amounts to a rereading of Kant. Lyotard shares Kant's desire to limit totalizing conceptions of reason to make room for practical reason. This involves transposing Kant's philosophy onto a theory of language. To begin with, Lyotard accepts the irreducible plurality of language games and their peculiar rationalities. At the same time, he observes that the rules of diverse language games are continually undergoing alteration in ways that undermine these differences. This process is treated in considerable detail in *The Postmodern Condition*. Written in the late seventies, this work displays its transitional character in its ambivalent attitude toward the inherent undecidability of discourse. On the one hand, Lyotard praised the undecidability of quantum mechanics as a prime example of what he took to be the paralogical or deconstructive tendency of modern rationality. At the same time he voiced reservations about the impurity of science, especially the implication that the distinction between its descriptive discourse and the prescriptive language of morality was purely relative. This issue was later explicitly addressed by him in *Just Gaming*, which appeared in 1979. Following Levinas's reading of Kant, Lyotard strenuously defended the radical heterogeneity of the moral imperative. Moreover, it was just this radical otherness, beyond all representation and determination, that he now took to be paradigmatic of rational undecidability.

If Lyotard defends an ethical universalism, it is a universalism shorn of ideology. For Lyotard, the moral imperative is an idea without content. Its regulative function is wholly indeterminate and incapable of representation. Indeed, it is prior to political notions of self-determination and cognitive notions of meaning and consistency. Consequently, attempts to represent or realize it commit a category mistake. As

Lyotard puts it, revolution "rests on a transcendental illusion in the political domain; it confuses what is presentable as an object for a cognitive phrase with what is presentable as an object for a speculative and/or ethical phrase."[12]

Nevertheless, we *are* obligated to act morally. However, on Lyotard's reading, the conditions of practical judgment would appear to be rationally unbounded. Indeed, Lyotard tells us that they are bounded only by competencies and conditions related to Aristotle's notion of *phronesis*, that is, habits and conventional criteria of taste possessing at most "local" validity. Still, "pagan" heteronomy, Lyotard realizes, is not unaffected by the unconditioned autonomy of "modern" reason. Lyotard now realizes that his earlier substitution of the small narratives of local practice for the grand narratives of the Enlightenment was premature. Practices in the modern age, unlike the mythic rituals of, say, the Cashinahua, are not legitimated solely by what they do. They must also be critically assessed in view of the indefinite and merely possible. In casting about for a formula that best captures this postmodern pastiche of conflicting styles, Lyotard thus ends up investing reason with the volatility and fluidity formerly ascribed to the libido.

In his most recent major work, *Le Différend* (1983), the relationship between theory and practice is itself formulated as a problem of justice. Once again, a strong ambivalence can be observed in the way Lyotard approaches this problem. This ambivalence is registered in his conviction that injustice is an unavoidable feature of political discourse. First, political language is essentially vulnerable to co-optation. One's interlocutor is always free to classify one's utterances under a regime different from that intended. Thus, the silence of Holocaust survivors in the face of historical challenges may be interpreted as lack of evidence for the existence of death camps rather than as moral indignation directed at the impertinence of the interrogator. Lyotard dubs such an injustice a *différend*. A différend occurs "whenever a plaintiff is deprived of the means of arguing and by this fact becomes a victim." In this instance the settling of a conflict between two parties "is made in the idiom of one of them in which the wrong suffered by the other signifies nothing."[13] Besides the injustice that occurs between interlocutors, Lyotard notes that a kind of injustice inhabits the structure of political deliberation. Injustice occurs, for example, when cognitive questions of means and consequences supersede and suppress moral questions of ends. Thus, far from being a medium of communicative reconciliation, language is reduced to a battleground of conflicting discourses, each having its separate telos.

But is there then no justice? Lyotard is not content to let the conflict rage without some intervention. In another surprising reversal he appeals to Kant's figuration of philosophy as a final court of appeal in which the claim of the weaker party is defended against that of the stronger. In *The Strife of the Faculties* Kant had argued that the critical philosopher was not a neutral spectator in the conflict between freedom and metaphysical dogmatism. Lyotard too wants to recover an advocacy role for critical philosophy. But by what authority is he entitled to do so?

In *Just Gaming* Lyotard acknowledged the irony of philosophy's pronouncing global judgments on the rightful limits of scientific and moral discourse. Did this not exemplify the very totalitarian reasoning he had criticized in others? What gives philosophy the right to prescribe the conditions and rules of other language games? By the early eighties Lyotard had decided that philosophy should not legislate over such matters in a prescriptive manner. Its regulative and critical function, he felt, could best be understood along the lines of Kant's aesthetic judgment.

For Kant, judgments of taste are reflexive rather than determinate. They are based upon feelings rather than concepts. These feelings, however, are not private. They are grounded in a common sense (*sensus communis*)—in this instance, the free harmony of cognitive faculties. In Lyotard this community of faculties is conceived as a community of conflicting discourses that manage to communicate with one another, despite incommensurabilities. If there is a regulative idea underlying this community, it is an agreement to disagree, to respect the autonomy of the other. Lyotard can only symbolize this community by appeal to the figure of an archipelago.

> The faculty of judging would be at least in part like a ship owner or an admiral who would launch from one island to another expeditions destined to present to the one what they have found (discovered in the old meaning of the term) in the other, and who could serve up to the first some "as-if" intuition in order to validate it. This force of intervention, war or commerce, hasn't any object, it has no island of its own, but it requires a milieu, the sea, the archipelago, the principal sea as the Aegean Sea was formerly named.[14]

The oceanic figure of an archipelago is supposed to provide Lyotard with that elusive higher ground for which he has been searching all along. Critical philosophy is not just one discourse among many but occupies a common ground in terms of which competing islands of discourse can be localized with respect to their particular domains of validity.

With this appeal to the oceanic, Lyotard's philosophy once again slips back into the dark void of the singular, the fluid, and the preconceptual. The higher ground on which Lyotard sought to place his justice ultimately proves to be as groundless and ephemeral as the shifting intensities of the libido. The abstract indeterminacy of the universal gives way to the material indeterminacy of the immediate, the singular, and the ever changing. In either case, critical judgment remains indiscriminate.

The yield of this philosophy for practice is rather meager. We are left with the spectacle of mutually canceling injustices, of never-ending conflict whose formlessness, boundlessness, and lack of finality can only indirectly signal a community based on true plurality. This is a justice whose sublimity is to be aesthetically appreciated rather than represented and acted upon. Justice can be judged but not prescribed. Thus, out of fear of transgressing the boundaries separating the ideal and the real, Lyotard is forced to conclude that "politics cannot have for its stake the good, but would have to have the least bad."[15] I'm not sure this *prescription* makes any sense. But then, Lyotard's political thought was never solely intended to convince rationally. Like the avant-garde work of art, it comprises a harsh rhetoric of provocation. As such, its effectiveness as political intervention must await the outcome of practice.

NOTES

This chapter is a composite sketch of some general themes that are developed at greater length in the following essays of mine: "Legitimacy and the Postmodern Condition: The Political Thought of Jean-Francois Lyotard," *Praxis International* 7 (Winter 1987–1988), pp. 286–305, and "The Postmodern Kantianism of Arendt and Lyotard," *Review of Metaphysics* 42 (September 1988), pp. 51–77.

1. See J. F. Lyotard, *The Postmodern Condition: A Report on Knowledge,* trans. G. Bennington and B. Massumi (Minneapolis: University of Minnesota Press, 1984).

2. See J. F. Lyotard, *Le Différend* (Paris: Les Editions de Minuit, 1983), p. 172; *Le Postmodern expliqué aux enfants* (Paris: Les Editions Gallee, 1986), pp. 40–41, 90–94, 105–15.

3. See T. W. Adorno and M. Horkheimer, *Dialectic of Enlightenment* (New York: Herder and Herder, 1947).

4. See T. W. Adorno, *Negative Dialectics* (New York: Seabury, 1973).

5. See J. F. Lyotard, "Adorno comme Diavolo," in *Des Dispositifs pulsionnels* (Paris: Les Editions des Minuit, 1973).

6. J. F. Lyotard, *Discours, Figure* (Paris: Klincksieck, 1971).

7. See H. Marcuse, *Eros and Civilization* (Boston: Beacon Press, 1972).

8. J. F. Lyotard, *Economie Libidinale* (Paris: Les Editions des Minuit, 1974).

9. See G. Deleuze and F. Guattari, *Anti-Oedipus* (London, 1984).

10. Lyotard explicitly criticizes the Deleuze-Guattari position in *Economie Libidinale,* pp. 54–55.

11. See J. F. Lyotard and J. L. Thebaud, *Just Gaming* (Manchester, 1986), pp. 89–90.

12. *Le Différend,* pp. 244, 246–48.

13. Ibid., pp. 24–25.

14. Ibid., p. 190.

15. Ibid., p. 203.

14

Elements of
a Derridean Social Theory

BILL MARTIN

T he work of Jacques Derrida has exercised broad influence in literary criticism, and more recently in philosophy. This influence, however, has yet to be felt in a comprehensive way in social theory. I will outline a social theory that uses Derrida's work as its methodological basis and demonstrate why a social theory of this type is needed. Though Derrida is not a social theorist, his work has profound implications for social theory in two respects: as the basis for the critique of contemporary social theories and as the basis for a social theory uniquely suited to a social situation that I call postmodern (the meaning and significance of this term will be explained in due course). In each case, Derrida's philosophy is the key to working through three basic problems (or complexes of problems): first, problems concerning the mediums of social interaction, in particular, systems of signification (systems in which meaning is generated); second, problems concerning the nature of subjectivity and the relation of subjectivity to human agency and responsibility; third, problems of social relations, intersubjectivity, and history.

These issues are central to many diverse social theories; that is why I take them to be the issues that "yet another" social theory has to deal with. Everything hinges, however, on what matrix the elaboration of these issues is arranged in and what line leads out of this arrangement to a new theory. With Derrida's work serving as a philosophical ground, a theory can be developed that addresses what I take to be the central questions of contemporary society, on the practical level of the problems of everyday life and on the broader plane of human relations in a thoroughly interconnected matrix of global social relations.

One thing that I want to emphasize is that this theory can be developed entirely out of elements taken from Derrida's work. I stress this point in connection with two concerns. First, I think that it may be important to remark on my own basic approach to Derrida's work. My view is that Derrida's work is systematic, rigorous, and argumentative. While this work at the same time undermines systems and teases out the limits of reason (by pursuing reason to its limits, I hasten to add), it is not the wild relativism portrayed in some hasty caricatures.[1] Second, it is also important to say a word or two about Marxism. A Derridean social theory must necessarily engage Marxism at many points. The purpose of my outline, however, is not geared toward foreshadowing a full-fledged systematic encounter between Derrida and Marxism. Though such an encounter is necessary and very important (and is in fact developing in the work of Gayatri Spivak, Michael Ryan, Gregory Jay, and others), I think it more worthwhile to explore first the possibilities of getting Derrida's philosophy onto the social theoretical terrain where any subsequent encounter with Marxism would more usefully be pursued.[2]

With these concerns in mind, we may turn to the matrix in which the aforementioned elements may be arranged. Since I am most interested in delineating a set of elements and their arrangement, page references to texts have for the most part been relegated to the footnotes. What follows, then, is a proposal for creating a Derridean social theory.

A specifically Derridean social theory must necessarily take problems of language and signification as central to understanding first subjectivity and then social relations in their historical setting. Derrida's approach to language stresses that language functions on the basis of a "system of differences" that in principle can unfold infinitely. This claim on Derrida's part is nothing more than the pursuit of the programs of Frege and (especially) Saussure to their logical conclusion. Each claimed that a word has meaning only within a linguistic context. For Saussure, a word means what it means by virtue of its distinguishability from other words—its difference. All that Derrida has added to this understanding is the notion that this process of differentiation is potentially endless.[3] But this is also to claim that there is no "final" context, which claim is a form of antifoundationalism. This antifoundationalism would have very significant practical consequences if it turns out that there is a basic relation among language (and other forms of signification—here I will use the term *language* as shorthand for all these forms), subjectivity, and social relations.

The arguments for a basic relation between language and subjectivity are many and diverse.[4] The position I take on this question will perhaps seem extreme, though it has had its proponents (again, a diverse group): Subjectivity is an *effect* of language.[5] I am less interested in pursuing this argument at great length (which responsibility I am relieved of by the fact that others have already engaged in this pursuit) than I am in drawing the conclusions that must necessarily follow if the language from which subjectivity emerges is itself not fully a "ground" in the traditional sense. Language may be supporting subjectivity, but what is supporting language?

The further ramifications of this question for social relations are clear: If subjectivity is not moored to a secure ground, then social relations would tend to be, if anything, on even less secure ground. If such conclusions were indeed the limit of a postmodern (using this term now in the loose sense promoted by Rorty, who equates antifoundationalism and postmodernism) understanding of things, then there would be no place for social theory (or even for morality) since there would be little more than a purely existential basis for fundamental notions such as responsibility and agency. More can be argued for, however, on the basis of Derrida's theory of language than mere indeterminacy.[6] In particular, there are two ramifications of that theory that are of prime importance for a Derridean social theory.

First, taken as a "medium," the social character of language ensures that subjectivity will also have a social character. On the basis of understanding that subjectivity in general is rooted in language, we may assert further that the social character of language grounds the view that intersubjectivity is prior to subjectivity in the order of explanation. Already, then, there is the basis for claiming that subjectivity exists in a social matrix and that regardless of whether this matrix is itself "ultimately" grounded (in a foundational sense), the expressions of individual agents have meaning at least insofar as this matrix is concerned. Though the effects of indeterminacy will have to be accounted for, there is the basis for a kind of social theory, though not a theory that claims to be foundational. Derrida's arguments concerning the relation of language to subjectivity, which are especially developed in *Speech and Phenomena*, are compelling.[7] However, it may safely be admitted that if the entire thrust of these arguments was geared only toward showing the necessity for practicing social theory in the pragmatic mode, there would already be a sufficient basis in quite a few other philosophers for moving ahead with this project. Among these would be the American pragmatists (especially Mead and Dewey), the later Wittgenstein, and the more naturalistic side of Marx. But there is another side to Derrida's approach to language that while not necessarily detracting from this pragmatic mode (and in fact that mode will be very important in developing a postmodern social theory), certainly augments that mode in a way not typical of (indeed, uncomfortable for) social theory in the pragmatic mode.

Second, then, I refer to Derrida's problematic of "the other." Given that this problematic is found in several different forms throughout the European traditions from Hegel to Heidegger and beyond, I think it important to spell out what I find to be Derrida's contribution to the notion of "the other." Derrida's problematic is closely associated with the fact, mentioned earlier, that there is no "ultimate context." Our participation in the world through particular systems of signification is what makes subjects feel and think that there *is* such a context, but this is a kind of metaphysical illusion. When we understand language as the product of difference,[8] we see that in both theory and practice, the "ultimate context" is simply a horizon that recedes as we approach it. There is always the infinite "beyond," or "other." As Derrida argues in a number of studies, including *Of Grammatology* and the essay, "Differance,"[9] this beyond is an "outside" that is also an "inside." The effect of this always-receding context is twofold and even paradoxical: The "other" makes language *impossible,* and yet it is the "other" that "calls" us to language by continually confronting the emerging subject with possibilities. The "impossibility" of language, as a foundational enterprise, is also, then, its possibility.[10]

The ramifications of this problematic for a Derridean social theory would be the following set of claims, which can be argued for on the basis of the framework now outlined. First, subjectivity, in addition to having its ground in intersubjectivity, is capable of hearing and responding to the call of the "other." This I take to be the basis of responsibility, including social responsibility.[11] Second, responding to this "call" is not, for Derrida, a quasi-mystical matter, as it seems to be for Heidegger. Rather, third, it is a question of pursuing systems of signification into their "margins," to their limits, to the point where their systematicity begins to break down.[12] One way to describe this Derridean pursuit is "reading against the grain," a formula that would figure prominently in any discussion of history and social relations undertaken in consideration of the elements outlined here.[13] Fourth, the notions of (forms of) subjectivity, social relations, responsibility, and history, as reconceived in a specifically Derridean antifoundational mode, can be distinguished from the notions that go by these names in other social theories. Fifth, these reconceived notions can be used to read against the grain of received history (by which I mean history that has been both created and reported from the perspective of foundational notions of subjectivity and responsibility) to reveal a different history that will be seen to have a different trajectory (one *without* an "outcome") than the mainstream (as opposed to the margins) of history. Finally, the possibility of reading against the grain will be seen as the beginning of a new practice of signification that could ground the practice of this "different history."

Wittgenstein argued for a similar possibility in both the earlier and later works (he had very different conceptions of what the possibility would mean in his early and later periods), namely, that a new politics would require a new language and that a new language would require a new attitude toward language. Where this possibility was merely glimpsed by Wittgenstein (it was one of his many undeveloped insights), Derrida's work lays the foundation for the systematic justification and articulation of this possibility. And it is a possibility that Derrida *practices* in his texts. While the framework just set out is in evidence in a number of Derrida's explicitly "political" writings (for instance, "No Apocalypse, Not Now," "Racism's Last Word," "The Ends of Man," etc.), it has not been fully elaborated in a social theoretical way. That is the task I hope this outline will contribute to.[14]

Beyond the fleshing out of such an outline, a Derridean social theory must take up a number of specific problems, which I will now set out. We need not claim that there is one and only one way of proceeding once we have a basic framework, but I would claim that these problems are indeed central to understanding and acting responsibly in post-modern society.

The first task in this regard, as I see it, is to contextualize the Derridean framework in an account of the social world that it must confront. This contextualization arises from my conviction that any convincing theory of contemporary social relations must be grounded in an understanding of the nature of *contemporary* society. Despite the obviousness of this claim—which is virtually no more than a truism—it is not clear that most contemporary social theories are formulated in light of it. Ironic as it may seem, this major proviso is in many cases not met in social commentaries that claim to be "postmodern." It is as though a style of theory called postmodern can be brought to bear on social questions that are conceived as essentially atemporal. My intuition, on the contrary, is that it is because society has entered a period, or phase, or *something* (perhaps something "out of phase," something that escapes the Hegelian sense of periodization) that is not simply "modern" but certainly *after* modernity that a style of theorizing called postmodern is appropriate. In attempting to come to grips with this only half-named "something," this "postmodernity," we should take Hegel at his word and read against the grain of that word. That is, from Hegel we inherit both the notion of periodization that has led to the formulation of the idea of postmodernity, and the notion of a "completion of history" that has seemingly not occurred.

My understanding of postmodernity is that it is the "period" (that is not exactly a period) in which the conditions for the completion of history (in Hegel's sense) are present but the end of history is forestalled, perhaps permanently. The sense of this impasse is captured in several of Derrida's essays, including "From Restricted to General Economy: A Hegelianism without Reserve," and, in a more atmospheric form, in *Glas*.[15] It remains for social theory to demonstrate how this impasse—which contains among its chief characteristics the suspension of received notions of subjectivity, responsibility, and praxis—is concretely the situation of contemporary society.[16] What is needed, then, is a "postmodern cartography." (And a distinction can be drawn between this type of social theory, which is "postmodern" because it aims at such a cartography, and those that claim to be "postmodern" for other reasons—not that this would in all cases be a hard and fast distinction.)

Within this historical contextualization (which is indeed the context of a historical impasse), the thematics of language, intersubjectivity, and responsibility can be taken up anew to argue that there is a way out of the impasse. As part of that argument, however, Derridean notions of language, subjectivity, and responsibility must confront the more typical notions that are found in "modern" social theories. As a key example here, consider the work of Jurgen Habermas. His social theory is exemplary in its comprehensiveness.[17] Furthermore, Habermas also takes the problem of language as central to the development of a contemporary social theory—and he is very attentive to what I earlier called the pragmatic mode.[18] However, Derrida and Habermas end in two very different places in pursuit of that mode. The comparison of the two thinkers has been undertaken thus far in piecemeal fashion, in part because Derrida is not a social theorist.[19] What needs showing is that a comprehensive social theory that takes a Derridean theory of language as its methodological basis would be a fit competitor to Habermas's.

It is important to note that there is a great deal of respect for Habermas, whom I regard as the most important social theorist writing today, embodied in this last claim. I see Habermas's theory as "the one to beat" and the one that has to be taken on. And here the whole question of a postmodern social theory enters in again, in two respects. First, Habermas, despite his pragmatic concerns, is foundational in ways a Derridean analysis can be specifically sensitive to (here Derrida's analysis of speech act theory, carried out in the essays "Signature Event Context" and "Limited Inc," is very important, as this form of philosophy of language motivates Habermas's arguments concerning communication).[20] Second, Habermas is concerned to press forward "the unfinished project of modernity."[21] At the center of that program is the rationalist paradigm that Habermas takes from Rousseau and Kant.[22] Here again, Derrida is especially important because unlike some "postmodernists," he does not simply throw the rationalist baby out with the bathwater. Derrida is concerned to read both with and against the grain of this Enlightenment heritage: he does not (despite what Habermas seems to think) simply want to turn reason, history, the subject, and so forth on their heads; he wants to understand how their marginal aspects both problematize and interact with, even to the point of making possible, their "central" aspects.[23]

In this regard we might make a useful detour through the work of Donald Davidson, which provides a bridge away from the philosophy of language found in Habermas and toward Derrida's approach to philosophy of language.[24] I see several reasons why such an engagement is practical. First, Davidson provides, in a way that is not always too clear (or at any rate accessible) in Derrida's work, a sense of what it means for language to have a nonfoundational structure.[25] Like Derrida, Davidson has a "minimal" conception of the sign.[26] That is, both Derrida and Davidson take it that there is nothing essential to the sign other than its repeatability.[27] Second, Habermas has admirably attempted to break out of the analytical-continental antinomy by engaging with analytical philosophy of language. I think this engagement is important for both philosophical and political reasons (even if of a merely "institutional" sort). Habermas would have been better served, however, by a truth-conditional theory of meaning, such as Davidson's, than a speech act theory, which actually has as a consequence (at least in the versions associated with Austin and Searle) the very relativism that Habermas wants to avoid.[28] Third, Davidson's theory, which also claims to be pragmatic (and antifoundationalist), does not recognize the problematics of otherness that I discussed earlier. Therefore, fourth, a critique of this pragmatic alternative to the philosophy of language taken up by Habermas serves as a further basis for showing why the problematic of otherness is essential to understanding language, subjectivity, and responsibility.[29] Finally, this comparison will also demonstrate that there are indeed different forms of antifoundationalism and why it is a matter of practical importance to distinguish among them. It seems to me that only an antifoundationalism of the sort that Derrida offers can allow us to gain access to the margins of history.

Through this matrix of language, subjectivity, and social relations, the move can be made toward more straightforward "political" questions, beginning with Supposing that we do have the basis for exploring the margins of history, what will we find in those margins? Not surprisingly, we will find marginal subjects; that is, those who have been written out of history but are also deeply inscribed in history, both written and lived. These subjects will be diverse, and the question of bringing their marginal voices to life will also be a question of radical diversity—but also a question of a radical *confluence*. I shall explain. Reading against the grain in Hegel in what I propose to call a post-modern cartography, we can take the Jews as an exemplary marginal subject. Hegel needs and takes what Jewish civilization had already created, namely, the very notion of narrative history and the basis for the concept of "civic altruism," which is found in the Jewish understanding that the relationship between the human person and God is actual only inasmuch as it is enacted in relationships in the human community.[30] What Hegel leaves behind are the Jews themselves. He also leaves behind the Jewish problematic of otherness in which the Absolute can never be seen or even named—and indeed the Absolute is always receding (the incarnation of God is always that which *will* come). This problematic is very much in evidence in Derrida (as in his essays "Shibboleth," "Des Tours de Babel," and "Violence and Metaphysics: An Essay on the Thought of Emmanuel Levinas").[31]

In any case, this simultaneous presence and absence of the Jews in Hegel can be taken as a model for reading other margins of history. On the basis of this reading, my further argument would be that these different margins, which include women, people of color, the poor, and other outcasts of history,[32] are not reducible to one another, even if, in terms of what I take to be the basic understanding created by the Derridean reading strategy, these outcasts conform to a certain model of marginality. The irreducibility of these marginalities has as a consequent the notion that a politics of the margins must depend on the possibility of confluence based in the model of marginality rather than on a monolithic politics based in reducibility to a single shared condition of life (as in some readings of Marx's notion of the proletariat). What unites these outcasts is, after all, their difference. The articulation of this radical-diversity–radical-confluence model will amount in practical terms to a philosophy of the new social movements.

Finally, then, we must ask what sorts of political engagements and solutions are made possible by this model. This questioning needs to be pursued on two levels: first, broad theoretical concerns relating to the question of the relation between responsibility and (1) capitalism, patriarchy, white supremacy, and industrialism; (2) communism, feminism, racial equality, and ecological concerns; second more "local" concerns—to put it crudely, the question of what people can *do*, what sorts of practice they can and should engage in, given the model outlined here.

Uppermost among my concerns is the question whether *community* is possible in postmodern society. This question can be raised only in the skeptical mode. That is, it will not do to assume from the start that community is possible and to proceed from there. A thoroughgoing analysis of postmodern society reveals that we cannot take it as an assumption that community is possible in contemporary society.

Four possibilities can be raised concerning the question of community. First, community is no longer possible at all; all the social conditions that have made community possible in the past are now irreparably shattered. I believe that this is a possibility that has to be seriously considered. No further possibilities can be considered apart from it. Second, some sort of community is possible in postmodernity itself. In setting out this possibility we incur the responsibility of showing what sort of postmodern community is possible. Third, community will be possible again only after the impasse of postmodernity is broken. Here we incur the necessity of showing that the time after postmodernity will in some sense be like the time before (and it will be an important question whether this would be a desirable thing). Fourth, community will be possible only after the impasse of postmodernity is broken *and* after the notion and the reality of community is recreated.

The outline I have presented here points toward the fourth possibility. The new community will be the community of radical diversity–radical confluence. This community will emerge by breaking the impasse of postmodernity, and in an interactive sense, the impasse of postmodernity will be broken by the emergence of this community. I should clarify what I mean by the word *will* in the last sentence. I mean that either this community will emerge and the impasse of postmodernity will be broken *or* that there will *not* be a future for humanity. The outcome of this disjunctive pair—which consists in a possibility and the negation of possibility—is far from certain, but with the outline offered here, I hope that we have the basis for some creative theoretical contributions to the furtherance of human possibility.

NOTES

At the 1988 Eastern Division meeting of the American Philosophical Society, several hundred members witnessed another chapter in the continuing saga of the nonengagement between the Habermasians and Derrida. Professor Derrida presented a paper on the politics of friendship, which worked through the philosophical discourse of friendship from Aristotle to the twentieth century. Derrida spoke of "a democracy that is yet to come, and which little resembles what goes by that name today." His analysis of democracy and community criticized the fact that throughout Western history friendship relations have been founded on a virile model. Future democracy depends on the replacement of this model by one that recognizes the possibility of sisterhood.

The respondent, Professor Thomas McCarthy, questioned whether Derrida's analysis was capable of founding a specific social program. McCarthy asked for a critique of specific institutions but did not really engage Derrida for what he *did* say. This I have found a typical trait of the Habermasian critique of Derrida. All the same, it is necessary to flesh out the elements of a Derridean social theory, and to show why such a theory is not only useful but necessary. This is the area of my research at present. I cannot claim that this chapter will make the Habermasians or other Marxists happy, but I think it will lay the ground for more productive engagements in the future.

1. Fortunately there are now some comprehensive, systematic studies of Derrida's work that begin to make such caricatures less feasible. Two studies in particular should be mentioned: Rodolphe Gasche, *The Tain of the Mirror: Derrida and the Philosophy of Reflection* (Cambridge: Harvard University Press, 1986), and Irene Harvey, *Derrida and the Economy of Differance* (Bloomington: Indiana University Press, 1986). Some have criticized these two books for being "too serious." My feeling is that the "seriousness" of these books is fully justified by some of the "playfulness" of some Derrideans, but even more so on independent grounds: that is, Derrida is a serious philosopher. Of course, for those analytic philosophers and others who do not feel that Derrida must be read in order to be condemned, there is little that even the work of Harvey and Gasche can do. My proposal is simply that whenever people of this bent say something negative about "Derrida" (i.e., something or someone they think of as Derrida), we should always challenge them to cite their source (and not let them off the hook with "I've *tried* to read Derrida—it's just not possible"). It's time to get serious with these people who are helping to destroy philosophy through promoting a proud illiteracy. There are enough forces outside of the academy promoting this; we don't need our colleagues adding to the anti-intellectual current. (I apologize for the sudden manifesto, but enough is enough!)

2. I do not consider this proposal, however, to be pitched in a *post-Marxist* direction—this term being presently fashionable among some members of the postmodern set. In particular, I think that there is a basis in Derrida for a kind of historical materialism (though not a "dialectical materialism"—although the dialectic is not nearly as absent from Derrida's work as some readers seem to think), though one that takes as its first task the "materialization of the signifier." The notion of marginal subjects in history that I will outline has a not coincidental resemblance to a certain reading of Marx's notion of the proletariat. Concerning the question of postmodernism, I think that we will need a notion of historical disjuncture that owes something to Marx and indeed Lenin. The Derridean strategy for reading against the grain might be seen as a form of immanent critique based in the materiality of the signifier. And both Marx and Derrida are well known as readers of Hegel. So Marx will hardly be absent from the elements outlined here—but then, I do not think that Marx is absent from either Derrida or the postmodern situation that a Derridean social theory must address.

3. Derrida has a far richer understanding of what it means for a word to "differ" from other words; it may be added that for a word to differ from another, it must also in some sense be "associated" with that other word, and here Derrida is foreshadowed by Freud, but also, interestingly enough, by Hume.

4. A very useful (as well as provocative) book that works through the interconnections of language and subjectivity is Paul Smith, *Discerning the Subject* (Minneapolis: University of Minnesota Press, 1988). An important book that puts forward the basic view that I am claiming here is Calvin O. Schrag, *Communicative Praxis and the Space of Subjectivity* (Bloomington: University of Indiana Press, 1986). Finally, a book in the analytic tradition that also outlines the language/subjectivity relation is J. N. Hattiangadi, *How Is Language Possible?* (La Salle: Open Court, 1987).

5. See, for example, Jacques Lacan, "The Agency of the Letter in the Unconscious, or Reason since Freud," in *Ecrits: A Selection,* trans. Alan Sheridan (New York: Norton, 1977); Jacques Derrida, "To Speculate—On Freud," in *The Postcard,* trans. Alan Bass

(Chicago: University of Chicago Press, 1987).

6. In the new afterword to the book version of *Limited Inc,* Derrida distinguishes what he means by *undecidability* from what is typically meant by *indeterminacy* in the analytic tradition. The former includes, but goes beyond, the latter. See "Toward an Ethic of Discussion," in *Limited Inc* (Evanston: Northwestern University Press, 1988).

7. See especially "Meaning as Soliloquy," in *Speech and Phenomena,* trans. David B. Allison (Evanston: Northwestern University Press, 1973).

8. Of course, for Derrida, difference is itself different, hence the grouping of all the possible effects of the system of differences under the general heading *differance.* The principle may be explained simply as follows: rather than "In the beginning was Identity" (substitute whatever name for *Identity* you like), it is "In the beginning there was difference—which really means that in the beginning there was no beginning, and before that there was no beginning either, etc." This is in a sense simply an archontological application of the context principle.

9. Jacques Derrida, *Of Grammatology,* trans. Gayatri Spivak (Baltimore: Johns Hopkins University Press, 1976); "Differance," in *Margins: Of Philosophy,* trans. Alan Bass (Chicago: University of Chicago Press, 1982).

10. This position on the coextensive possibility and impossibility of language is perhaps not so different from a certain reading of Wittgenstein's *Tractatus.* This kind of reading is evidenced in Russell Nieli, *Wittgenstein . . . From Mysticism to Ordinary Language* (Albany: SUNY Press, 1987), though I think the author goes a little overboard on some of the mystical aspects of the problems that Wittgenstein was raising concerning language (though Nieli is undoubtedly fair to what seem to have been Wittgenstein's mystical leanings). Nieli would have been well served by a better sense of the problematics of language and otherness in Heidegger, Levinas, and Derrida. It is noteworthy that Henry Staten does not deal with the question of the possibility of language in his *Wittgenstein and Derrida* (Lincoln: University of Nebraska Press, 1984).

The other point that may be mentioned at this juncture is that Derrida's problematics of otherness is certainly indebted to Heidegger's, as the reader might expect. The chief difference that I would claim for Derrida's view is its *materialism.* That is, Derrida's problematic arises from pursuing the pragmatic mode of language study to its limit and by raising questions at that limit. On this pursuit, see John Llewelyn, *Derrida on the Threshold of Sense* (New York: St. Martin's Press, 1986).

11. Here it is imperative that the connection with Levinas be stressed. On this matter, see especially the essays by Steven G. Smith, Theodore de Boer, and Robert Bernasconi in Richard A. Cohen, ed., *Face to Face with Levinas* (Albany: SUNY Press, 1986). Also see the chapter on Levinas, "Infinity," in Mark Taylor, *Altarity* (Chicago: University of Chicago Press, 1987).

12. This line of reasoning is clearly evident in the first presentation that Derrida made in the United States, "Structure, Sign and Play in the Discourse of the Human Sciences," in *Writing and Difference,* trans. Alan Bass (Chicago: University of Chicago Press, 1978).

13. Here it is necessary to stress the affinities of this reading strategy with the thought of Walter Benjamin. On the questions of textuality and the mixture of Judaism and Marxism in Benjamin, see Terry Eagleton, *Walter Benjamin, or Towards a Revolutionary Criticism* (London: Verso, 1981), pp. 114–30. For a commentary that links Benjamin more with Jewish sources than Marxist sources, see David Biale, *Gershom Scholem: Kabbalah and Counter-History* (Cambridge: Harvard University Press, 1982).

14. "No Apocalypse, Not Now (full speed ahead, seven missiles, seven missives)," trans. Catherine Porter and Philip Lewis, *Diacritics* 14(2)(Summer 1984), pp. 20–31; "Racism's Last Word," trans. Peggy Kamuf, *Critical Inquiry* 12(1)(Autumn 1985), pp. 290–99; "The Ends of Man," in *Margins,* pp. 109–36.

15. *Glas,* trans. John P. Leavey, Jr., and Richard Rand (Lincoln: University of

Nebraska Press, 1986); "From Restricted to General Economy," in *Writing and Difference*.

16. These notions of suspension and impasse owe a great deal to the analysis in Fredric Jameson's well-known article *"Postmodernism, or the Cultural Logic of Late Capitalism," New Left Review* 146 (July–August 1984).

17. Comprehensiveness is part of what distinguishes a "social theory" from a "political philosophy." The other main point of distinction, not unrelated to comprehensiveness, is that a social theory contains an understanding of the broader culture the theory hopes to address. The difference is demonstrated by a comparison between, say, Habermas's *Theory of Communicative Action* (especially as understood in the context of his ongoing project of social critique) and John Rawls's *A Theory of Justice*. The latter is not without merit, of course, but it is in the tradition of the kind of liberal social philosophy that is not particularly culture-specific in any deep sense (though Rawls has claimed that his theory is more or less specific to "Western" societies, one does not get from his theory any interesting sense of what *Western* means).

18. See "An Alternative Way out of the Philosophy of the Subject: Communicative versus Subject-Centered Reason," in *The Philosophical Discourse of Modernity*, trans. Frederick Lawrence (Cambridge: MIT Press, 1987), pp. 294–326).

19. Habermas's noncritique of Derrida is found on pp. 161–210 of *Philosophical Discourse*. To say that these pages do not begin to engage the philosophical project of Derrida would be an understatement (they are really a bit of a disappointment, not really up to the caliber of critique Habermas is capable of). Derrida comments on this nonengagement in *Limited Inc*, pp. 156–58.

20. See Jurgen Habermas, "What is Universal Pragmatics?" in *Communication and the Evolution of Society*, trans. Thomas McCarthy (Boston: Beacon Press, 1979), and *The Theory of Communicative Action*, trans. Thomas McCarthy (Boston: Beacon Press, 1984), vol. 1, chap. 3.

21. See Jurgen Habermas, "Modernity versus Postmodernity," *New German Critique* 22 (Winter 1981). Also see the useful collection edited by Richard Bernstein, *Habermas and Modernity* (Cambridge: MIT Press, 1985).

22. On Kantian themes in Habermas's thought, see Rick Roderick, *Habermas and the Foundations of Critical Theory* (New York: St. Martin's Press, 1986), pp. 17–19, Harry van der Linden, *Kantian Ethics and Socialism* (Indianapolis: Hackett, 1988).

23. A useful project here, not yet pursued (to my knowledge), would be a reading of Derrida's "Ends of Man" in the context of the discussion of humanism in Sartre ("Existentialism Is a Humanism") and Heidegger ("Letter on Humanism"). A further project which suggests itself here would be a reading that moves historically and politically "forward" from Sartre, through structuralism (esp. Althusser), to Derrida. These readings would be useful for establishing Derrida's relationship to the Enlightenment in a more contextually secure way.

24. See especially Donald Davidson, *Inquiries into Truth and Interpretation* (Oxford: Oxford University Press, 1985), and "Language and Reality," in Ernest LePore, ed., *Truth and Interpretation: Perspectives on the Philosophy of Donald Davidson* (Oxford: Basil Blackwell, 1986).

25. Here the question is especially the use and modifications that Davidson has made of Tarski's semantic conception of truth. See essays 1–5 in *Inquiries*. Often the subtleties of Davidson's pragmatic reading of the semantic conception are missed, in part because analytic and "Continental" philosophers sometimes have different foci concerning the metaphysics of language and interpretation. Tarski's conception is an attempted end run around problems of metaphysics. In Davidson's reworking, there is no attempt to avoid metaphysics, only to minimize recourse to metaphysics and to define clearly the scope of metaphysics. Whether this attempt succeeds or not, one important aspect of the attempt is that it struggles against metaphysics "from the inside" in a way that is not so foreign to

Derrida's attitude toward metaphysics.

26. See S. Pradhan, "Minimalist Semantics: Davidson and Derrida on Meaning, Use and Convention," *Diacritics* 16(1)(Spring 1986), pp. 65–77.

27. It should be added that the term *repeatability* does not cover the range of possibilities that Derrida signifies with the term *iterability*. On this point, see the afterword to *Limited Inc* and Gasche, pp. 212–17.

28. Two points need to be raised here. First, Habermas's conflation of the views of language in the work of Michael Dummett and Donald Davidson indicate that there is a bit of confusion and perhaps carelessness in Habermas's investigation of theories of communication; see *Theory of Communicative Action*, pp. 276, 316–18. (This reminds one of the way that analytic philosophers often lop diverse Continental figures such as Derrida, Habermas, and Foucault together. Davidson and Dummett are really quite different in their views of language; see Michael Dummett, "What is a theory of meaning?" in Samuel Guttenplan, ed., *Mind and Language* [Oxford: Oxford University Press, 1975], pp. 97–138, in which Dummett discusses his differences with Davidson.) Second, there is the problem that speech act theories tend to be both foundationalistic and relativistic: foundational in their positing of a self-present subject who knows and speaks, relativistic in what Dagfinn Follesdal and others have tagged a "Humpty-Dumpty theory of meaning" ("a word means just what I say it means").

29. This understanding must intersect at points with Heidegger's thought on language, even though I prefer to stick to a "pragmatic" track as much as possible. The point that I think needs emphasizing is that if language is the "house of being," what is the place of humanity? I would argue that humanity is in a sense a guest, sometimes an uncomfortable guest, in this house. This status of humanity is complicated by the fact, or what I accept as fact, that language is at least in part a human creation (the role played by alterity in the creation of language cannot be merely ascribed to human invention), but I do not think that fact changes the basic picture. See Joseph J. Kockelmans, ed., *On Heidegger and Language* (Evanston: Northwestern University Press, 1972).

30. Among the many important references here would be Levinas, Buber, and Fackenheim. See especially Emil Fackenheim, "The Shibboleth of Revelation: From Spinoza Beyond Hegel," in *To Mend the World: Foundations of Future Jewish Thought* (New York: Schocken Books, 1982). A pair of articles that articulate the point I am making here are Richard L. Rubenstein, "Civic Altruism and the Resacralization of the Political Order," and Manfred H. Vogel, "The Social Dimension of the Faith of Judaism: Phenomenological and Historic Aspects," in M. Darrol Bryant and Rita H. Mataragnon, eds., *The Many Faces of Religion and Society* (New York: Paragon House, 1985).

31. "Shibboleth," trans. Joshua Wilner, in Geoffrey H. Hartman and Sanford Budick, eds., *Midrash and Literature* (New Haven: Yale University Press, 1986); "Des Tours de Babel," trans. Joseph F. Graham, in Joseph F. Graham, ed., *"Différence" in Translation* (Ithaca: Cornell University Press, 1985); "Violence and Metaphysics: An Essay on the Thought of Emmanuel Levinas," in *Writing and Difference*.

32. We may include here representatives and representations of outcast issues in history; for example, the romantic rebellion against the Enlightenment notion of progress.

15

The Critique of Marxism in Baudrillard's Later Writings

TONY SMITH

T he politics of postmodernism is a variant of the politics of post-Marxism. At least most of the figures associated with the postmodernist movement have declared that they are "beyond" Marx in some fundamental fashion. This is certainly the case for Jean Baudrillard.[1] He first presented his case against Marxism in his early work *The Mirror of Production.*[2] I shall examine some of the major objections to Marxism formulated in his later writings. First, however, a brief summary of the Marxist position must be given.

On the most abstract level, Marx's position can be formulated in terms taken from Hegel.[3] Both Hegel and Marx interpret sociopolitical reality in terms of a dialectic between the moments of universality, particularity, and individuality. For Hegel, these poles are in principle reconciled in the modern capitalist state. In this sense, for Hegel, the real has become rational. For Marx, in contrast, capital is an alien form of universality. It involves the exploitation of particular classes and does not allow true individuality to flourish. Therefore, for Marx, the real is not rational. However, there are structural contradictions in reality that create the objective possibility of a transition to a social order where the universal (i.e., the community as a whole), particular groups within the community, and individuals can truly be reconciled. This is the dialectic of history.

With these contradictions, we arrived at the more concrete dimension of Marx's theory. The most basic contradiction is between the class with a fundamental interest in maintaining the given institutional framework and the class with a fundamental interest in attaining a new set of institutions. The former class benefits from the labor of others, although ideologies will be generated that attempt to mask this. The latter class is exploited at the point of production and enjoys a precarious and incomplete satisfaction of its needs, although here too ideologies will be generated that distort this state of affairs. The task of Marxist theory is to undermine these ideologies.

For Marxism, some forms of activity are privileged. Praxis that is devoted to the resolution of this contradiction in a direction favorable to the interests of the exploited furthers the struggle to attain the next stage in social evolution. In the present historical context, this theoretical schema orients and justifies revolutionary struggles to replace capitalism with socialism.

For Baudrillard, all of the above is hopelessly out of date. The Marxist account utterly fails to appreciate the specificity of our postmodern condition. Baudrillard's rejection of Marxism can be summarized under five headings.

Beyond the Dialectic

In Baudrillard's view, we live today in the epoch of simulation. The real event has been replaced by the simulacra of a real event, simulacra that multiply themselves endlessly in all directions. The world we dwell in is dominated by images that pretend to depict a reality but depict only themselves. When we come to see "reality" in terms of these images, these images have become our reality. But it is a reality more real than reality itself, a hyperreality that "substitutes signs of the real for the real itself."[4]

In this new epoch, any dialectic connecting universal, particular, and individual is ruled out. On the one side, the universal is dissolved ("the universal no longer exists");[5] specifically, "capital" no longer functions as a universal once we are within "the hyperreal, which no longer has anything to do with either capital or the social."[6] On the other, the individual is dissolved into "the anonymous and perfectly undifferentiated individual, the term substitutable for any other . . . the end products of the social, of a now globalised abstract society."[7] A world dissolved into undifferentiated individuals has no room for a dialectic between the real and the rational. "There is no longer any critical and speculative distance between the real and the rational. . . . Neither realised nor idealised: but hyperrealized."[8]

Beyond the Productivist Paradigm

For Baudrillard, "Marxism's assumption in its purest form" is "productivity regarding as a discourse of total reference."[9] Marx's concern with production simply reflected that of nineteenth-century capitalism itself, which focused on production with a maniacal obsession. However, Baudrillard holds that a fundamental shift has occurred since Marx's day. The rupture took place when the system developed to the point where so much could be produced that consumers had to be molded to absorb more and more products. We are now in a radically new period from that described by Marx, one in which the old language of capitalism has been put out of play: "Everything changes with the precession of the production of demand before that of goods. Their logical relationship (between production and consumption) is broken, and we move into a totally different order, which is no longer that of either production, or consumption, but that of the simulation of both, thanks to the inversion of the process."[10]

Another way of putting the reason why a theory of modes of production is outmoded is that the molding of consumers takes place through cultural images. In other words, there is now a complete interpenetration of the cultural realm and the realm of production. Things have moved to the point where there no longer are mere means of production. "We live everywhere already in an 'esthetic' hallucination of reality."[11]

The Marxist concern with production extends to the production of theory, the production of meanings that make sense of the world. Here Baudrillard claims that Marxism has fallen into a trap set by capitalism. Ironically, it provides a support for the very system it intended to undermine, for "it is the production of this demand for meaning which has become crucial for the system,"[12] even if this is but the simulation of a production of meaning.

Beyond Needs; Beyond Truth

Marxist discourse essentially involves truth claims that are supposedly grounded by objectively existing referents. The theory of needs was a crucial component of Marx's critique of capitalism. "Unmet social needs" provided a natural reference point in terms of which the failures of capitalism could be objectively measured. In this manner the truth of the critique could be grounded. Postmodern thinkers, however, reject the notion that there is some transcendental referent for the signs we use, grounding the truth of our assertions. Baudrillard speaks of the "liquidation of all referentials."[13] "Needs," for example, are not naturalistically given and thus cannot ground the truth of Marxist discourse.

Beyond Ideology

The concept of ideology implies that some reality has been falsely presented. The concept of an ideology critique implies that it is possible to present the truth of that reality. If reality has been replaced by hyperreality and if the notion of truth must be abandoned along with that of reference, it follows at once that the concepts of ideology and ideology critique cannot be retained. Baudrillard does not shy away from drawing this conclusion. "It is no longer a question of the false representation of reality (ideology), but of concealing the fact that the real is no longer real."[14] Here too, Marxism must be rejected, for "it is always a false problem to want to restore the truth beneath the simulacrum."[15]

Beyond Revolution

From all that has been said thus far, it follows that the project of revolutionary action oriented by the rational understanding of a dialectical social reality must be completely abandoned. Any attempt to escape from the simulations of hyperreality only further entraps us in it. Where does this leave us? Baudrillard seems to propose two answers.

First, a radical project today does not attempt to struggle against the ceaseless production of hyperreality. Instead, the radical today is like a judo master who accepts the force thrown against her and even reinforces that force, thereby throwing it off. Baudrillard's advice to us is to amplify the hyperreality around us, to give in to its fascination rather than attempt to resist it. "The strategic resistance is that of . . . the hyperconformist simulation of the very mechanisms of the system, which is a form of refusal and of non-reception."[16] This amplification may then lead to the "implosion" of the hyperreality, to a catastrophe whose dimensions cannot be predicted or imagined at this point. Anything short of this implosion does not count as a radical act in the present context; anything else would not go to the root of the matter.

A second option seems to involve a more active form of resistance. It involves a "challenge" to the production of hyperreality: "Challenge is the opposite of *dialogue:* it creates a nondialectic, ineluctable space. It is neither a means nor an end: it opposes its own space to political space. It knows neither middle-range nor long-term; its only term is the immediacy of a response or of death. Everything linear, including history, has an end; challenge alone is without end since it is indefinitely reversible."[17] "Challenge" in this sense counts as the purest form of defiance, for "defiance always comes from that which has no meaning, no name, no identity—it is a defiance of meaning, of power, of truth."[18]

For Baudrillard, the greatest moments of working-class rebellion were not the goal-directed attempts to seize state power but those revolts that fit this notion of challenge. Here too, what was sought was an "implosion," not a revolution: "[In] the *real* history of class struggle . . . [its] only moments were those when the dominated class fought on the basis of its self-denial 'as such,' on the basis of the sole fact that it amounted to nothing. . . . When the class itself, or a faction of it, prefers to act as a radical non-class, i.e. to act out its own death right away within the explosive structure of capital, when it chooses to implode suddenly instead of seeking political expansion and class hegemony. . . . The secret of the void lies here, in the incalculable force of the implosion (contrary to our imaginary concept of revolutionary explosion)."[19]

But for Baudrillard, even this seems to be a matter of the past. The socialist project of a class-based revolution is ruled out today because in a world of hyperreality there cannot be any real classes to serve as revolutionary agents. From this perspective, the very project of socialism is dissolved: "The social will never have had time to lead to socialism, it will have been short-circuited by the hypersocial, by the hyperreality of the social."[20] In a world of undifferentiated individuals, "the concept of class will have dissolved . . . into some parodic, extended double, like 'the mass of workers' or simply into a retrospective simulation of the proletariat."[21]

How should we evaluate Baudrillard's writings? In a certain sense, Baudrillard has undercut all possibility of objecting to his position by insisting that he does not have a position. He has insisted that he is not in the least interested in presenting truth claims. His objective is to use the language of thought to make himself and his readers "dizzy" with the experience: "My way is to make ideas appear, but as soon as they appear I immediately try to make them disappear . . . nothing remains but a sense of dizziness, with which you can't do anything."[22] However, there is more going on in his writings than the attempt to evoke that one emotion. Baudrillard's writings are also meant to *persuade* us of various things, from the bankruptcy of Marxism to the characteristics of the postmodern world. This implies, however, that it is legitimate to raise the question whether Baudrillard's points are persuasive.

My thesis is that there is a built-in tension between the project of making the reader experience dizziness and the project of persuading the reader of the correctness of a given interpretation. A plausible case for the correctness of a specific insight generally involves things such as spelling out carefully the implications of accepting the insight, discussing the range of cases to which it applies and the range to which it does not, considering alternative insights that attempt to account for the same range, and so on. In contrast, intellectual dizziness is most reliably evoked when one begins with a specific insight and then wildly extrapolates to the most extreme thesis that could possibly be connected to that insight. Given the obvious divergence in both method and purpose of the two projects, it would be most unlikely for a single author to combine the two successfully. As far as Baudrillard is concerned, there can be no doubt that his writings successfully evoke dizziness in the reader. However, his success in presenting us with reasons to regard his critique of Marxism as plausible is much more doubtful. With this thesis in mind, we can go through Baudrillard's key claims in turn.

Beyond Dialectics?

In terms of the dialectic of universality, particularity, and individuality, the moment of individuality is certainly present in his thought, even if in the debased form of "the anonymous and perfectly undifferentiated individual."[23] And the various codes or models repeated over and over in the production of hyperreality form a moment of particularity. At first it may appear that this is all that there is. Baudrillard writes, "The universal no longer exists, there is nothing left but a singularity which can take on the aspect of totality."[24] But this is not quite right. It turns out that for Baudrillard no less than for Marx, the form of capital is an alien universal above individuals. If anything, capital for Baudrillard is even more of a universal than for Marx. Its scope extends to the innermost depths of our existence:

This compulsion toward liquidity, flow, and an accelerated circulation of what is psychic, sexual, or pertaining to the body is the exact replica of the force which rules market value: capital must circulate; gravity and any fixed point must disappear; the chain of investments and reinvestments must never stop; value must radiate endlessly and in every direction. This is the form itself which the current realization of value takes. It is the form of capital, and sexuality as a catchword and a *model* is the way it appears at the level of bodies. . . . It is capital which gives birth in the same movement to the energetic of labor power and to the body we dream of today as the locus of desire and the unconscious. . . . To rediscover in the secret of bodies an unbound "libidinal" energy which would be opposed to the bound energy of productive bodies, and to rediscover a phantasmal and instinctual truth of the body in desire, is still only to unearth the psychic metaphor of capital.[25]

Baudrillard thus cannot claim that his thought does not involve the abstract categories of universal, particularity, and individual. His claim that "the universal no longer exists" is a wild extrapolation from the fact that the alien universal of capital is more extensive and intensive in its scope than ever before.

Turning to more concrete matters, are there objective dialectical tendencies in the present configuration? At first it might seem that this question, of such central importance to Marx, is no longer relevant. After all, Baudrillard has written that "dialectical polarity no longer exists."[26] But a closer look at Baudrillard's position reveals that this cannot be maintained. On the one hand, he points to the endless and impersonal production of a meaningless hyperreality. On the other, there is the "silent majority" that dwells in this hyperreality. On his view, the production of hyperreality generates the preconditions for an ironic hyperconformism in the silent majority or for a challenge and defiance of the present order. Either way, Baudrillard has argued in effect that there is a "dialectical polarity" between hyperreality and the silent majority. From this he derives an objective structural tendency toward what he terms implosion. Like it or not, with this he has in effect hypothesized regarding a dialectical development. Whatever the plausibility of this scenario, it is the unfolding of a historical dialectic. Baudrillard has made a wild extrapolation from the fact that the dialectic he sketches is quite different from other accounts to the conclusion that the very category of dialectical tendencies must be abandoned.

Beyond Production?

Baudrillard begins with an interesting insight. Capitalism has become so productive that the danger of producing commodities that are not absorbed by the market is ever present. This means that great effort must continually be made to create demand for products. When products are cultural signs, the demand for them will not be limited by any functional use those products may have. In this sense there is no longer (if there ever was) any sphere of production separate from the sphere of culture.[27]

From this observation Baudrillard extrapolates to the claims that any attempt to consider production independently of culture is mistaken and that any attempt by critics of capitalism to produce cultural meanings supports the very system they meant to oppose. Neither of these claims withstands scrutiny.

Production and culture are certainly mediated together. But this does not necessarily imply that they are fused. It may be the case that they are united-in-difference. If so, it would be legitimate to consider production apart from culture, as long as one realizes that the mediation of the two spheres must be comprehended if the level of concretion is to be attained.

The proof that the two spheres are distinguishable in their unity comes from the fact that there are some things that can be comprehended only if production is considered in abstraction from its connection to culture. The hyperreality of which Baudrillard speaks is itself produced. Even if it were the case that the production of images is now more crucial to the present stage of capital than the production of material products, we cannot extrapolate from this to the conclusion that the question of the ownership and control of the means of production is not of crucial significance.

There is a tremendous concentration of capital in the ownership and control of the means of producing messages. Robert Maxwell and Rupert Murdoch have created global media empires that spread through book, magazine, and newspaper publishing; TV station ownership; TV program planning; cable TV network ownership, satellite TV distribution; and electronic hardware production. *Time* and Warner have merged into a media conglomerate with revenues of $10 billion a year. The next Madonna wannabe will be signed by Warner, given an HBO special, reviewed in *Time,* and appear on the cover of *People* in an hyperreal blitz, all as a result of a decision made by headquarters in New York. Surely a consideration of such matters cannot be avoided if we wish to understand the dynamics of our hyperreal postmodern world. Baudrillard cannot possibly provide any sort of argument that his thought leads us beyond Marx's concern with the ownership and control of the means of production. Marxism has not suddenly become outdated with the rise of the electronic mass media. The age of hyperreality confirms Marx's essential insight that the concentration and centralization of control of the means of production is inherent in the logic of capital and that this generates alien social forces standing above the members of society.[28]

Turning to the other issue to be considered here, Baudrillard begins with a very plausible insight into the connection of capitalism and the production of meanings. He points out that the capitalist order must continually produce meanings if for no other reason than to hide how much the workings of this order have produced generalized meaninglessness. From this insight, however, he goes on to extrapolate wildly to the thesis that *any* production of meanings serves the interests of capitalism, those that reject the logic of capitalism no less than those that accept that logic: "All that capital asks of us is to receive it as rational or to combat it in the name of rationality, to receive it as moral or to combat it in the name of morality."[29] He claims that Marxism's commitment to produce theories that make sense of the social world is just another form of the production of meanings by means of which capitalism continues.

With one wave of his magisterial hand, Baudrillard rules out *any* possibility that Marxist accounts of the social world might contribute to a counterhegemony that seriously threatens the stability of the capitalist order. One need not assert that the meanings produced by Marxist theory are presently about to have this effect to dismiss Baudrillard's extrapolation. He has not presented any reasons to believe that it is impossible in principle that they *ever* have this effect.

Beyond Needs and Truth?

Baudrillard is quite correct to insist that all needs are socially and culturally defined. But he is mistaken if he believes that Marx was not aware of this.[30] More important, he is wrong when he extrapolates from this to the conclusion that needs are *solely* a matter of codes, systems of signifiers that refer to no referent. In its own way, the view that states that human needs have no natural or biological basis is as one-sided—and therefore false—as the sociobiological position that ignores the historical and cultural components of our nature. Rather than developing this point, however, I would like to concentrate on Baudrillard's more general claim.[31] The denial that we can say anything true about the nature of our needs is just a specific case of a general rejection of the referent, a rejection of our being able to formulate truth claims regarding the signified in language.

At this point it would seem that Baudrillard is yet another victim of the old trap Aristotle set for the skeptics. A writer who is attempting to persuade us of the correctness of his or her views cannot consistently claim that the question of correctness is now irrelevant in our post-modern age. For this reason, someone like Habermas, who recognizes that validity claims are built into our speech, formulates a more plausible view than the French postmodernists who deny it.[32] However, this point does not consider Baudrillard's case on its own terms. A more immanent critique can be given by considering some of the examples Baudrillard discusses.

Baudrillard has a very plausible insight into the Watergate saga of the Nixon era. The *Washington Post* employed precisely the same undercover methods in breaking the story as the Nixon administration employed in planning the initial break-ins. Also, the source for the *Post*'s stories, "Deep Throat," may well have been someone within the Nixon administration. All of this is interesting enough. But at this point Baudrillard heads for the stratosphere and extrapolates from the fact that in this case we may never know the truth of the matter to the conclusion that the very category of "truth" must be abandoned.[33] Or take another of Baudrillard's cases. In the Franco years, Franco ordered the public execution of some Basque nationalists. Baudrillard points out that this was Franco's gift to Western Europe. Western Europe could piously complain about Franco, thereby indulging in pompous and pointless self-congratulations regarding its liberalism. And this response in turn was Western Europe's gift to Franco. The attacks on Spain allowed him to solidify his rule by appealing to Spanish national unity. It is certainly true that in this complex web it is hard to distinguish posturing from facts. But Baudrillard derives a much stronger conclusion: "Where is the truth in all that, when such collusions admirably knit together without their authors ever knowing it?"[34] This implies that the category "truth" would have validity only if states of affairs corresponded to the subjective intentions of the social actors who brought them about. This is surely a wild extrapolation. Baudrillard has illuminated what the facts of the matter probably were. He has captured at least an essential part of the truth of this situation, so he is hardly in a position to claim that this sort of situation undermines the category of truth. Anyone deriving this conclusion from the case being considered ought to feel dizzy. But anyone attempting to reject on these grounds a theory such as Marx's that makes truth claims ought to think twice.

Beyond Ideology?

Marx's category of ideology depends upon an underlying reality that has been masked. In the age of hyperreality, Baudrillard insists, this cannot be the case. When it comes to the question of social reality, there is no doubt that Baudrillard once again begins with an important insight. Baudrillard's notion of simulacrum illuminates our contemporary fate. An Italian girl from Michigan with a fairly ordinary voice has become an icon because of her sophisticated manipulation of the signs of sexuality in countless MTV videos.[35] The producers of colored sugarwater have built vast corporate empires by associating that sugarwater with the signs of youth in endlessly repeated commercials. In both cases these signs do not refer to the commodity in question; they refer to nothing at all. Yet they are more real than real—hyperreal.

Baudrillard is at his best when he shows how contemporary politics is also nothing but a series of meaningless simulations. "Propaganda and advertising fuse in the same marketing and merchandising of objects and ideologies."[36] A better description of our redempubocratic system could not be given that his: "Simulation of opposition between two parties, absorption of their respective objectives, reversibility of the entire discourse one into the other."[37] Politics too has been taken over by the hyperreal. Consider the way Bush wrapped himself in the American flag. What did this signify? To what did it refer? Obviously it had no connection to Bush's record as a Texas oil millionaire, CIA director, or vice president, little to do with the values most of the U.S. electorate associates with the flag. There was no reality to which his employment of the flag as sign referred, and yet the employment of the flag as sign had a reality of its own. It too was more real than real; it was hyperreal. Or consider the Willie Horton ads. These ads functioned as signs that were clearly designed to be perceived as referring to hordes of black rapists leniently treated by liberal administrators. But the social effect of these ads, these signifiers, had nothing to do with the question whether there was any reality signified to which they referred. The only thing that mattered was that they were taken to refer to the real. In this sense the ads took on a power that made them more than real. They also created a hyperreality.

We are surrounded by signs that have profound effects in the social world without referring to anything real. In forcing us to confront this, Baudrillard makes a significant contribution to contemporary social theory. But he is not content to leave things there. He pushes the wild extrapolation button and comes up with the thesis that the very notion of reality must be abandoned now that we have entered the epoch of the simulacrum. The "decisive turning point" that marks our age is "the transition from signs which dissimulate something to signs which dissimulate that there is nothing."[38]

This induces the sought-for dizziness, but it does so at the cost of coherence. To know that Bush's appeal to the flag created a hyperreality rather than referring to anything real about Bush, one must *already* know that *in reality* Bush's career reflects a commitment to values quite different from those most of the populace associate with the flag. To know that the Willie Horton ads created a hyperreality rather than referring to anything real in the social world, one must *already* know that *in reality* the myth of the black rapist is just that, a myth,[39] and that *in reality* the U.S. legal system is guilty of massive and systematic discrimination against black males. The category of hyperreality thus cannot be a *replacement* for the concept of reality, as Baudrillard holds. We must presuppose the validity of the latter term to determine instances where the former term is exemplified.

The signs around us do not hide from us that there is nothing; they hide from us that Madonna's poses oversimplify human sexuality, that Pepsi is colored sugarwater, that Bush is a hypocrite and a racist. These signs distort and mask an underlying reality, a reality that thought in principle can appropriate, as many of Baudrillard's writings show.[40] This implies that the age of simulacra is another stage *within* the age of ideology and not some radically new epoch where the Marxist concept of ideology has become irrelevant.

Beyond Revolution?

Two points can be considered under this heading: (1) Does Baudrillard present a compelling case against the project of revolutionary class struggle? (2) Does he present an acceptable alternative?

We have seen that Baudrillard holds that the idea of a revolution furthering the interests of the working classes is senseless today. His argument was that in the age of hyperreality the very concept of class becomes a "parody," a "retrospective simulation." However, Baudrillard grants that there is exploitation in the present order. This seems to imply that we are able to distinguish the exploiting classes from those that are exploited without resorting to parody or simulation. Baudrillard seems to acknowledge this. However, he simply denies its interest: "Exploitater and exploited do in fact exist, they are on different sides because there is no reversibility in production, which is precisely the point: nothing essential happens at that level."[41]

Of course, this argument depends entirely on the unstated premise that "reversibility" is the distinguishing characteristic of what is "essential." Why should one grant this premise? Baudrillard doesn't attempt to argue for it in any way. It is true that many significant social relations are "reversible"; it is often possible to observe the observer, to dominate the dominating, and so on. But why extrapolate from this to the claim that "nothing essential happens" unless there is reversibility? Isn't the essentiality of a phenomenon a function of its importance within a given social order?

At any rate, Baudrillard does not really claim that there are no classes but only that class struggle is useless. He holds that there is no dialectic in the present epoch that could possibly point to socialism's being on the historical agenda. "Once capital itself has become its own myth, or rather an interminable machine, aleatory, something like a *social genetic code,* it no longer leaves any room for a planned reversal; and this is its true violence."[42]

Arguments for the inevitable success of socialism are surely suspect.

But are arguments for the inevitability of the failure of socialism any less suspect? Baudrillard's case for the thesis that capital "no longer leaves any room for a planned reversal" appeals to the fact that in the industrialized West the labor-union apparatus has been integrated into the bourgeois order. "Strikes . . . are incorporated like obsolescence in objects, like crisis in production. . . . There is no longer any strikes or work, but . . . a scenodrama (not to say melodrama) of production, collective dramaturgy upon the empty stage of the social."[43]

The wild extrapolation here is transparent. From the present relative passivity of the labor movement, Baudrillard jumps to the conclusion that all capital–wage-labor confrontations in principle can never be more than the mere simulation of conflict. He completely rules out in principle any possibility of there ever being dissident movements within the labor movement that successfully unite workers with consumers, women, racially oppressed groups, environmental activists, in a common struggle against capital. He completely rules out in principle the possibility of a dynamic unfolding of this struggle to the point where capital's control of investment decisions is seriously called into question. He makes a wild extrapolation from the fact that these things are not on the agenda today to the conclusion that in principle they can never occur. To say that he fails to provide any plausible arguments for such a strong position is to put things far too mildly.

Baudrillard's alternatives to organized struggle against capital are hyperconformism and defiance. Examples of the former range from yuppies who accumulate the latest electronic gadgets with the proper demeanor of hip irony to the crack-dealing B-boys whose obsession with designer labels and BMWs simulates the hypermaterialism of the very system that has destroyed their communities. Rampant hyperconformism of this sort may very well lead the system to implode, from the waste, environmental damage, and community disintegration imposed by hyperconsumerism. The only problem is that by the time this implosion occurs, it may be too late for the human species to pick up the pieces.

Baudrillard's cryptoexistentialist odes to defiance perhaps present a more attractive option. However, these odes romanticize defeat. They honor the memory of rebels not for the heroism exemplified in their defeats and not for the lessons that can be learned from those defeats. It is the defeats themselves that meet with Baudrillard's approval, the fact that the rebels were "acting out (their) own death right away . . . instead of seeking political expansion and class hegemony." This form of implosion is like fireworks that brilliantly illuminate the landscape when they go off only to dissolve at once, leaving everything immersed in darkness as before. And this form of implosion is an option for suicide. In my view, neither of Baudrillard's proposals provide a satisfactory alternative to revolutionary Marxism, however unfashionable the latter may be today.

NOTES

1. Arthur Kroker has proposed that Baudrillard should be seen as a Marxist, albeit one who has grasped the necessity of reading Marx in terms of Nietzsche. On Kroker's reading of *Capital,* the principle underlying the circuit of capital is the will to will of which Nietzsche spoke. *The Postmodern Scene* (Montreal: New World Perspectives, 1986). This is an interesting suggestion, but it cannot be accepted. For one thing, for every fundamental Marxist thesis that Baudrillard turns out to share, there are a multitude that he rejects. For another, Baudrillard himself has explicitly rejected this sort of suggestion. When asked if he is a person of the Left or the Right, he answered "I can no longer function according to this criterion." "Intellectual Commitment and Political Power: An Interview with Jean Baudrillard," *Thesis Eleven* nos. 10, 11(1984–1985), p. 171. Most importantly, there is the substantive dimension of Kroker's case. Kroker interprets the Marxist category of capital in terms of Nietzsche's will to will. But Marx's concern was with two specific sorts of will, the will to accumulate (forced upon capitalists by the logic of market competition) and the will to resist capital accumulation (forced upon wage laborers by that same logic). The "will to will" is abstract, and it covers over class distinctions. Categories with these two features were consistently rejected by Marx.

2. *The Mirror of Production* (St. Louis: Telos Press, 1975).

3. I have developed the connection between Hegel and Marx at length in *The Logic of Marx's Capital: Replies to Hegelian Criticisms* (SUNY Press, 1990). See also my "Hegelianism and Marx: A Reply to Lucio Colletti," *Science and Society* 50(2)(1986).

4. "The Precession of Simulacra," in *Simulations* (New York: Semiotext(e), 1983), p. 4.

5. "Forget Baudrillard," in *Forget Foucault* (New York: Semiotext(e), 1987), p. 90.

6. " . . . Or the End of the Social," In *In the Shadow of the Silent Majorities . . . Or the End of the Social; and Other Essays* (New York: Semiotext(e), 1983), p. 89.

7. "In the Shadow of the Silent Majorities," in *In the Shadow,* p. 56.

8. "End of the Social," p. 84.

9. "Forget Foucault," in *Forget Foucault,* p. 27.

10. "End of the Social," p. 89.

11. "The Orders of Simulacra," in *Simulations,* pp. 147–48. Also see the passage quoted in note 27, below.

12. "In the Shadow," p. 27. "All the movements which only bet on liberation, emancipation, the resurrection of the subject of history, of the group, of speech as a raising of consciousness, indeed of a 'seizure of the unconscious' of subjects and of the masses, do not see that they are acting in accordance with the system, whose imperative today is the overproduction and regeneration of meaning and speech." "The Implosion of Meaning in the Media," in *In the Shadow,* p. 109.

13. "Precession of Simulacra," p. 4. The rejection of the specific referent "needs" goes back to Baudrillard's earliest writings, collected in *For a Critique of the Political Economy of the Sign* (St. Louis: Telos Press, 1981), especially "The Ideological Genesis of Needs" and "Beyond Use Value." See also *The Mirror of Production,* pp. 28, 32.

14. Ibid., p. 25.

15. Ibid., p. 48.

16. "Implosion of Meaning in the Media," p. 108. There is no positive act here;

instead it is an "absence of response" that is lauded as a counterstrategy of the masses in the age of simulation. Ibid., p. 105.

17. "Forget Foucault," p. 56.
18. "End of the Social," p. 70. See also *Mirror of Production,* p. 158.
19. "Forget Foucault," p. 58.
20. "End of the Social," p. 85.
21. Ibid., p. 86.
22. "Forget Baudrillard," pp. 127–29.
23. "Shadow of the Silent Majorities," p. 56.
24. "Forget Baudrillard," p. 90.
25. "Forget Foucault," pp. 25–26.
26. "Precession of Simulacra," p. 31.

27. In our world, "art and industry exchange their signs. . . . Production can lose all social finality so as to be verified and exalted finally in the prestigious, hyperbolic signs that are the great industrial combines, the ¼ mile high towers or the number mysticism of the GNP . . . art is everywhere, since artifice is the very heart of reality." "Orders of Simulacra," p. 151. Mark Poster's "Semiology and Critical Theory: From Marx to Baudrillard" provides a good overview of this aspect of Baudrillard's thought. In *The Question of Textuality,* ed. Spanos, Bové, and O'Hara (Bloomington: Indiana University Press, 1982). Its importance for an understanding of contemporary culture has been explored by Victor Burgin in *The End of Art Theory: Criticism and Postmodernity* (London: Macmillan, 1986).

28. I would like to note in passing that developments in information technology that confirm the Marxist position undermine a number of other currents that proclaim themselves post-Marxist. Lyotard, who also claims to be beyond Marx, calls for the means of producing information to be made available to all. In this era of ever-increasing concentration and centralization of information technology in the hands of capital, the naiveté of this position is staggering. See his *The Postmodern Condition: A Report on Knowledge* (Minneapolis: University of Minnesota Press, 1984), p. 67.

29. "Precession of Simulacra," p. 28. "The liberating practices respond to *one* of the aspects of the system, to the constant ultimatum to make of ourselves pure objects, but they don't respond at all to the other demand, which is to constitute ourselves as subjects, to liberate ourselves, to express ourselves at any price." "The Implosion of Meaning in the Media." Ibid., p. 108.

30. Marx pointed to "the discovery, creation and satisfaction of new needs arising from society itself; the cultivation of all the qualities of the social human being, production of the same in a form as rich as possible in needs, because rich in qualities and relations—production of this being as the most total and universal possible social product, for, in order to take gratification in a many-sided way, he must be capable of many pleasures, hence cultured to a high degree—is likewise a condition of production founded on capital. . . . The development of a constantly expanding and more comprehensive system of different kinds of labour, different kinds of production, to which a constantly expanding and constantly enriched system of needs corresponds." *Grundrisse* (New York: Vintage, 1973), p. 409. This is very far from the crassly naturalistic theory of needs Baudrillard imputes to Marx.

31. For critical discussions of Baudrillard's rejection of the category of needs, see Robert Hefner's "Baudrillard's Noble Anthropology: The Image of Symbolic Exchange in Political Economy," *Sub-Stance* (1977) and Patrick Murray and Jeanne Schuler, "Postmodernism in a French Context," *History of European Ideas* 9(1988). A clear exposition and defense of Baudrillard's position is found in William Bogard, "Sociology in the Absence of the Social: The Significance of Baudrillard for Contemporary Thought," *Philosophy and Social Criticism* 13(1987).

32. I discuss Habermas's theory of truth at length in "The Scope of the Social Sciences in Weber and Habermas," *Philosophy and Social Criticism* 8(1)(1981), and "Ethics and Politics in the Work of Jurgen Habermas," *Interpretation* 11(3)(1983).

33. See "Precession of Simulacra," pp. 26–27.

34. Ibid., p. 34.

35. This element of repetition is a crucial component of Baudrillard's definition of simulacra, which are "produced from miniaturised units, from matrices, memory banks and command models—and with these it can be reproduced an indefinite number of times." Ibid., p. 3. "For the sign to be pure it has to duplicate itself: it is the duplication of the sign which destroys its meaning." "Orders of Simulacra," p. 136. The paradigm is the genetic code, meaninglessly producing endless derivations of itself without any finality. Ibid., p. 105.

36. Ibid., p. 125.

37. Ibid., p. 133.

38. "Precession of Simulacra," p. 12.

39. Angela Y. Davis, *Women, Race and Class* (New York: Vintage, 1983), chap. 11.

40. Never one to be overly concerned with elementary consistency, Baudrillard has recently said, "I hold no position on reality. Reality remains an unsinkable postulate." Now he insists that his point is that reality is like seismatic shifts of plates of the earth: "The seismatic is our form of the slipping and sliding of the referential. . . . Nothing remains but shifting movements that provoke very powerful raw events. . . . Things no longer meet head-on; they slip past one another." "Forget Baudrillard," pp. 125–26. With this return of the repressed referent, however, any attempt to justify a rejection of Marxism on the grounds that it holds to a reality principle dissolves. For Marx's project was precisely to understand these shifting movements.

41. "Forget Foucault," p. 44. We have seen that elsewhere Baudrillard writes that "dialectical polarity no longer exists." But does not the fact that the position of exploiter and exploited cannot be reversed suggest that there indeed is a "dialectical polarity" in this relation?

42. Ibid., p. 112.

43. Ibid., p. 48.

Contributors

KATHRYN PYNE ADDELSON is a professor in the philosophy department and the program in the history of the sciences at Smith College. She is the author of *Impure Thoughts* and numerous articles on moral theory, feminism, and the sociology of knowledge. Dr. Addelson is a founding member of the Society for Women in Philosophy and a member of the board for the Conservation Land Trust. She is currently working with the Shelter for the Homeless.

JOSEPH BIEN did his doctoral studies in philosophy under the direction of Jean Hyppolite and Paul Ricoeur at the University of Paris. He has been on the faculties of the Ecole Centrale de Paris, the University of Texas at Austin, Texas A&M University and is currently professor of philosophy at the University of Missouri–Columbia. In 1991 he served as a director of the *Sozialphilosophie und Lebenswelt: M. Merleau-Ponty* at the Inter-University Centre for Postgraduate Studies in Dubrovnik. Professor Bien is an author, editor, or translator of six philosophy volumes. He is currently completing a book manuscript on Lukacs's social ontology.

FRED EVANS is an assistant professor of philosophy at Duquesne University. His recent publications include "Language and Political Agency: Derrida, Marx, and Bakhtin" (*Southern Journal of Philosophy*), "To 'Informate' or 'Automate': The New Information Technologies and Democratization of the Workplace" (*Journal of Social Theory and Practice*), and *Cognitive Psychology and Modern Nihilism: A Genealogical Critique of the Computational Model of Mind.*

JOHN EXDELL is associate professor of philosophy at Kansas State University where he teaches courses in social philosophy and the philosophy of law. His most recent publication is "Ethics, Ideology, and Feminine Value," in *The Canadian Journal of Philosophy.*

ANN FERGUSON is professor of philosophy and women's studies at the University of Massachusetts–Amherst. She has been a socialist-feminist activist for many years and is presently a member of Feminist Aid to Central America

211

and the University of Massachusetts Coalition on the Middle East Crisis. When her daughter was in grade school, she was involved in the parent-cooperative third-world socialist Che Lumumba School. She has published *Blood at the Root: Motherhood, Sexuality and Male Dominance* and *Sexual Democracy: Women, Oppression and Revolution.*

STEVEN JAY GOLD is assistant professor of philosophy, Southern Connecticut State University. He has written articles on Marxism, politics, and law for *Rethinking Marxism, Nature Society and Thought, The Critical Criminologist,* and *Philosophy Research Archives.* Dr. Gold is currently working on analytical Marxist methodology, police brutality, and criminal-justice issues.

ROBERT HOLLINGER is associate professor of philosophy, Iowa State University. His main interests are in nineteenth- and twentieth-century European philosophy, cultural history, and sociological theory. Dr. Hollinger's recent writings are on Heidegger, Habermas, Rorty, and hermeneutics; he is the editor of *Hermeneutics as Praxis, Postmodernism and the Social Sciences,* and *The Dark Side of Liberalism: Elitism Versus Democracy.*

DAVID INGRAM is associate professor of philosophy, Loyola University of Chicago. He is the author of *Habermas and the Dialectic of Reason, Critical Theory and Philosophy,* and the editor of *Critical Theory: The Essential Readings.* He has published articles on Hegel, Marx, hermeneutics, philosophy of history, and philosophy of law. His studies of contemporary French political thinkers include "The Postmodern Kantianism of Arendt and Lyotard" (*Review of Metaphysics*) and "Legitimacy and the Postmodern Condition: The Political Thought of Jean-François Lyotard" (*Praxis International*).

WILLIAM LANGENFUS is an assistant professor of philosophy, John Carroll University in Cleveland. Dr. Langenfus has published articles on ethics in *American Philosophical Quarterly, The Southern Journal of Philosophy,* and *Philosophy Research Archives.* He is currently working in the consequentialist tradition on the moral status of character traits, most importantly moral conscience.

BILL MARTIN teaches in the philosophy department at DePaul University of Chicago. He is the author of *Matrix and Line: Derrida and the Possibilities of Postmodern Social Theory.* He is also the editor of *Deconstruction and Social Theory* and, with George Trey, *Left Without Ground: Radical Possibilities of Postmodernity.* His articles have appeared in *The Journal of Philosophy, Philosophy and Literature, The Canadian Journal of Political and Social Theory,* and elsewhere.

EDWARD SANKOWSKI is associate professor of philosophy at the University of Oklahoma. Dr. Sankowski specializes in ethics and social and political philosophy and has published in *The Southern Journal of Philosophy, Inquiry, The Canadian Journal of Philosophy, Philosophical Studies, Mind,* and others.

DANIEL W. SKUBIK is a lecturer in the Division of Asian and International Studies, Griffith University in Brisbane, Australia. He has published numerous articles on legal, political, and moral philosophy and is the author of *At the Intersection of Legality and Morality*.

TONY SMITH is associate professor of philosophy, Iowa State University. Dr. Smith is the author of three recent books, *The Logic of Marx's Capital, The Role of Ethics in Social Theory*, and *Dialectical Social Theory and Its Critics*.

J. K. SWINDLER is associate professor and chair of the philosophy department, Westminster College, Fulton, Mo. He is the author of *Weaving: An Analysis of the Constitution of Objects* (Rowman & Littlefield, forthcoming) and articles in *The Thomist, Nous*, and *Southwestern Philosophical Studies*.

IRIS MARION YOUNG teaches ethics and political theory at the Graduate School of Public and International Affairs, University of Pittsburgh. She is the author of *Justice and the Politics of Difference* and numerous articles on feminist theory and political theory. Dr. Young has been an activist for reproductive rights, anti-intervention, and housing issues. She is currently involved in civil-rights activism in Pittsburgh.

Index

Abortion, 6
Acceptance conditions, 13–14
Adams, John, 84
Adorno, Theodor, 141, 143, 160, 175, 180
Affirmative-action, 103–4
Arafat, Yasir, 51
Arendt, Hannah, 157, 162, 172
Aristotle, 43, 145, 174, 178
Arneson, Richard, 5, 10
Aspect theory of self, 109–13
Atomism, 108
Austin, J. L., 187
Autonomy, 5, 34–48

Bakhtin, Mikhail, 80–82, 93
Baudrillard, Jean, xvii, 169, 194–209
de Beauvoir, Simone, 114n
Becker, Howard, 120, 121, 137
Benhabib, Seyla, 152–53
Benjamin, Walter, 168–69, 191
Bivalence thesis, 24–26, 28–29
Blum, Lawrence, 145
Blumer, Herbert, 120, 122–23
Bush, George, 204–5

Cartesian ego, 143
Chodorow, Nancy, 106, 114n
CIA, 204
Class balance, 62
Class consciousness, 69–79
Class struggle, 198
Cohen, G. A., xi, 60–61, 67–68
Cohen, Marshall, 22
Collectives, 50–56
Communicative ethics, 152–58
Coparenting, 109
Copp, David, x, 50

Daly, Mary, 105, 114
Davidson, Donald, 187, 192, 193
Davis, Angela, 209
Deep Throat, 203
Deleuze, Gilles, 176, 180

Delphy, Christine, 114n
Democracy, 79–97
  liberal, 85–86
Deontology, 144–45, 151
Derrida, Jacques, xv, xvii, 153, 167, 173, 181–93
Descartes, René, 166
Dialectic, 195–96
Difference theory, 104–9
Dinnerstein, Dorothy, 106, 115
Dostoyevski, Fyoder, 80
Dworkin, Andrea, 6, 114
Dworkin, Ronald, ix, 8, 22–33

Egalitarianism, 45
Elshtain, Jean, 156
Elster, Jon, xi, 60–61, 63, 67
England, 83–84
English Civil War, 84
Enlightenment, 156–57, 159, 168, 174–89
Essentialist theories, 108–9, 113
Existential process, 110–11

Fair play, 11–22
Feinberg, Joel, 3, 4, 6, 9, 47, 49
Feminism, xii–xv, 101–62
  anarchist, 116
  lesbian, 116
  liberal, xiii, 116
  psychoanalytic, 105, 118–20
  radical, xiii, 101, 105, 116
  socialist, xiv
Foucault, Michel, xi–xii, xv, 59–67, 171–73, 207, 208–9
Franco, Francisco, 203
Freedom, 5, 44
Frege, G., 182
French, Peter, x, 50–51
Freudian, 177
Fuller, Lon L., 15–16, 18, 21–22
Functionalism, 59–68

Gasche, Rodolphe, 190
Gender, 101–62

Gilligan, Carol, 106, 109, 115n, 118–20, 134, 136, 141
Gouldner, A., 84–85, 93
Gramsci, Antonio, 172
Guattari, Felix, 176, 180

Habermas, Jurgen, xv, xvii, 141, 146–47, 151–58, 161–62, 167, 169, 170–73, 186–87, 189–90, 192, 202, 209
Harding, Sandra, 114n
Harm principle, 46
Hart, H. L. A., 11, 21, 22
Hartmann, Heidi, 114n
Hartsock, Nancy, 114n
Hegel, Georg, xv, 70, 72, 76–77, 141, 148–49, 166–67, 175, 185–86, 188, 194
Hegelian, 50, 185, 186
    logic, 70–79
Heidegger, Martin, 167, 170, 184, 191–92
Hempel, C. G., 61, 67
Heterosexual, 107–13, 127
Hobbes, Thomas, viii, 147
Hodson, John, 5, 9
Hollingdale, R., 95
Holocaust, 178
Homosexuality, 158
Horkheimer, Max, 175, 180
Horton, Willie ads, 204
Hughes, Everett, 120
Hume, David, 190

Identity, 143
Ideology, 195, 197, 203–5
Institutions, 34–49
Instrumentalism, 62–63

Jameson, Frederic, 192
Jay, Gregory, 182
Jay, Martin, 94
Jefferson, Thomas, 102, 150
Jews, as subject, 188

Kant, Immanuel, xvi, 6, 37, 54, 174, 177, 179, 187
Kantian, xvii, 3, 6, 9, 37, 50, 144, 170, 192
Kaufman, Walter, 93–96
Keane, John, 139, 154, 160
Kierkegaard, Søren, 166–67
Klosko, George, 14, 21
Knowledge, theory of, 69–79

Kohlberg, Lawrence, 118–20, 134
Kripke, Saul, 52
Kristeva, Julia, 155–56
Kroker, Arthur, 207

Lacan, Jacques, 190
LaCapra, Dominick, 154
Ladd, John, x, 50, 52
Laos, 81–82
Lefebvre, Henri, 77
Levinas, Emmanuel, 188, 191, 193
Levine, Andrew, 60, 66, 160
Liberalism, vii–x, 3–58, 116, 139–62, 175
    and democracy, 139–42, 175
Locke, John, viii, 6, 102
Lukacs, Georg, xii, 69–79
Lyotard, Jean-Francois, xv, xvi–xvii, 169, 174–93, 208

MacIntyre, Alasdair, 49n
Marcuse, Herbert, 49n, 177, 180
Marx, Karl, x–xii, xvi, 59–97, 148, 183, 188, 194–209
Marxism, x–xii, 38, 59–115, 174, 182, 194–209
May, Larry, 50
McCarthy, Thomas, 189–90
Merleu-Ponty, 77–78, 176
Mill, J. S., 4, 6, 41, 46–47, 167
Mills, C. Wright, 119, 136
Mode of production, 62
Modernity, 166–209
Morris, R. B., 93
Mothering, 106–7
Murphy, Patrick, 208

National Organization for Women, 117
New Right, 111–12
Nicholson, Linda, 149
Nietzsche, Friedrich, xii, xv, 61, 79–97, 170, 174, 207
Nixon, Richard, 202–3
No-right-answer answers, 23–33
Nozick, Robert, viii, xi

Obligation, 11–22, 27
O'Brien, Mary, 105, 114

Paternalism, legal, 3–4, 6, 7–9
Patriarchy, xii, 188
Piaget, Jean, 118
Pluralism, 43

Polanyi, Karl, 10
Poster, Mark, 208
Postmodernism, xv–xvii, 163–209
  politics of, 165–73
Power, 62–67, 102, 159
Praxis, 69–79
Prima facie duty, 24–25
Primary benefit, 17–18
Primary good, 14, 17, 18
Psychotherapeutic explanation, 128–29
Public, the civic, 12, 13, 139–59
Public-private split, 101

Rains, Prudence, 121–25
Rational-maximizer theory of self, 102–
  4, 107–9
Rawls, John, viii, xi, 8–9, 11–12, 14, 19,
  21, 48–49, 160
Raymond, Jan, 105–6
Raz, Joseph, x, 32, 34–49
Reason, 142–59
Reductionism, 50–56
Reich, Wilhelm, 60–61
Ressentiment, 87
Revai, Josef, 78
Revolution, 197–99, 205–7
Rich, Adrienne, 138
Roemer, John, xi
Rorty, Richard, 166, 172, 183
Rousseau, Jean-Jacques, viii, xv, 139,
  141, 147, 149, 187
Ruddick, Sara, 106–7, 115
Ryan, Michael, 154, 182

Sartorious, Ralph, 7, 10
Saussure, Ferdinand, 182
Schrag, Calvin, 190
Schuler, Jeanne, 208

Searle, John, 187
Secondary benefits, 17
Self, 101–15
Sennett, Richard, 81, 93, 146–47, 161
Sensitizing concepts, 122–23
Simmons, A. John, 13–14, 19–21
Smith, Adam, 6
Smith, Paul, 190
Sociology, 119–24
Sokoloff, Natalie, 114n
Spain, 203
Spivak, Gayatri, 182
Structuralism, 62
Symbolic interactionism, 120

Taylor, Charles, 66, 68
Testosterone, 105
Time, 201
Tucker, Robert, 96

United Way, 117
Unwed mothers, 123–36
Utilitarianism, 142–43

VanDeVeer, Donald, 5, 7–8, 10n
Voice, 79–97
Voluntary risk-takers, 4

Warner, 201
Washington Post, 202–3
Watergate, 202–3
West, Cornel, 160n
Wittgenstein, Ludwig, 183, 191
Wolin, Sheldon, 156
Wollstonecraft, Mary, 140

Young, Robert, 5, 10